About the Author

Born to Christian Arab parents in Nazareth, Israel and brought up and educated in Kufur Yasief Yanni School, Israel, Emil Shehadeh came to the UK in 1975, where he studied at St Andrews University, obtaining a BSc (Hons) in Medical Biology, followed by an MSc in Biochemistry. In 1985 he moved to Glasgow University and after three years at the School of Medicine he obtained his MB ChB. He qualified as a GP and member of the Royal College of General Practitioners in 1995. He then undertook some training in Dermatology and obtained a diploma from Cardiff University in 1997. Throughout this time, he has been an active member of the church and has maintained his interest in history since his school days.

Dedication

I dedicate this book to people and places dear to me: to my birth parents Saleem and Nasrah Shehadeh, my surrogate parents Owen J and Peggy Thomas, for their immense love and care; to my numerous brothers and sisters for their love, support and guidance through life; to my teachers who have inspired me: my late brother Antione Shehadeh, who encouraged me to write in my early teens, to my cousin and headmaster Nadeem Naim Shehadeh who kept my childhood compositions in a treasure box alongside his son's (now Professor Naim Nadeem Shehadeh), a unique expression of faith. To Mary Sabbah, my sister and private tutor; to my teachers, Jameel Shehadeh and Naif Farah for helping me to appreciate history, and my teacher and friend Waleed Hazzan, for being the best English language teacher I could have ever had; to my Arabic teacher Gabriel Jiryes for his brilliant encouragement; to my Hebrew teacher Ahmad al-Haj for his unique teaching abilities. Finally, I dedicate this bok to my wife Carol for her incalculable support. I dedicate this to two places, my place of birth Nazareth which being the home town of my Lord and Saviour Jesus Christ and home to many of my friends and relatives, will always hold a special place in my affection; to Kufur Yasief, my home town, of whose people I am very proud as a model of co-existence between Christians and Muslims. May it forever shine as a beacon of tolerance and peaceful co-existence.

Emil Saleem Shehadeh

THE OTHER ANTI-SEMITISM

THE PLIGHT OF THE CHRISTIANS OF THE MIDDLE EAST

A Personal and Historical Perspective

AUSTIN MACAULEY
PUBLISHERS LTD.

A CIP catalogue record for this title is available from the British Library.

ISBN 978 1 78455 203 9 (Paperback)
ISBN 978 1 78455 204 6 (Hardback)

www.austinmacauley.com

First Published (2015)
Austin Macauley Publishers Ltd.
25 Canada Square
Canary Wharf
London
E14 5LB

Printed and bound in Great Britain

Contents

Preface

The purpose of this work, my first ever, is to bring to the attention of all thinking men and women, of all colours and creeds, the plight of the Christians of the Middle East. It has been written over many years, during the busiest period of any man's life, as a father, a busy physician and an educator. Though this did not make the work any easier, it did turn it into an enjoyable diversion from my daily toils.

I recall watching a film once, whose title evades me, in which a young writer was determined to get published. After several refusals, she was advised to write something with which she was familiar. That advice has stayed with me, and I have been determined ever since to make my first work conform to this sound piece of advice.

An Arab by race, a Christian by religion, Israeli and British by nationality, I have chosen a subject close to my heart. One of my main self-criticisms as an Arab is that we Arabs are guided more by feelings and emotions than we are by reason and intellect. I have therefore attempted to be more rational than emotional, not an easy task when dealing with two thousand years of persecution of the Christians of the Middle East, mostly by their own Semitic brethren, initially the Jews, then the Muslim Arabs, and last but not least by their own spiritual brothers and sisters in the West.

In doing so, I am aware I have embarked on a difficult journey fraught with potential pitfalls. Emotions and prejudice, amongst some of the readership, may confuse and obscure the intent and the sense of this book. My approach has been candid, perhaps relatively confrontational in some sense. But as a physician I have learnt that most human beings prefer candour. As a physician I have always been careful to define the problem in hand and to take a detailed history of the presenting complaint followed by a thorough examination, before embarking on a diagnosis let alone any treatment or cure. Sometimes I have had to ask offensive questions, perhaps about patients' social or sexual habits. Offensive, but necessary.

Historical material has been key to this work. However, I do not claim be an expert, but simply a student of history. It is my hope, nonetheless, that anyone with an interest in history would find enough in this book to satisfy their appetite for historical fodder.

Just as a physician cannot always make a diagnosis without causing "offense", they can less often offer a treatment that smells sweet, tastes savoury or feels pleasing. Indeed some treatment may involve cutting flesh and causing blood loss. It may cause pain initially. But no physician sets out to cause discomfort or suffering; they may cause it inadvertently and only if the end is to achieve relief.

We Arabs are famous for our honeyed tongue. Our language developed to suit this Arab attribute. Our communications are full of flattery, adulation and sweet nothings. Whilst it may be pleasing to the ear to hear lovely words, when twinned with insincerity, which is often the case, it becomes more than just hypocritical bordering on sycophancy. I prefer candour.

The situation of the Christians of the Middle East is too dire to pussy foot and equivocate or prevaricate. Indeed in a situation in which the very existence of the Christian community in Iraq and Syria is in peril, it is not only wrong to practice sycophancy, but it is cowardly and immoral. Candour is the answer. I have never shirked from telling a patient that they are terminally ill, despite many pleads from emotionally guided concerned relatives. How else is the poor patient going to prepare. Indeed what of the dignity of that dying person. One can fool them for a while. But even simple people know that they are dying. Candour is a moral responsibility. How candour is employed, is a personal matter, a matter of style and personal preference.

The relative inertness of the world to the plight of the Church in the Middle East bears no silence. This book is a voice on behalf of the voiceless, a cry from those too exhausted to cry for help. In this book, their welfare has been given priority over the sensitivity or indeed the oversensitivity and unwarranted protests of their aggressors.

Mindful of the ethnic variations to be found in the Churches of the Middle East, when describing the subject matter, it has been difficult to decide on whether to refer to the persecuted Christians of the Middle East as Christian Arabs or simply as the Christians of the Middle East. In an attempt to avoid the appearance of excluding them by the use of one expression or offending them by the use of another, I have often resorted to the happy medium of using the expression "Arabic-speaking Christians". The Assyrians and Chaldeans of Iraq and Syria may speak Arabic, and are cousins to the Arabs, but they are not Arabs. Ashur, the father of the Assyrians, was brother to Arphaxad the father of both Jews and Arabs. I have the utmost respect for the individual identities of the Assyrian, Coptic and other non-Arab Christians in the Middle East, though the latter have every right to call themselves Arabs, despite their mixed blood.

This brings me to the next dilemma. We often, if not only subconsciously, take racial purity for granted. However, in my opinion, there is no such thing as racial purity. The Arabs of South Arabia have mixed with the Japhetites of Africa and the peoples of Persia and India through trade. The Arabs of north Arabia have mixed with the Assyrians, the Persians, the Medes and the Lydians, the Romans, and the Greeks. The Assyrians have mixed with the Babylonians, also Semite. If one throws into the melting pot the fact that 10% of the Roman Empire was Jewish, mainly by conversion, and that the early church was predominantly Jewish, and that the Northern Arab tribes most of whom espoused the Christian faith, intermarried with Jewish Christians and Greeks and Phoenicians, one can see that the concept, more so the pursuit, of racial purity is a mirage. Brotherhood is far more attainable a dream and loftier a cause.

It is brotherhood, especially of the Semitic peoples, I have tried to highlight. The persecution of the Christians of the Middle East is a bitter rivalry between brethren. It is this brotherhood that gives me hope that despite the bitter past, the future could be sweet. Therefore, I have chosen to end this book with a plea. Having employed the mind to survey history and theology at the outset, I employed emotions, mixed with reason, at the close in the hope that Semitic cousins, amongst the greatest peoples of the earth, should see that to persecute one's brother is to injure one's own flesh. The current persecution of the Christians of the Middle East by Muslim Arab fundamentalists is a form of self-mutilation. If I were to employ humour in this situation I would say it is no wiser than a monkey sawing off the tree the very branch on which it is perched. However the matter is too painful and too serious and an emotional plea is a fitting penultimate section to this work.

If I may wear my physician's coat again, especially when conveying bad news or recommending some unpalatable medicine, it usually helps to give hope or inject a dose of positivity. In no other condition is such an injection more apt than when dealing with depression. It is said that the most effective treatment of depression is a positive new start, such as a new friendship or a repaired human relationship. This brings hope into a desperate situation. My Semitic dream is that hope, that faint glimmer of light that may, with prayer and hard work, become a bright flame of Semitic mutual love and respect, of fruitful co-operation between brothers for the common good of the Semitic peoples and the rest of the world.

In all of this, I have intended to do least harm and do most good. If there is to be a Semitic reconciliation, the truth must be spoken and heard first. Truth is the only unshakeable foundation to any lasting peace and reconciliation. In speaking the truth, I apologise for any unintended offence and call upon the reader to keep an open mind and be prepared to change their mind.

Introduction

This book has been born out of many conversations with Jews, Muslims, Christians and fellow Evangelicals in the UK, Europe and the USA about the Israeli-Arab conflict over many years. Most such conversations have left me downhearted, disappointed and even frustrated. I do not mind admitting that at times I have felt angry, even furious at some Western Evangelicals, in particular, because of their level of ignorance, stark insensitivity towards Arabic-speaking Christians, their tunnel vision of the geopolitical situation, and their almost cultic adherence to some rigid and illogical Zionist interpretation of Scripture. The obsession of some Western Evangelicals with Israel and the end times has led some to completely lose sight of the central issue of the Christian faith, and to abdicate the duty of brotherly love towards suffering Christians in the largely Muslim Middle East.

Some Evangelical attitudes, particularly the blind support for Israel and the associated occult, sometimes overt, hatred for Arabs is one of the biggest obstacles against Evangelism in the Middle East. *"As I daily witness ignorant Christian conversations, and watch ignorant Christian soldiers, blindly marching off to war, arrogantly boasting about the killing of 'rag-heads' and the total annihilation of 'Habib,' I often wonder: Where is your Christian compassion, Christian?"* writes an American Muslim (Sunday, February 11, 2007 courier-journal.com). This Muslim has far greater insight into Christianity than most Evangelical Zionists.

Repeated conversations with some Western Evangelicals have often caused me to feel totally numb. If you cannot feel pain, you cannot be affected by it. It is an effective defence mechanism, often seen in victims of PTSD. Two of the cardinal symptoms of PTSD are numbing and avoidance. I have been so traumatised by these repeated arguments that I decided not to get involved in them, and when I heard them I made myself deaf to them. Eventually I decided that one day I should write a book dealing with issues commonly raised in such conversations.

The last straw, however, was a conversation I enjoyed with some of my American relatives in the summer of 2006, through which I was reminded of how little Western Evangelicals knew about their fellow Evangelicals in the Arab world at large, and more specifically in the Israeli Arab community.

This book will contain material which may shock and disquiet some Western Evangelicals, Jews and Muslims. I am also aware that some may feel offended. No offence is intended in this book. I have merely attempted to present arguments rarely expressed, let alone heard. I am the voice of a silent minority in the Christian Arab Church, a minority that has been forgotten and neglected. Within that Christian minority, there is a smaller minority of Evangelical Arabs, who have for years suffered in silence. The time has come for someone to sound the trumpet.

The title of this book conveys a sense of fundamental injustice. This injustice has been partly committed by those who like to portray themselves as victims, namely Zionist Jews. The victims have been Arabic-speaking Christians, who have equally been persecuted by Muslim Arabs, and ignored by fellow Christians for centuries.

The author is a Christian Israeli Arab, who considers himself to be pro-Jewish and certainly pro-Western. My family have been good Israeli citizens since the inception of the State. Yet we have not been treated equally. Though I am critical of the State of Israel, I am by no means bitter. Nor do I believe that being critical amounts to hostility. The Bible says "faithful are the wounds of a friend". When your friend loses their capacity to be critical, they have become a stooge and a charlatan.

As a Christian, I acknowledge that God has a plan for the Jewish nation. However, I take issue with the way this is applied in practice by some fellow Western Evangelicals, who have totally ignored the feelings and needs of their fellow Evangelicals in the Middle East, and specifically in the Israeli-Arab and Palestinian community and have been so blatantly and unabashedly pro-Zionist to the hurt of their own brothers and sisters in the faith.

The contrast between the favourable Western Evangelical treatment of Zionists and their wanton treatment of Arabic-speaking Christians and Evangelical Israeli-Arabs at best reflects a deeply negative attitude towards Arabs in general. There is a whiff of racism about such an attitude.

I have been blessed with four beautiful sisters, the youngest of whom is also cute and cheeky with it. When we were children, she would muse that when she grew up she wanted to be a teacher and would let naughty beautiful children off the hook, but would always punish aesthetically challenged children. Whilst this may be funny in a jocular child, it is a serious character flaw in an adult, and a gaping fissure in the theology of a church. The Arabs, to Western Evangelicals, are the ugly children, whilst the Zionists are the beautiful children. According to some Western Evangelicals, Israel can get away with murder, quite literally, whilst Arabs will never measure up, or make the grade.

Another personal experience which mirrors Western Evangelical attitudes towards Arabs in general was the German police classification of non-Germans. This is something I personally experienced in 1994, having sacrificed a career as a junior psychiatrist in the United Kingdom and moved to Germany to look after my elderly German in-laws. My wife and I had made copious and extensive enquiries about the prospect of working in Germany as a general practitioner. My German wife and I left nothing to chance. All the signs were encouraging. Our move to Germany, with our three children, was planned with Teutonic precision. To my disappointment, however, I found that I had to be registered with the German police, even though I was a citizen of the EU. Though I resented the idea, I was prepared to go through with it for the sake of my in-laws. I recall going to the local police station in Villingen (Black Forest). I stood in queue and when I reached reception I was told I had been standing in the wrong queue, the *Schoene Auslaender* (beautiful foreigner) queue. Since I was black-haired and olive skinned, I had to queue in the *Haesliche Auslaender* (ugly foreigner) queue. This was one of the worst instances of racism I have experienced outside of Israel. Shocking as it is, such racist treatment by a heathen nation with a recent Nazi past is less hurtful than similar treatment by the people of God, the church. Evangelical Arabs in general feel that some Western Evangelicals treat them as if they were "Haesliche Auslaender". What is more disheartening is that some Evangelicals have built a system of theology to justify their disdain, hatred and racism towards Arabs in general, evangelicals included. Measure this up against the following Scripture:

"Do not marvel, my brethren, if the world hates you. We know that we have passed from death to life, because we love the brethren. He who does not love his brother abides in death. Whoever hates his brother is a murderer, and you know that no murderer has eternal life abiding in him." (1 John 3:13-15 NKJV)

Israeli Arabic-speaking Christians do not expect the Zionist State to love them. We do not marvel at our ill-treatment by the Zionists. But we do expect love from fellow Christians elsewhere, if not for their own sake, according to the sobering divine word above. There is a serious warning for Western Evangelicals: you cannot claim to be born again and you cannot be part of the Kingdom of Heaven if you continue to mistreat and hate your Arab brethren!

It is my view that generalisations can be dangerous and may reflect an unrefined mind, but they cannot be dismissed wholesale. I have tried not to tarnish all evangelicals or all Jews or Muslims with the same brush. I have attempted to make a distinction between Zionists and Jews. Whilst Zionists may be Jews, all Jews are not Zionists. Israeli Jews are largely Zionist. It also has to be stated that not all Western Evangelicals are pro-Zionist. However, I have rarely encountered Western Evangelicals who are sufficiently aware of the plight of Israeli-Arab Evangelicals, let alone Arabic-speaking Christians in general.

Therefore, the aim of this book is to shed some light on some injustices committed by the Zionist State, Muslim fundamentalists, and some Western Evangelicals against Arabs in general, and more specifically, against Arabic-speaking Christians. I hope this revelation will result in some changed attitudes.

Finally, and equally importantly, I hope there will be a metanoya, a turning round, a conversion of the Western Christian mind towards their spiritual kith and kin in the Middle East. This should mean palpable moral, political and financial support akin to that now enjoyed by Israel. Western Evangelicals, particularly those from the USA, should remind the Zionist State on which side her bread is buttered and use their influence for the improvement of the lives of Arabic-speaking Christians in particular, and Arabs in general. Western Evangelicals should use their influence to increase the liberty granted by Israel to the local Christians, especially amongst the Arabs.

By highlighting the persecution of Arabic-speaking Christians in Muslim Arab countries, it is hoped that the church in the West will mobilise to stand up for the human rights of Arabic-speaking Christians. How else can we expect the secular world to support Christian Arab minorities in their pursuit of basic human rights?

The reader will find an admonition, some rebuke and much remonstration with Western Evangelicals, Zionists and Muslims. It is a call to cast some self-doubt, if not just for a couple of hours. Is it possible that Western Christians have been mistaken all these years? Have they been guilty of neglect and unfairness towards their fellow Christians in the Holy Lands? For those with an open mind, I say *"read on, and read on not only with an open mind, but also with an open heart. Think not how hurt you may feel for the next two hours, but rather think how you have hurt your brothers and sisters for the last century or longer."*

For those unflinching hardened pro-Evangelical Zionists, I would say, you may not feel inclined to read on, but do so nonetheless. Put yourself through the hardship of reading the unpalatable, as an athlete would run a few miles, or as a sick man may take his medicine. The hardship of the next two hours may be character-building, and the medicine may cure you of your bigotry. Read this rebuke now from a fellow evangelical or else face your creator on the day of judgement.

If you are too cowardly to read on, then remember the Word of God, when it says: *"Honour all people. Love the brotherhood. Fear God."* NKJV1 Peter 2:17

You cannot claim to fear God if you despise "the brotherhood", turn a blind eye to their suffering, and act unjustly and discriminate against them.

Prepare an answer now for the question *"what have you done to your brethren? Have you loved your brethren as Christ has loved you?"* Just remember one more thing; on the day of judgement, no amount of theology will suffice. Less so any money you may have donated to the Zionist State.

The contents of this book will inevitably grate with some readers. If there is a sense of anger in this book, it is just righteous indignation at the injustices committed by one group of Christians, who should know better, against another, who is vulnerable. There is a sense of abandonment of the needier brother for the sake of the less needy stranger. I have not set out to arouse or provoke any sense of hatred or plant any root of bitterness. If the contents of this book are judged to be disturbing, one must enquire as to how much more disturbing it is for those who have had to endure persecution, neglect and injustice for many years. The experience is always much more difficult to bear than the account is to read.

Yes, I have a bone to pick with some Western Evangelicals, Jews, and Muslim Arabs. This book is a challenge for them to stand before the mirrors of history and of the Word of God, basic justice and fairness, to gaze closely and realize their errors of omission and commission, and the injustices they have committed against the Arabic-speaking Christians in the Holy Lands. It is a call from the heart, born out of pain and suffering, and out of jealousy for the body and bride of Christ.

When I shared the concept of this book with some family members and some friends, many reacted with a warning *"They will call you anti-Semitic... they will be after you... watch your back... are you sure you can handle their reaction?"* I am well aware that closed-minded people will react unfavourably. I am aware that some will refer to me with a range of unflattering adjectives. This would only scare me if I had claimed to be perfect and sinless, which I have never done. Nor do I believe that one has to attain perfection before they express their views. If so, no word could have ever been uttered, or any book written by any human being.

Chapter I

A Historic Perspective of Anti-Semitism

"I shall induce anti-Semites to liquidate Jewish wealth... The anti-Semites will assist us thereby in that they will strengthen the persecution and oppression of Jews. The anti-Semites shall be our best friends" (Theodore Herzl).

"Interestingly, whilst these words were being uttered, my maternal grandmother, Miriam Kahaz Musallam, a Christian Palestinian midwife, was probably delivering a calf or a baby for her Jewish neighbours near Affoula, free of charge. Who is the anti-Semite, Mr Herzl or midwife Miriam Kahaz Musallam?"

The simplest definition of an anti-Semite is someone who is not overly fond of Semites. Therefore it may be prudent to begin by asking who the Semites are.

The Semites are descendants of Shem, one of the three sons of Noah. See the tree on the next page.

One of Shem's descendants was Eber, who is the father of all True Arabs, Arabised Arabs and Jews. Eber begat Pheleg, who after several generations produced Abraham. Eber also begat Yoktan (Qahtan), one of whose descendants was Yarub, after whom Arabs are called. Therefore Arabs and Jews are both Semites. Other Semites include the Edomites (descendants of Esau), the Moabites and the Ammonites (descendants of Lot through his two daughters). The great Assyrian nation, descendants of Ashur, son of Shem have an equally valid claim on the Semitic title. The Ethiopians, at least partly Semitic, can also make a valid claim to the Semitic title. The Elamites of Persia, direct descendants of Shem may have been engulfed within the Persian Empire, but their blood still flows in the largely Indo-European Persians. The Lydians of Asia Minor, also direct descendants of Shem, whose blood has intermixed with the invading Mongols, can lay a legitimate claim to the Semitic title. (George David Malech, *History of the Syrian Nation and the Old Evangelical-Apostolic Church of the East*; Gorgias Press p.1-2)

The Genealogy of Shem

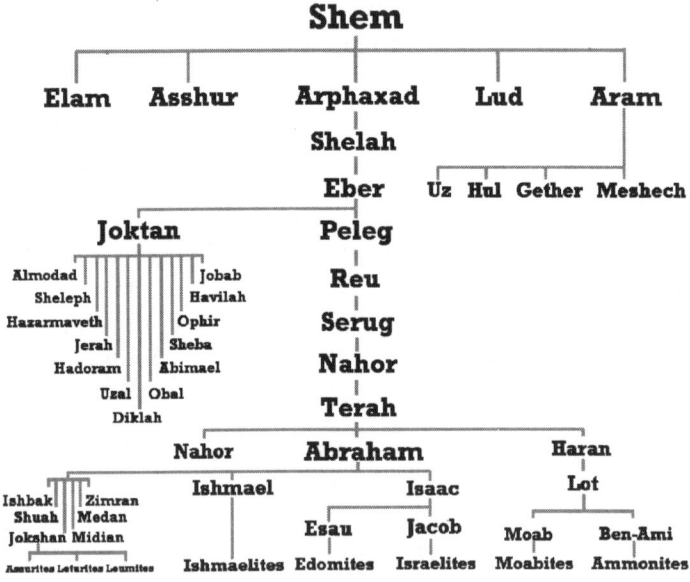

It should be hardly surprising therefore to read that Jews and Arabs have been found to be genetically closely related. *"In a recent study of 1371 men from around the world, geneticist Michael Hammer of the University of Arizona in Tucson found that the Y chromosome in Middle Eastern Arabs was almost*

indistinguishable from that of Jews." ("Jews and Arabs Share Recent Ancestry" by Ann Gibbons on 30 October 2000.)

Therefore, strictly speaking, an anti-Semite should be someone who is not awfully fond of all the above Semites, be they Jews or Arabs.

Yet the term "anti-Semite" is mainly used to encompass any thought, word or action reflecting or inciting disrespect, hatred or violence against the Jews, and the Jews alone.

The term *Antisemitismus* was first coined by German political agitator Wilhelm Marr. In his book *"The Way to Victory of Germanicism over Judaism"* published in 1879, he referred to *Antisemitismus* as meaning *Judenhass* (hatred of Jews). As his book gained popularity, he founded the "*Antisemiten-Liga*", a league of anti-Semites, whose aim was to fight against the Jews and expel them from Germany, believing the Jews to have plotted a takeover of Germany.

The term comes from the fact that Jews are a member of the Semitic group of nations, the descendants of Shem, one of the three sons of Noah. In that sense anti-Semitism is a misnomer. Yehuda Bauer articulated this view in his writings and lectures: *"[the term] Anti-Semitism, especially in its hyphenated spelling, is inane nonsense, because there is no Semitism that you can be anti to."*

Bernard Lewis, Professor of Near Eastern Studies Emeritus at Princeton University, says that *"Anti-Semitism has never anywhere been concerned with anyone but Jews."*

Holocaust scholar and City University of New York professor Helen Fein's definition has been particularly influential. She defines anti-Semitism as *"a persisting latent structure of hostile beliefs towards Jews as a collective manifested in individuals as attitudes, and in culture as myth, ideology, folklore and imagery, and in actions – social or legal discrimination, political mobilization against the Jews, and collective or state violence – which results in and/or is designed to distance, displace, or destroy Jews as Jews."*

It is worth noting that whilst some naïve people assume that anti-Semitism against the Jews is something of which only non-Jews are guilty, history proves the opposite to be true.

Zionists are amongst the worst anti-Semites (in the Jewish sense of the word). *"Anti-Semites will become our surest friends, anti-Semitic countries our allies."* (Th. Herzl, "Der Kongress", *Welt*, June 4, 1897. Reprinted in: *Theodore Herzl's Zionistische Schriften* (Leon Kellner, ed.), ester Teil, Berlin: Judischer Verlag, 1920, p.190 and p.139). Herzl made no bones about his collaboration with the Nazis to entice Jews to immigrate to Palestine: *"It is essential that the sufferings of Jews... become worse... this will assist in realization of our plans... I have an excellent idea... I shall induce anti-Semites to liquidate Jewish wealth... The anti-Semites will assist us thereby in that they will strengthen the persecution and oppression of Jews. The anti-Semites shall be our best friends."* (From his Diary, Part I, p.16.)

What Herzl and the Zionists did to their own people had never even been imagined by ordinary Palestinians. Interestingly, whilst these words were being uttered, my maternal grandmother, Miriam Kahaz Musallam, a Christian Palestinian midwife, was probably delivering a calf or a baby for her Jewish neighbours near Affoula, free of charge. Who is the anti-Semite, Mr Herzl or midwife Miriam Musallam?

Chaim Weizmann, speaking in Berlin in 1920, long before Hitler had put pen to the paper of *Mein Kampf*, stated openly: *"Germany... has too many Jews."* He later became the first President of the Zionist State.

There are many Jews who believe that Zionism is at least as responsible for Nazism as Hitler, whose Mr Streicher once said: *"I did no more than echo what the leading Zionists had been saying".*

The Zionists co-operated with Hitler in order to transfer Jews, and more importantly, Jewish wealth to Palestine. This is well detailed in an excellent book by Edwin Black, *The Transfer Agreement* (2nd edition, 1999). According to an agreement concluded in 1933 between Zionists and the Third Reich, the German economy, which was choked by embargoes from the allies, would be given new oxygen by Zionists who would purchase equipment and material from the Germans to support the fastest growing economy in the world, namely Palestine, particularly the Jewish sector.

The Zionist attitude to Jews is little short of anti-Semitic. Zionists did not bat an eyelid about shedding innocent Jewish blood in order to achieve their personal dream of a Jewish State. Ben-Gurion said on December 7, 1938, *"If I knew it was possible to save all the children in Germany by taking them to England, and only half of the children by taking them to Eretz Israel, I would choose the second solution. For we must take into account not only the lives of these children but also the history of the people of Israel."* (Yvon Gelbner, *Zionist policy and the fate of European Jewry*, in Yad Vashem studies (Jerusalem, vol. XII, p.199).

He has also been quoted as saying *"... not always and not everywhere do I oppose anti-Semitism."* Why? Because it was the catalyst for the Zionist formula, nay a guarantor of the fulfilment of his Zionist dream, regardless of the cost in terms of lost Jewish lives.

"To attain its practical objectives, Zionism hopes it will be able to collaborate with a government that is fundamentally hostile to the Jews." (Lucy Dawidovitch, *A Holocaust Reader*, p.155).

Zionists have not only participated in actions of anti-Semitism, but have forever kept the term alive in the consciousness of the Jews, if not the rest of the world, as a means of ensuring more Jewish immigration to their state. *"The best solution to anti-Semitism is immigration to Israel. It is the only place on Earth where Jews can live as Jews,"* ("Sharon Urges Jews to go to Israel", BBC News, 17 Nov. 2003.)

It is therefore no surprise that the Jewish Edwin Samuel Montagu, who was Lloyd George's Secretary of State for India, objected to Zionism by telling Prime Minister Lloyd George: *"All my life I have been trying to get out of the ghetto. You want to force me back there."*

Montagu regarded Zionism as a *"mischievous political creed, untenable by any patriotic citizen of the United Kingdom."*

Montagu, who married a Gentile, was opposed to Zionism, partly in fear that the creation of a national home for Jews in Palestine would overnight lead to the loss of the huge liberties Jews had been enjoying in Christian Britain. *"I have always recognized the unpopularity... of my community. We have obtained a far greater share of this country's goods and opportunities than we are numerically entitled to. We reach on the whole maturity earlier, and therefore with people of our own age we compete unfairly. Many of us have been exclusive in our friendships and intolerant in our attitude, and I can easily understand that many a non-Jew in England wants to get rid of us.*

"But just as there is no community of thought and mode of life among Christian Englishmen, so there is not among Jewish Englishmen. More and more we are educated in public schools and at the Universities, and take our part in the politics, in the Army, in the Civil Service, of our country. And I am glad to think that the prejudices against inter-marriage are breaking down. But when the Jew has a national home, surely it follows that the impetus to deprive us of the rights of British citizenship must be enormously increased. Palestine will become the world's Ghetto."

Was he an anti-Semite? Only unrefined minds would entertain such a notion. He regarded himself a Jew to the end. It is the Zionists who are anti-Semites for their co-operation with Nazis.

And what of the Hassidic Jews who denounce Zionism and the State of Israel? Are they anti-Semitic? Joel Teitelbaum, a famous Orthodox Jewish religious leader, was totally opposed to the Zionist movement and was unambiguously damning of it: *"Zionism forestalled the Messiah... brought the Holocaust and other calamities on the Jewish people."* His views, typically Orthodox, are based on the belief that Zionists have attempted to usurp God's role, who would miraculously return the Jews to the land of their forebears. Zionists, many of whose leaders were non-believers, rather than wait for divine intervention, relied on their own deceitful works to return the Jews to the Promised Land. These Jews do not believe in the legitimacy of the State of Israel. Their stance is offensive to Zionist Jews. Are they anti-Semites?

The Jews and the Catholic Church often unfairly and wrongly attribute the German Nazi Holocaust to Martin Luther, who in 1523 wrote an article entitled, *"That Jesus Was Born a Jew,"* in which he invited Christians to be kind and clement with the Jews, hoping that Christian love would lead them to Christ. He thought that Jews would appreciate the contrast between hundreds of years of persecution by the Catholic Church and his new approach. However, no great conversion of Jews took place and Luther defaulted to his old Catholic position recommending that all synagogues be burnt and their properties confiscated amongst other things. It would be ignorant to blame almost 1700 years of persecution of the Jews in Europe on one such isolated event, when history shows that Rome and the Orthodox churches taught and practised persecution of Jews on a large scale with a well-developed, though misguided, system of theology to justify it. In this respect, some Evangelicals foolishly accept blame for something that is not their fault. The Zionists are clever enough to exploit this self-imposed guilt to their advantage.

It was the Catholic Church's Fourth Lateran Council in 1215 that proclaimed the requirement for Jews to wear something that distinguished them as Jews. It could be a colored piece of cloth in the shape of a star or circle or square, a hat (*Judenhut*), or a robe. In many localities, members of medieval society wore badges to distinguish their social status. Some badges (such as those of guild members) were prestigious, while others were worn by ostracized outcasts such as lepers, reformed heretics and prostitutes. Jews sought to evade the badges by paying what amounted to bribes in the form of temporary "exemptions" to kings, which were revoked and re-paid whenever the king needed to raise funds.

Both economically and socially, the crusades were disastrous for European Jews. They prepared the way for the anti-Jewish legislation of Pope Innocent III, and formed the turning-point in the medieval history of the Jews.

Semites, or speakers of Semitic languages include: the Arabs, Jews, Amharic People (living in Ethiopia, Eritrea and Abyssinia), the Chaldeans (who live in Iraq and speak Aramaic), and the Syriacs who speak Syriac and live in Syria.

Therefore it is a clear misnomer to apply the term "anti-Semitic" exclusively to those who hate the Jews.

The exclusive application of the term anti-Semitic to the Jews is not only misleading, but reflects a subtle implication that of all the sons of Shem, the Jews are the only people who have been persecuted, or who are worth taking note of or protecting from persecution.

This reflects total disregard for the existence, dignity, rights and needs of other Semitic nations. Historically, this attitude amongst Evangelicals has led to unjustifiable prejudice against Arabs, Muslim and Christian alike.

Though the term "anti-Semitic" was coined by Gentiles, the term has been adopted and developed by Jews and their allies. It has, amongst other things, come to mean any mode of behaviour or way of thinking and making utterances that cause discomfort to Jews or their allies, usually Evangelical Zionists. In reality, it has come to mean any speech or behaviour with which Jews and Evangelical Zionists disagree. In that respect, the term anti-Semitism has become a weapon with which the Jews can curb the liberty of innocent people from making valid justifiable observations about the Jews, which though not flattering may be entirely and historically true. Indeed, the term has become a tool for curbing the rights and liberties of majorities in post-Christian Western countries.

This is best exemplified in an event to which I allude later in greater detail. When a journalist witnessed an Israeli soldier confiscate a Palestinian vehicle for driving on a road intended for Jews only, but not signposted so, she challenged the soldier who replied: *"What do you want us to do, put up a sign here and let some anti-Semitic reporter or journalist take a photo so he that can show the world that Apartheid exists here?"* The use of the term "anti-Semitic" in this context betrays the meaning that anti-Semites are people who dare criticise Zionists, whether rightly or wrongly.

A case in point is an incident in which a British Evangelical paid the post office a considerable sum of money in return for a simple statement stamped on every envelope delivered by the post office around Easter, which says "Jesus is risen". The outcry from the Jewish community in the UK and particularly from their Chief Rabbi was disproportionate. The Chief Rabbi likened this exercise to the Holocaust in that both threatened the identity of the Jews. The simple statement that Christ is risen during Easter, in a largely Christian country, during the most important festival in the Christian calendar, has been taken as an expression of anti-Semitism. This unreasonable outcry by the Jewish community in England went largely unchecked. And yet Israeli TV and radio and newspapers flaunt things Jewish all the time and no one accuses them of threatening the identity of Israeli Arabs, be they Christian or Muslim.

In that sense, the use of the term "anti-Semitism" by Jews has done the Jewish nation a disservice. To put Hitler's anti-Semitism on par with an Evangelical paying the post office a fee for stamping "Jesus is risen" on every envelope at Easter, in a Christian United Kingdom, is tantamount to an insult to all those Jews who perished in the Holocaust. Jews were not victimised by such an expression of faith in a Christian country at Easter. The Chief Rabbi's reaction not only demeaned the Holocaust, but amounted to a brazen assault on the liberties of the majority of Britons who choose to be called Christian. If Jews were the only Semites, this Jewish over-reaction would justifiably be called Semitic Christophobia.

What is noteworthy here is the self-centredness of some Jewish minds. When Evangelicals support their claim to the land of Palestine, they are greeted warmly. When Evangelicals, who earn their name from evangelising, vaguely appear to be doing what they should be doing, evangelising, they are labelled anti-Semites. How quickly the pendulum swings!

In his book *The Idea of Israel*, Ilan Pappe also criticises the Zionist manipulation of world sentiment by overusing the Holocaust card. *"From vindication of the brutal killing of Palestinians in 1948 and subsequently, in the war against*

Palestinian infiltrations, through the instigation of public panic on the eve of the 1967 war, to the justification of intransigent official positions on peace following the war, to the present oppressive policies against the Palestinians in the occupied territories – Holocaust memory has been a supremely useful and accessible means of silencing criticism and pushing a policy of belligerence."

Those Jews who are too quick to flag up the "anti-Semitic" card, in the face of any criticism of Zionism or Jewry, do the victims of the Holocaust a huge disfavour. President Carter's book *Palestine, Peace Not Apartheid* was met by a barrage of criticism by some Jews; some of it came even before his book was published. President Carter, a Christian and a Baptist Sunday School teacher in his former persona, expressed his disappointment at some Jewish response to his work: *"My most troubling experience has been the rejection of my offers to speak, for free, about the book on university campuses with high Jewish enrollment and to answer questions from students and professors."* (*Los Angeles Times*, by Jimmy Carter the 39th President of the United States. His newest book is "Palestine: Peace Not Apartheid," December 8, 2006.)

The use, indeed manipulation, of the term "anti-Semitism" has gone so far as to reflect total disrespect by Jews for what is sacred to others. The New Testament to Christians is God inspired and unchangeable. It cannot be changed through political pressure, by an influential group, who feel slighted by its content. Yet the Jews call certain parts of the Scripture anti-Semitic.

Jesus speaking to a group of Pharisees: *"I know that you are descendants of Abraham; yet you seek to kill me, because my word finds no place in you. I speak of what I have seen with my Father, and you do what you have heard from your father. They answered him, "Abraham is our father." Jesus said to them, "If you were Abraham's children, you would do what Abraham did.... You are of your father the devil, and your will is to do your father's desires. He was a murderer from the beginning, and has nothing to do with the truth, because there is no truth in him. When he lies, he speaks according to his* own nature, for he is a liar and the father of lies. But, because I tell the truth, you do not believe me. Which of you convicts me of sin? If I tell the truth, why do you not believe me? He who is of God hears the words of God; the reason why you do not hear them is you are not of God." (John 8:37-39, 44-47, RSV)

Stephen speaking before a synagogue council just before his execution: *"You stiff-necked people, uncircumcised in heart and ears, you always resist the* Holy Spirit. *As your fathers did, so do you. Which of the prophets did not your fathers persecute?! And they killed those who announced beforehand the coming of the Righteous One, whom you have now betrayed and murdered, you who received the law as delivered by angels and did not keep it."* (Acts 7:51-53, RSV)

"Behold, I will make those of the synagogue of Satan who say that they are Jews and are not, but lie – behold, I will make them come and bow down before your feet, and learn that I have loved you." (Revelation 3:9, RSV)

Imagine the furore of Jewish communities around the World if non-Jews demanded that the Old Testament were altered in favour of Ishmael. If Arabs protested that the treatment of Ishmael and his mother Hagar was anti-Arab, would the Jews think it fair to change their scriptures out of respect for Arab sentiment? I think not! Yet Jews will not desist from constantly protesting about parts of the New Testament, for every time they complain, they are practising Christophobia. It should not be forgotten that the Jews persecuted the early Church when the former were in the ascendancy. Indeed Paul, previously Saul of Tarsus, was on his way to Damascus, armed with a letter from the high priest in Jerusalem to the synagogue in Damascus, authorising him to bind and bring to Jerusalem any converts to Christianity. Paul, the Jewish Pharisee, was a master persecutor of Christians.

Paul miraculously converted to Christianity. The persecutor of the Christians became a passionate propounder and propagator of the Christian faith. When Paul left Thessalonica having preached there for a while, he moved to Beroea, a peaceful city, where he was received warmly.

However, Thessalonian Jews followed him to Beroea to cause him trouble, and stir the people up against him (Acts 17:13).

In 2005, the European Monitoring Centre on Racism and Xenophobia (EUMC), a body of the European Union, developed a more detailed working definition for the term "anti-Semitic", which listed examples of anti-Semitism such as: *Making mendacious, dehumanizing, demonizing, or stereotypical allegations about Jews; accusing Jews as a people of being responsible for real or imagined wrongdoing committed by a single Jewish person or group.*

The first three examples are of great interest to me, as they bear a personal relevance to a shocking event in my childhood. My father was a free Evangelical pastor, and as such we were often visited by Christians from the West, some of whom had never conceived that Christian Churches could exist amongst the Arabs, especially in Israel. One day, we were visited by a Norwegian lady, who not unlike others kept staring at me. I was shocked to learn from my mother that the Norwegian Christian could not believe that I had no tail! She was brought up to believe that Arab children, like monkeys, had tails. I wonder why she did not think my mother had a tail! This lady was brought up in an anti-Semitic environment in which *"mendacious, dehumanizing, demonizing, or stereotypical allegations"* against the Arabs (a Semite nation) were made on a regular basis. Do I have the right to make that claim, or is anti-Semitism a Jewish preserve?!

Interestingly, soon after the 1967 war was over and the borders with the West Bank were opened, my father took us to visit an old acquaintance of his, a successful businessman from Nablus (Shechem). I must have been just over ten years of age when Uncle Adel's daughter told us that her teachers taught her that Jews had tails and were subhuman. This was anti-Semitism too.

To return to my point about the application of the term anti-Semitism, the point must be made that the Jews are not the only descendants of Shem who have suffered racial discrimination. Arabs too, especially Arabic-speaking Christians including Assyrians and Chaldeans and Copts, have and continue to suffer from racial discrimination, which often emanates from sheer ignorance and blind loyalty to a people who appear to be friends, but in reality are foes.

Zionists are so engrossed in their own painful experiences in Europe that they cannot see their own excesses, and unpalatable deeds. On 06.02.06, the Church of England called for divestment from companies who provide military parts for Israel, such as caterpillars and bulldozers, which are used against the citizens of the Palestinian territories. Israel called the Anglican position a *"moral outrage"*. The whole international community, including many Jewish Israeli citizens, was opposed to the wall erected around Palestinian communities. Why are Zionists surprised by the Anglican stance?! Because they are so engrossed in their own fears and anxieties that they cannot see the suffering they are inflicting on their Palestinian cousins. Rather than engage in some soul-searching and self-criticism, Zionists have started asking *"Where has this ideology of divestment come from?"* They should be asking *"Why are our friends turning away from us?"* Is it because Zionists are too arrogant to listen to their friends?

Even a leading Israeli architect has called the wall illegal: *"Eyal Weizman, the Israeli director of the Centre for Research Architecture at Goldsmith's College in London, urged action. 'A boycott would be totally legitimate,' he said. 'The wall and the settlements have been deemed illegal by the International Court of Justice and we should boycott any company which does business, any architects that participate – anyone facilitating these human rights violations and war crimes.'"* (*Independent*, London, 25 February 2007.)

The South African Archbishop Tutu has visited Israel and seen at close quarters how Israel treats Palestinians. *"I've been very deeply distressed in my visit to the Holy Land; it reminded me so much of what happened to us black people in South Africa. I have seen the humiliation of the Palestinians at checkpoints and roadblocks, suffering like us when young white police officers prevented us from moving about."* (Desmond Tutu, *Guardian*, Monday April 29, 2002)

I have witnessed and personally experienced this sort of humiliation. You are ordered out of your car. You are addressed in such a tone of voice that says you are inferior, and I am boss. You feel the hatred darting out of the Israeli soldiers' eyes and the disrespect is so tangible you could catch a handful and keep it in a jar. You are told to do things that make no sense and are asked questions that are simply meant to annoy, humiliate and provoke you. Fear of terrorism cannot be cured by building a wall around a community. Terrorism can come from without that wall. What then?! What if such maltreatment led to the radicalization of Muslim Israeli Arabs, who took over the suicide bombing campaign?! What wall would Israel build to prevent such attacks?! Yes, Israel has reduced the number of suicide bombings, but who is to say whether the suffering they have caused in the process is not causing a nascent volcano of reprisals ready to erupt at the first available opportunity?!

If forty-five nations, including Sweden, the Red Cross, seventy members of the American congress and Amnesty International, opined that Israel is violating international laws by incarcerating Palestinians on a small part of Palestinian land, why are the Zionists outraged at the Anglican stance of divestment?! Is it because they have no regard for the feelings and sufferings of their neighbours and cousins, the Palestinians? Or is it because to Zionist thinking, as Ben-Gurion once said, what matters is not what the world thinks of the Jews, but rather what the Jews do?! Or have the Jewish minds come to expect automatic unquestioning support from the West on pain of being branded anti-Semitic?

Not wishing to belittle Jewish suffering, particularly at the hands of the Catholics and Orthodox of Europe, it is my conviction that Zionists have whined so much about the Holocaust that people may stop taking them seriously. The Holocaust has become a trump card they flash too readily whenever they find themselves in a moral dilemma, and

34

whenever the morality of their own action is scrutinized. This both makes a mockery of anti-Semitism and lessens the credibility of such Zionists.

Christian Western nations, and their Evangelicals in particular, have relentlessly supported the Zionist State financially, and buttressed it politically and militarily and have never represented the interests of their Christian brethren, the Arabic-speaking Christians, who have suffered from racial discrimination from the beginning of the church and for the entire duration of the existence of the modern State of Israel. Christian Israeli Arabs watch in amazement as American churches send hundreds of millions of dollars, and the American authorities send tens of billions of dollars to Israel with little and disproportionate consideration for the Christian Israeli Arabs, much less for Arabic-speaking Christians elsewhere in the Middle East.

For the Christian Israeli Arabs, the acceptance of the State of Israel is not the problem. The maltreatment by Jews and the Zionist State is a relatively minor problem. One learns to take Zionist anti-Arab practices in one's stride. The worst problem is the way we have been forgotten by our kith and kin, the Western Churches. Whilst I do not condone Israel's stance towards its Arab citizens, particularly the Christian section of the population, I believe that Israel has little choice in the matter. The die was cast at least a century ago. Once one commits to a Zionist ideal, one must anticipate the bitter consequences that will inevitably ensue. The Zionist ideals inherently lead to discrimination, racism and apartheid against Gentiles, in this case Arab citizens of Israel.

It is no coincidence that the UN reached a resolution that Zionism is racism, though it was repealed under pressure in 1991.

I will show in this book how the Arabs of Israel, and more specifically Arabic-speaking Christians in Israel and the wider Middle East, have suffered a sort of anti-Semitism at the hands of Jews and Western Christians, particularly Americans. This anti-Semitism has consisted of: Denial of the existence of Arabic-speaking Christians, disrespect for their standing, total ignorance of their plight, and turning a deaf ear to their cries for help.

Chapter II

Who Are These Arabic-speaking Christians?

"Although some people think that the term 'Palestinian' implies a person is a Muslim, Palestinian Christians also exist and their ancestry in the Holy Land goes back to the earliest days of Christianity." ("Israel and the Territories – Disappearance, Disappearing Christians of the Middle East", by Daphne Tsimhoni, *Middle East Quarterly*, Winter 2001, pp. 31-34.)

Living in London and working in the kitchen of the London Bible College at the age of eighteen, I was delighted to rub shoulders with theological students from one-hundred countries, whilst living with my British surrogate parents, Rev Owen and Mrs Peggy Thomas. My surrogate parents' deep knowledge of the history of Arabic-speaking Christians stood in sharp contrast to the international students' shallow knowledge, even perhaps ignorance of the subject. What authority do I have to make such a harsh judgement? Personal experience; I was often asked how my parents had reacted to my conversion to Christianity.

I loved accompanying my surrogate father to churches where he preached. He would introduce me as his Arab son, and would enunciate the word Arab slowly and carefully. At the end of these church services, many fellow Christians would come to greet me and again would assume I had been converted from Islam. When some heard that I hailed from Israel, they would assume that I had been converted from Judaism. My surrogate father would smile patiently as if to say: "Give them a chance. They know not what they are saying."

These recurrent questions revealed three mistaken assumptions often made by non-Arab Christians, and non-Christians, worldwide: the first is the erroneous assumption that Arab is synonymous with Muslim. The second assumption, a consequence of the first, is that the only way an Arab can be a Christian is by personal conversion from Islam. The third mistaken assumption is that Israeli is synonymous with Jewish. Clearly the events of the twentieth century in Palestine are not well taught to Christians.

The amazement expressed by international theological students when disabused of these misguided assumptions remains fresh in my memory. It never occurred to them, even to students of church history, that Arabs were amongst the first recipients of Christianity. I was amazed at their amazement, which is a roundabout way of saying that I was amazed at their knowledge deficit, for want of a kinder expression.

Daphne Tsimhoni attests to the antiquity of Christian Palestinians (Israeli Arabs) thus: *"Although some people think that the term 'Palestinian' implies a person is a Muslim, Palestinian Christians also exist and their ancestry in the Holy Land goes back to the earliest days of Christianity."* ("Israel and the Territories – Disappearance, Disappearing Christians of the Middle East", by Daphne Tsimhoni, *Middle East Quarterly* Winter 2001, pp. 31-34.)

The acceptance or otherwise of a minority within a nation, by the majority, depends on numerous factors. Some factors are minority-dependent, some factors are majority dependent, whilst others belong to historical fact and fiction in equal measure. We are talking here about the identity of the Christian Arabic speaking minority in the Middle East, both real identity and perceived identity. The latter is as varied as the observer.

Arabic-speaking Christians are racially Semitic descendants of Eber, cousins to the Jews. Religiously speaking, they have adopted the Christian faith at its inception. They are my people, of whom I am both fond and proud, and for whose suffering I shed tears before God. They are a forgotten remnant, despite their direct connection to the source: Nazareth, Bethlehem Jerusalem, and Pentecost. My aspiration is that this work will induce many international Christians to begin to share my love and compassion for this small member of the body of Christ, and for any non-Christian to become aware of the continuous breach of human rights of a silent minority, simply because their cause has found no voice, or at best, a feeble voice.

Christian Arabs Preceded the Advent of Islam

Pre-Islamic Arab history has largely been recorded by Muslim Arabs, and is often referred to in Arabic as Aljahiliyya (the age of ignorance of God or folly or even stupidity). The concept is based on the idea that Islam is the only true faith, before whose advent the Arab world lay in spiritual darkness. This concept is unjustifiably and unreasonably dismissive of the Christian faith, already adopted by not a few Arab tribes. The Islamic concept of Aljahiliyya has become so dominant and deeply rooted in Arab sub-consciousness that often Arab equals Muslim. To many Muslim Arabs, Arabic-speaking Christians may as well not exist. As far as they are aware, pre-Islamic Arabia consisted of those who worshipped idols, with a handful of Jews and Christians, who are sometimes called infidels, and sometimes "people of the book" depending on which way the wind blew on the day (Tanasokh).

Yet an objective survey of history shows that nothing could be further from the truth. Arabic-speaking Christians were a force for good and a force to be reckoned with from the advent of the Christian faith.

Paul the Apostle, shortly after his conversion, and probably due to the cold reception he was given by Jews and Christians in Palestine, went to Arabia. We are told of this fact in his letter to the Galatians 1:17.

Scholars may argue about where Arabia was. Some say Arabia was synonymous with Sinai. Factually speaking, Sinai was part of Arabia, and not Arabia. But even if he had gone to Sinai, it was clear that he had gone to the Arab world. And even if he had gone into seclusion, extremely unlike Paul who was fired up with missionary zeal, he would have had an impact in Arabia.

Also on the day of Pentecost, Jews from Arabia were present and were converted. They went back to Arabia and as others did elsewhere, we have no reason to disbelieve that they started their own churches in Arabia.

Paul Yule (*Spiegel* online 21.12.2012) confirms that Zafar, in South Yemen, had a church built in 354 AD.

"The first recorded text in the Arabic alphabet was written in 512. It is a trilingual dedication in Greek, Syriac and Arabic found at Zabad in Syria." (arabic-greek-etymology.blogspot.com 20.06.2013.)

Clearly, this predates Islam. Evidence suggests that Arabic writing preceded Islam, which means that the concept of Jahiliyyah is purely religious and has little to do with culture, literacy or education.

In the Acts of the Apostles (6:1-6) we are told that the church appointed seven men to serve as deacons. The seven were chosen because of their piety and wisdom, one of whom was Timon, who is said to have brought the Gospel to Alghassanids, the first Christian Arab Kingdom.

There is a big gap between those early days of the church and the first record of Christian Arab tribes. However, Arab history is rife with evidence that whole tribes were happy and proud to acknowledge Christ. They had abandoned their heathen Arab religions, the worship of idols, and followed Christ. Indeed the positive influence and rich cultural heritage of some of the Christian Arab tribes is attested to by all and sundry, including Muslim scholars. I am referring here to Ghassan, Kinda, Tanukh, Salih, Judham, Camila, Balqayn, Bahraa', Kalb, Bali, Taghlib, 'Iyad, Al-Namir, Tayy, and Cudhra.

It is also widely attested that the first Arabic script was found in Syria (home of the Ghassanids) and dates back to 512 AD, long before Islam. This belies the hollow claim that the period preceding Islam was a period of ignorance. Indeed, if it were not for the pre-Islamic Arabs, most probably Christian Nubians, the Qur'an would have never been written, certainly not in Arabic.

The significance of the Namara inscription is aptly expressed by a fellow Christian Arab historian, Yasmine Zahran, in her excellent work *The Lakhmids of Hira*: *"The Namara inscription in Nabatean Aramaic with the lines in Arabic in Nabatean alphabet is the most ancient Arabic script, and shows the emergence of Arabic in a period of transfer from the long dependency from various dialects of Aramaic (Nabatean and Palmyran) and the spread of North Arabic writing to the detriment of the Himyarite south Arabian script."*

The other significance of this inscription is its portrayal of the extent of Imru's influence: Syria, Iraq and the Arab peninsula. Imru being the first Lakhmid King to have converted to Christianity (Tabari vol 4 p.45), wherever Imru went, so went his faith and Christian practices, which includes his wearing the cross, the Sunday procession to Church and the relationship with church and monastery.

In this regard, it is essential to resort to Muslim tradition for a testimony to how key the Christians were even to Muhammad and the Qur'an. Muhammad is known to have befriended Bahira, who was a Nestorian Christian monk, who lived in Syria, but who had been expelled by his monastery. His Christian name was Sergius or Georgius. He travelled to Mecca on a mission where he became acquainted with Muhammad. It is widely believed that the Qur'anic sections dealing with Christianity were heavily influenced by Bahira.

It is also well known that Muhammad had conversations with a Christian slave called Ibn Qumta. *'A more ancient historian, Wakidi, has the following sentence in which it is suggested that 'Abdallah b. Sa'd b. Abi Sarh, and a Christian slave, ibn Qumta, had something to do with the Qur'an. And ibn Abi Sarh came back and said to Quraish: "It was only a Christian slave who was teaching him (Muhammad); I used to write to him and change whatever I wanted."'* (Alphonso Mingana, "The Transmission of the Qur'an", *The Origins of the Qur'an*, p.103.)

The Hadith confirms this: *"A Christian who converted to Islam wrote Muhammad's revelations; then he reverted back to Christianity and claimed that Muhammad knew nothing and he wrote the Qur'an for Muhammad; when this man died his body was repeatedly thrown out from the grave..."* (4.56.814)

Waraqa, the Cousin of Muhammad's first wife, Khadija, was a Christian. He would have shared his faith with Muhammad. Waraqa apparently translated the Gospel into Arabic.

Sahih Bukhari claims that the Gospel had been translated into Arabic during Muhammad's life. He also writes that Waraqa read the Gospel in Arabic.

Volume 4, Book 55, Number 605:

Narrated 'Aisha:

"The Prophet returned to Khadija while his heart was beating rapidly. She took him to Waraqa bin Naufal who was a Christian convert and used to read the Gospels in Arabic. Waraqa asked [the Prophet], "What do you see?" When he told him, Waraqa said, "That is the same angel whom Allah sent to the Prophet Moses. Should I live till you receive the Divine Message, I will support you strongly."

Volume 6, Book 60, Number 478:

Narrated Aisha:

"... Khadija then took him to Waraqa bin Naufil, the son of Khadija's paternal uncle. Waraqa had been converted to Christianity in the Pre-lslamic Period and used to write Arabic and write of the Gospel in Arabic as much as Allah wished him to write..."

Volume 1, Book 1, Number 3:

Narrated Aisha:

"... Khadija then accompanied him to her cousin Waraqa bin Naufal bin Asad bin 'Abdul 'Uzza, who, during the Pre-Islamic Period became a Christian and used to write the

writing with Hebrew letters. He would write from the Gospel in Hebrew as much as Allah wished him to write…"

Thus we have seen that Muslim tradition strongly attests to the existence and influence of the Gospel in Arabic and to the fact that many Arabs were Christian, before the advent of Islam.

It behoves us then to look at the religion, culture, achievements and influence of these pre-Islamic Christian Arab Tribes.

The Lakhmids

Having ruled Yemen in the second century AD (hence the Lakhmid Kingdom), this was a tribe whose members, also known as Al-Munthirs (Al-Manathirah), Qahtani Arabs, emigrated in 266 AD and settled in Al-Hira (Southern Iraq). Al-Hira had been developed by the Lakhmids to such a degree of beauty that Arab poets likened it to heaven. Indeed scholars believe that the Muslim description of paradise is based on Al-Hira, whose ruins lie a mere 3 km south of Kufa, on the west bank of the river Euphrates.

The son of the founder of the dynasty, Imru' al-Qais, apparently converted to Christianity. His ambition was a unified Arabia, which ambition fuelled his conquests. His tomb in Syria provides evidence that he enjoyed the title of "King of all the Arabs"

Though the Lakhmids shared the Christian faith of Al Ghassanids, they belonged to the diaphysite Nestorian camp who believed that Christ had two separate natures. The Lakhmid Nestorians were renowned for their Evangelistic zeal and sent missionaries to India and Iran. Their confessions were zealous and reflected a deep seated loyalty to the Christian faith.

Though the Sassanids allowed their clients the Lakhmids the freedom to practice their Christian faith, politically, the Lakhmids had to dance to their master's tune, which is what might explain their willingness to fight their Christian Ghassanid neighbours.

In 325 AD, the Lakhmids were attacked by the Sassanids (Persians) upon which Imru' al-Qais sought the protection of the Romans. However, Constantius was unable to help. The Persian victory was final and their treatment of the Lakhmids was cruel and harsh. The Lakhmids became vassals and were given the responsibility of buffering the zone between the Persians and Rome/Byzantium.

The Lakhmids are thought to have been the first to use modern Arab script. It is believed to have been the cradle of the Arabic alphabet. 'Amr ibn Hind (554–569) who was a Christian, was patron of one of the most renowned pre-Islamic Arabic poets known as Ṭarafah, whose poetry forms an essential part of *Al-Mu'allaqāt.*

The Lakhmid Christians of Al-Hira were also known as the Ibad, which is the plural of Abd, an Arabic name meaning servant or slave. This is because of Abd being a popular part of composite Christian names, such as Abd Elmasih (servant of Christ), Abd Yasu' (Servant of Jesus), or Abadallah (servant of God).

Yasmine Zahran, describes the wealth of Hira thus: *"Merchants of the Ibad Chastain Aristocracy built palaces (qusur) like forts, with rich furnishings. They ate from gold and silver plates and slept in beds spread with silk sheets, and had incense, perfumes of musk and amber burning in silver censors. The city achieved a level of luxury not known before in an Arab capital."*

The Lakhmids did not only celebrate their wealth. They also expressed their Christian faith. Zahran continues: *"Nu'man, the last king who rode on Sundays and feast days to a church or a monastery accompanied by the royal family dressed in garments of silk... Preceded by banners with the sign of the cross. After prayer, the king and his court feasted on delicacies and rare wines."*

The Lakhmid Christians of Hira expressed their faith by their traditions, by adopting the name of Christ, by wearing crosses, and also by evangelism. *"The Lakhmids sent missionaries to evangelise the Arabian Gulf and peninsula."* (Rabbath, *L'Orient, p.*147). Christian mission is not an imperial Western invention. It is active obedience of all Christians to the last commission, whereby Christ commanded *"Go ye into all the world, and preach the gospel to every creature"* (Mark 16:15, King James version). The Arabic-speaking Christians of Hira took their Christianity seriously enough to want to share it with their kith and kin.

The Lakhmid Christians excelled in building churches and monasteries, not by sheer number only, as it was the custom of members of the royal family to build churches and monasteries, but also in the unique architecture which reflected central Christian beliefs. The walls of their churches were covered with Kufic Inscriptions (the Kufic script of the Ibad Christians), with painting of leafed crosses. *"The leafed cross was the motif of the Christian art of Hira and spread outside of Iraq."* (Yasmine Zahran, p.71.)

Lakhmid kings, always careful not to incur the displeasure of their Persian paymasters, would conceal their Christianity behind their Christian daughters and wives. Hind, the Christian Kindite princess, wife of the Lakhmid king and mother of Amr Ibn Hind, erected Deir Hind al-Kubra with the following inscription, which is rich with Christian expressions of faith, and which reflects the doctrine of the early Arabic-speaking Christians: *"This church has been erected by Hind, daughter of Harith ibn Amr ibn Hujor, the queen daughter of kings and mother of the king Amr Ibn al-Munthir, the handmaid of Christ and mother of his servitor under the reign of the king of kings. Kisra Anushurwan, in the time of bishop Mar Ephraim. May the Lord for whom she built this monastery pardon her sins; may He have mercy on her and her son; may He receive her into the security of His truth and may the Lord be with her son for ever and ever."* (Trimingham, p.196, Salem, Abd al-Aziz, p.279.)

To name and describe the numerous other monasteries built by the Lakhmids is beyond the scope of this book. Suffice it to add that many of the monasteries and palaces built by the

Christian Lakhmids were loved by the Umayyads and Abbasids who dwelt in them for hundreds of years to come. The palace of Khawarnaq is a case in point.

Hira was also a patron of arts, such as singing. The Hira style of singing became famous and survived into the Umayyad era. Hunayn, a famous Christian singer of the Umayyad period, was famous for his Hira singing style.

Hira was also responsible for developing the Arab script. Men of the tribe of Tayy who came from Boqa, near Hira, based Arabic orthography on the Nabatean alphabet in the fourth century AD. The first Lakhmid to write in the Northern Arabic script was Hamad Ibn Zayd, who was a courtier. Writing was taught to the Lakhmid children in a church in the village of Al-Nuqayra, near Hira. Although we have no evidence yet, and archaeological finds are only a matter of time, of what material these children were taught, most probably, and most credibly, they were taught to write the Scriptures and prayers in Arabic.

By the date of the Namara script (the earliest Arabic script in existence), the alphabet had been developed into the North Arabia joined style. This script eventually reached Hijaz through the tribe of Iyyad, who passed it onto the tribe of Anbar, who took it to Hijaz (Salem Abd Al-Aziz p.268). The tribe of Muhammad, Quraysh tribe, were taught the Hira Arabic script by two of its members, namely Sufyan Ibn Umayya and Abu Qays Ibn Abd Manaf. (Amin, Ahmad, p18)

In 602 Numaan III was defeated by the Sassanids, and the Lakhmids were annexed. Eventually most of them were Islamised at the defeat of Hira, when they surrendered to the Muslim armies of Abu Bakr.

The Lakhmids are known to have also settled in Northern Egypt. Apparently Jamal Abd Elnaser, president of Egypt, comes from the Bani Mur, a branch of Bani Lakhm. His daughter has confirmed that their family comes from Hijaz.

It is also believed that most Druze in Jabal Lebanon are descendants of the Banu Lakhm. The tribe also gave birth to the Abbadid, a ruling family in Andalucía, Abadi, Ubadi and Banu Bahr dynasties in Spain

Alghassanids

These are a number of related Christian Arab tribes, the children of Azd, who originated from South Yemen (Ma'arib). It is believed by some scholars that a damaged dam, causing a flood and loss of life and livelihood, forced some of these Arabic-speaking Christians to migrate north, settling initially in Houran (Syria) under the Sabean King Jafna bin 'Amr (220-265 AD), then expanding their territory to Lebanon, Jordan, Palestine and North of the Arabian peninsula. However, the dam was damaged in 570 AD. Yet other scholars believe the migration began with *Jafna bin Amr* founder of the Ghassanid Kingdom in 220 AD.

They are sometimes referred to as Helenized, or Romanised Arabs. Their first mention occurred in AD 473, when they became Roman Foederati, signed up by their chief Amorkesos to defend the eastern borders of Christendom from the invading Persian armies. Not only were the Ghassanids Christian, but they chose their denomination, initially siding with the Chalcedonians, and eventually in 510 becoming monophysites.

Al-Ghassanids survived Islam and settled mainly in Syria, Lebanon, Jordan and Palestine. Many families from that region are proud descendants of al-Ghassanids. One such family is the Haddad family of which the Shehadehs are a branch.

The term Helenized or Romanized Arabs may put into question the Arab identity of the Ghassanids. This raises the question of what are the pre-requisites of an Arab? Who can call themselves Arabs? What attributes must they confer upon themselves to be entitled to call themselves Arabs?

Generally speaking there are three kinds of Arab tribes:

1. True Arabs which includes the Al Qahtan, from which Alghassanids descended;
2. Arabized Arabs (thought to be the descendants of Ishmael, the Son of Hagar and Abraham);

3. The Destroyed (extinct) Arabs, consisting of tribes that have vanished either through genocide or disease.

Muslims often pride themselves on the claim that their prophet Muhammad is a descendent of Ishmael, the son of Abraham (Ibn Ishak). If that were true, then the Ghassanids are more Arabic than the prophet of Islam himself.

The Battle of Yarmuk in 636, in which the Muslim Arab tribes defeated the weakened Byzantine Empire, is often hailed as the end of the Alghassanids. However, nothing could be further from the truth. Alghassanids continued to practise their Christian faith, and avoided proselytization to Islam by agreeing to pay special taxes. There were some converts to Islam under king Jabalah. However, he soon returned to his Christian faith when he felt he had been unjustly treated by Umar ibn-al-Khattab. He and 30,000 of his followers left Syria and settled on the Byzantine borders. One of their most famous sons is Nikephoros, who established the Nikophoros Byzantine dynasty which ruled the Byzantine Empire from 802 AD to 813 AD.

Nikophoros was the first Byzantine Emperor to refuse to pay tax to the Caliph of Baghdad, though he was eventually forced to do so. He also defended Anatolia (where other Ghassanids had settled) and the Balkans.

The Son of Jabala, king al-Harith ibn Jabalah (529-569 AD) supported the Byzantines against Sassanid Persia and was given the title "Basileus" (Augustus or 'Imperial Majesty') and 'Patricius' (Noble of the Byzantine Empire) in 529 by the emperor Justinian I.

The Byzantine Empire relied on Alghassanids to defend its eastern borders. Were it not for the valour of Alghassanids, Byzantium would not have survived as long as it did, and the Christian faith would have vanished from parts of the Middle East and Eastern Europe at least.

The Christian values and practices of the Ghassanids are attested to in the poetry of Hassan, one of the most prominent poets of pre-Islamic Arabs. In one of his eulogies of Jabala, the last Ghassanid king, he says: *"Easter draws near – the maids are preparing the feast. Prayers to Christ rise in that monastery with the incantations of monks and priests.... Their shoes are soft. They salute with hands full of basil on Palm Sunday."*

Writing of his king and master, Jabala, whom he calls Lord and King of Bilad al-Sham (modern Syria), he continued *" He did not forget me as a Christian with the Rum."* (*Ghassan Resurrected*, Yasmine Zahran, p.15.)

The Ghassanids' love for life and poetry attracted many a poet. Amongst them was the Christian poet al-Nabigha, whose full name was al-Nabighah al-Dhubyani, real name Ziyad ibn Muawiyah (c. 535 – c. 604), one of the last and finest poets of the pre-Islamic era. His genius as a poet is permanently etched in his name, his name literally meaning genius. He will always be remembered as one of the poets of al-Muallakat, the odes hung on the walls of Ka'ba in Mecca, in pre-Islamic Arabia.

Al-Nabigha's poetry reflects knowledge of figures of the Old Testament, such as David and Solomon. He also describes the Christian practices of the Ghassanids, such as his reference to the cross of Zawra. (*First Encyclopaedia of Islam*: 1913-1936 p.805.)

The Ghassanids made pilgrimages regularly to various shrines, the commonest amongst them were the Tomb of St Sergius and that of St John the Baptist in Jawlan. (Dauphin C 1998 Vol. 1 p.272.)

The Lakhmids, who also came from South Yemen, occupied Mesopotamia and allied themselves with the Persians, whilst al-Ghassanids allied themselves with the Byzantines. Though the two tribes were united by their Christian faith, they were divided by the unfortunate Monophysite controversy of the Chaldean Council.

The Ghassanids were renowned for their love of monastery building and have built numerous monasteries around their capital city, Houran. Some of these monasteries were later converted to alternative use by the Muslims, though some have survived as monasteries to the present time. The monastery built by Mundir in Himayr was later converted by the Umayyads to a palace.

History records in detail the contributions the Ghassanids have made to the Arab world, and even to Islam. However, before we launch into this interesting line of discovery, and in view of the title of this book, it is worth noting that early Greek and Roman scholars referred to Arabs in derogatory terms. Arabs were often referred to as Saracens or Bedouins. Indeed, many scholars claimed that Arabs were pastoral and unsettled. Yet the famous Arab poet Hassan, in his detailed descriptions, shows that the Ghassanids were anything but pastoral. The history of the Ghassanids belies these unflattering descriptions.

Nihayat Al Arab, a work prepared for the Caliph Harun Al-Rashid, includes a description of Ghassanid culture and tradition. It includes a description of a Ghassanid wedding at Antioch, studded with revelatory jewels for any earnest enquirer into Ghassanid life.

I will summarise the salient features of the wedding based on Irfan Shahid's excellent work:

1. The bridesmaid's name was Dhalfa, which is a feminine Arabic word for one with a beautiful nose. The Ghassanids were Arabs who therefore had traditional meaningful Arabic names.
2. She was the sister of the bride, a tradition that has survived to date.
3. The Ghassanids, like most Arabs, believed in endogamy. In this wedding, the bride and groom were cousins.
4. This tradition has survived to date. Many of my cousins are intermarried. Indeed nephews and nieces have intermarried.
5. It is hard to imagine an Arab wedding without dancing. The Ghassanids were no different.
6. The use of "Al-Daff" (a tambourine) in Ghassanid weddings survives to-date in the Levant.

An account by the Arab poet Hassan of Qiyan dancing for King Jabala shows the King's conduct to be absent of any vulgarity or obscenity, as one would expect from a Christian. This is in keeping with other accounts of Ghassanid chastity and decency. (Diwan al-Nabighaal-Dubyani) (Irfan Shahid p. 125).

The Ghassanids built palaces, lived in luxurious accommodation, enjoyed beautiful gardens, and had developed water technology beyond any of their contemporary Arab tribes. Their technological and architectural superiority was known to all Arabs, so much so that the Qur'anic description of paradise may have been a description of a Ghassanid banquet. Irfan Shahid quotes from Hassan's description of a Ghassanid banquet and compares it with the Qur'an's description of paradise. The similarities are uncanny, from the reference to the throne (sarir) to the types of fruit and drink served at Ghassanid banquets and the use of green silk. This is hardly surprising given the close trading relationships between the Meccans and the Ghassanids.

The Ghassanids did not only build palaces for themselves to inhabit, but they also signalled their Christian faith by building churches and monasteries all over Syria, Lebanon, Jordan and Palestine.

Arthur Voobus (Irfan Shahid p. 291) demonstrates the use of monasteries by the Arab Byzantine Foederati as centres of education, teaching children and adults to read and write, transcribing and translating ancient works, all this occurring before the rise of Islam. The main language was Syriac, from which Arabic script derived, the Ghassanids playing a significant role in its development.

The most ancient Arabic inscription in existence is the Namara inscription (the epitaph of Imru al-Qays), dating back to 328 AD. It was written in Nabatean script. Arabic inscriptions of the 5th century AD are attributed to another Christian Arab tribe, the Salihids, who also had settled in Syria.

The Ghassanids of the 5th century AD played an important role in the development of the Arabic script, well before the rise of Islam. Their contribution is illustrated by two extant inscriptions, the Usays inscription of 529 written by a

Ghassanid military commander (Ibn al-Mughira). The second inscription was written by a Ghassanid phylarch, a carving in a church in Harran, a dedication to St John. The spread of monasteries and monasticism allied with a flourishing Ghassanid kingdom would have been a perfect impetus for the advance of Arabic as a language with its own script.

Whilst Islam can take credit for developing Arabic calligraphy, it was Christians who first introduced the Arabic script and calligraphy. The destruction of Arabic churches and monasteries since the advent of Islam, as well as the restriction by modern Islamic regimes on archaeological exploration, leave us wondering about the extent of such development preceding Islam. I say wondering not because we are completely bereft of evidence. Indeed the church of St George on Mount Nebo, Madaba, Jordan, contains a Mosaic dating back to 536 AD, which contains the Arabic word "bisalam" (in peace). Prior to the Ghassanids, Madaba was ruled by another Christian tribe, the Salihids, who also built monasteries.

To those who may wish to attribute the "bi-salam" script to the Nabataeans, it should be recalled that they mainly wrote in Syriac or Aramaic. The Ghassanid ownership of "bi-salam" is supported by the discovery of the mosaics of the church of St Sergius in Nitil near Madaba. Besides, the Nabateans were eventually governed by the Ghassanids with whom they shared the same origin. The two tribes mixed congenially as described in the Petra Papyrus

The idea that Arabic calligraphy was widespread in Ghassanid times should not be difficult to believe as the Ghassanids had close fellowship with their Greek and Roman Christian brothers, who were renowned for their religious art and calligraphy.

An examination by Hikmat Kashouh of almost 200 Arabic Gospel Manuscripts dating back to the 9th century AD concludes that, judging by the language used, some of these manuscripts originated before Islam. The use of pre-Islamic words such as" Arbaa", instead of "Talameeth" (post-Islamic) to refer to the Disciples of Christ supports this conclusion. The name form of Elijah in some of these manuscripts predates Islam.

Bausmark argues for three characteristics of some of Arabic Gospel Manuscripts, which places their origin prior to the advent of Islam.

These are namely:

1. The liturgical marks and signs used in these AGMs are identical to those used in the Jerusalem church in the sixth century AD before the rise of Islam.
2. The mission of the church to Arabia had preceded Islam by a long time. Al-Hira for one was a centre of culture and learning. It is inconceivable that the most important manuscripts in Christendom were not translated into Arabic for the local population's usage.
3. Biblical citation in Muslim writings: Ibn Ishaq quoted the scriptures in Arabic, as did al-Tabari and Ibn Qutayba. It is conceivable that they translated these quotations from a Syriac source. But it is not inconceivable that they quoted directly from an Arabic version which pre-dated Islam.

The Arabic language as a whole and the Ghassanid's influence on the language, poetry being its main aspect, did wonders for Arabic. Poetry flourished under the Ghassanids. Poetry was their preferred vehicle of communication, celebration, mourning, reporting and a record of their history.

Amr Ibn Kulthum is one of the poets whose poetry was honoured by all early Arabs in al "Mu'allakat". His poetry, along with six others, was hung or suspended on the Kaabah, which is now the most holy place for Islam. The Ghassanids introduced the concept of the poet laureate, as they built palaces and gardens where poetry was recited almost like a religious rite. The poet laureates of the Ghassanids reflect the Christian character of the tribe. Hassan often referred to the monasteries and churches in his poetry.

The ninth century author, Al-Jahiz made extensive reference to the Christian poetry of the Ghassanids. Hassan refers to "salawat Al Masih" (the prayers of Christ)". Key words such as qissis, deir and "rubban" appear meaning priest, monastery and monks. Al-Nabigha in his poetic work known as Ba'iyya, speaks of the Ghassanids thus:

"Their home the Holy Land; their faith upright
They keep the Feast of Palms, when maidens pale."

It is inconceivable that the Ghassanids, who built hundreds of monasteries and churches and fostered Arabic poetry, did not have Arabic hymns and liturgy, especially knowing that they had contributed to the development of the Arabic script.

One advantage of a desert homeland is that it hides secrets for hundreds and thousands of years. We know of promising archaeological finds that may provide new evidence of Arabic liturgy and Scriptures preceding Islam. In the 1990s remains of a Christian monastery were found on the island of Sir Bani Yas. *"Academically, it's fascinating and really important,"* *said Peter Hellyer, the excavation's project manager and a* *columnist for The National. "It explains a lot more about the* *heritage of this country. Most people wouldn't know that* *history, that there was Christianity here before Islam."* (The National 12.12.2010.)

The discovery of the Jubail Church in Saudi Arabia is another reminder of the spread of Christianity in the Arab peninsula long before Islam. The church was found in the region of Najran, once populated by two prominent Christian tribes, namely Banu Taghlib and Tamim. The church dates back to the 4th century AD. It was discovered in 1986 and has typical Christian symbols such as the cross. The Saudi Arabian authorities have banned further excavations under the guise that Islam prevents imagery, and Christian churches were known to include images in worship.

"They should be left in the ground," said Sheikh Mohammed al-Nujaimi, a well-known cleric, reflecting the views of many religious leaders. *"Any ruins belonging to non-Muslims should not be touched. Leave them in place, the way they have been for thousands of years."*

In an interview, he said Christians and Jews might claim discoveries of relics, and that Muslims would be angered if ancient symbols of other religions went on show. *"How can crosses be displayed when Islam doesn't recognize that Christ was crucified?"* (Donna Abu Nasr, Associated Press Writer.)

The above should not come as a surprise. It reflects the usual prevailing negative attitudes in Muslim countries towards Christianity. Sheikh Abdul-Aziz ibn Abdullah, the Grand Mufti of Saudi Arabia, when asked by his Kuwaiti guests what they should do about churches in Kuwait, he apparently responded, *"There should be no Christian churches on the Arabian Peninsula"* (*Charisma News* "Saudi Arabia Declares Destruction of All Churches in Region", 12:30PM EDT 4/1/2013). Such a stance is completely predictable, depicting total open uncompromising hostility by Muslim leaders towards Christians. In March 2012 he had already announced that in his opinion, it is necessary to destroy all the churches in the Arab peninsula.

Is this a genuine reason for preventing further excavations, or is it an excuse? If it were a genuine reason, one would have to assume that symbols are forbidden and evaded in Islam. Is that the case? What about the crescent, one of the most powerful symbols of Islam, which graces many a mosque dome, and many an Islamic country's flag. Not only does the ubiquitous presence of the crescent in Muslim lands belie the claim that Islam does not encourage the use of symbols, it begs the question of why the moon was chosen as a symbol.

Some Christians, in their eagerness to confute Muslims, falsely claim that the crescent in modern-day Islam comes from the pre-Islamic Arabic worship of the moon. However, this is historically untrue and is tantamount either to ignorance or cheap point-scoring which serves no cause.

To be fair to Muslims, the crescent became a symbol of Islam under the Ottomans, several hundred years after the advent of Islam, who apparently adopted it from the Byzantines. However, it would be ludicrous to blame the Byzantines for such a breech in Islamic standards. The Byzantines neither had the power nor the inclination to force

Muslims to adopt the crescent. Indeed, many ancient cultures used the crescent as a symbol, not least the pre-Islamic Arabs who were worshippers of idols. One of the Gods Arabs had worshipped was the God of the moon. This may explain why the Qur'an says: *"Do not worship the sun or the moon, but worship Allah who created them."* (Qur'an 41:37.)

Once more, I must take issue with Christians who are too eager to score cheap points against Muslims, who claim that because the Moon was referred to as Allah, that Muslims worship the Moon. The fact is that the word Allah is a Semitic word meaning deity. It is a generic term which even Christian Arabs use to refer to the God of the Bible. That said, I wish to reiterate the dichotomy and inconsistency of the Saudi authorities' position, who have barred further excavations of ancient Christian archaeological sites in their country under the pretext of Islam forbidding the use of images in worship, when they are happy to widely adopt the crescent as a symbol of their Muslin faith. This smacks of thinly disguised phobia of Christians.

And what of the holy relics of Islam? These consist of Muhammad's mantle, a piece of his tooth, his holy banner, Muhammad's footprint and the swords of his companions. These Islamic sacred relics (Turkish: *Kutsal emanetler*), are kept in Topkapı Palace in Istanbul, and venerated by Muslims.

Spiegel International (Matthias Schulz, December 21, 2012) carried a piece about a German archaeologist, Yule of Heidelberg, discovering a statue in Zafar, Yemen, representing a Christian king/priest. The settlement in that region must have resulted from a Christian Ethiopian invasion of Yemen in 524 and Zafar must have become home to approximately 25,000. However, there had already been a Christian community in Zafar, as there is evidence of a church being built there in 324 AD. The city was multi-faith with also some Jews resident in the oasis. The increased threat from Western Christians caused many heathen Arabs to convert to Judaism.

Matthias Schulz notes that mention was made, by the Arab historian Asraki, of a Christian cemetery in Mecca preceding Islam.

The prevention of further excavations of Christian archaeological sites in the Muslim world rests upon one thing, and one thing only. Islam has an official stance towards building and renovating churches well rooted in the Conditions of Omar. Many fatwas have been issued on the subject, leading to specific demolitions of churches. Many excuses are given in Egypt by planning authorities to prevent the building of new churches, whilst the destruction of Churches by Muslims is rarely punished.

The reason is exemplified in this work by Sheikh Ismail bin Muhammad al-Ansari in his authoritative work "Ruling on building churches in Muslim countries" in 1979. The grand Mufti of Saudi Arabia gave the following resumé of the book: *"... in it the author documents all mention concerning churches, monasteries and other places of idolatrous worship as found in the prophetic hadith and other books and the words of the ulema of the four schools of law..."*

If the reader were to visit the archaeological find on the internet, he or she will find the cross is the only extant image on the site. So if Muslim opposition to further excavation on the ground of repugnance by images in worship, the cross is the object of that repugnance. This is in keeping with Muhammad himself, who apparently had such distaste for the cross that he would break any object that was brought to him bearing the cross. (Sahih al Bukhari – *The book of the Stories of the Prophets*, 40:60:3448.)

Khalid bin Al-Walid, the vanquisher of Byzantium, the so called "Sword of Allah", was also known for his repugnance of the cross. He was renowned in battle for giving Christians the choice of surrendering and breaking their crosses, or dying in battle. Was his repugnance for the cross based on any theological ground? If so, why did he like alcohol so much that not only did he get drunk habitually, but also was known to bathe in wine. Is that not forbidden by Allah?!

Banu Taghlib

These were a large powerful Christian Arab tribe of Mesopotamia and eastern Arabia. They are thought to be descendants of the Adnanite Arabs (Arabized Arabs; this distinction is not supported by any reliable evidence).

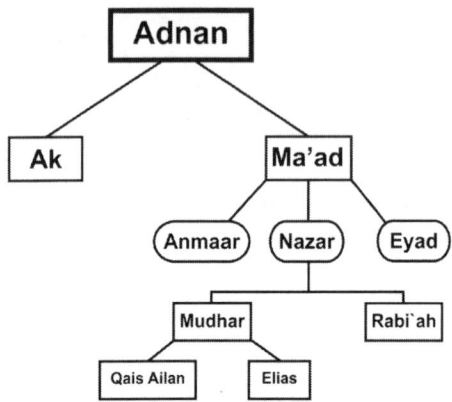

The largely Christian tribe moved from Nejd in Central Arabia to Mesopotamia in the 6th century, as a result of a 40 year war (War of Basous) with their Adnanite cousins, Banu Bakr.

The Taghlib tribe produced two renowned Poets, Amr ibn Kulthum Ibn Malik Ibn A'tab Abu Al-Aswad al-Taghlibi, one of whose odes was hung on the walls of Ka'aba in Mecca, in recognition of its superior quality. Al-Akhtal was another renowned Christian Arab poet from Taghlib.

Taghlib was one of the most powerful Arab tribes of the pre-Islamic period, originating from the line of Adnan, son of Ishmael, son of Abraham and Hagar. It was said of them that *"had Islam come a little later, the Banu Taghlib would have swallowed up all mankind"* (Lammens, Chantre p.79; mo'awiya p.398, Omayyades p.267).

They are one of the four branches of Kindah, who eventually settled in Mesopotamia and eastern Arabia. More significantly, they were mostly Christian under the Patriarchy of Antioch, the first town where the followers of Jesus of Nazareth were called Christian.

One of their kings was called Abd El-Maseeh, meaning servant of Christ, a common name amongst Christian Arabs. The last Taghlibi Bishop listed in church records was appointed in the 10th century AD.

It is known that their patron saint was Sergius, and that they made pilgrimage to his place of burial at Al-Rusafa. They went to war under St Sergius' banner, which drew contempt from other Arab tribes (Lammens, Omayyades p.214, 217, 239-242; Moawia, p.435; Musil, Palmyrena, p.267, 269; Cheikho al-Nasraniya p.99).

Taghlib resisted conversion to Islam, and due to their magnitude and wealth, which comes from the various trade routes that traversed their territory, they managed to persuade Mohammad that they need not convert to Islam, as long as they paid a fee and refrained from baptising their children.

The fee Taghlib negotiated was not the usual Jizya. They were too important to be humiliated in that way, as Jizya means punishment, which in effect is "protection money". Instead, they agreed to pay Sadakah (Alms), which more aptly befitted their lofty estate.

They continued to baptize their children despite the agreement with Muhammad and subsequently Omar. In the days of Ali, there were calls for their decimation because of their on-going practice of baptising their children (Baladhurt, p.183).

Taghlib's relationship with Muslims was typified by the poet laureate Al-Akhtal having secured Hurmah from the Caliphs. He was known by his adherence to his Christian tradition, particularly wearing a chain round his neck, bearing a golden cross.

Al-Akhtal was a widely respected classical poet, well versed in classical poetry. He endeared himself to Muawiyah, and his Son Yazid. He fell out with Walid, but found favour with his successor. Of note is Muawiyah's wife, Maysun, who was a devout Christian, whose son Yazid, renowned for his close relationship with Al-Akhtal, also married a Christian

Ghassanid, Umm Ramla. The Caliphs employed many Christians in high offices, and dwelt in Palaces built by Christians, especially the Ghassanids.

The Christian tribe produced many renowned poets other than Al-Akhtal. One of his predecessors was Amr Ibn Kulthum (died 584), who is the author of one of the seven hung poems, which were hung on the walls of al-Ka'aba, in pre-Islamic times.

Taghlib were on good terms with the Lakhmids, another Christian Arab tribe, until Amr Ibn Kulthum killed their king, Amr Ibn Hind.

Taghlib's last mention as an entity occurred in the 14th century AD. Notwithstanding, two tribes, namely Shammar and Dawasir, claim descent from Taghlib (Fuad Hamza, Kalb Djazirat Al Arab Mecca 1352 p.150)

The previous few pages can be neatly summarised by the words of The Oxford Islamicist, Bishop Kenneth Cragg, who in *The Arab Christian, A History in The Middle East*, wrote: *"Arabism is so deeply involved in being Muslim, for reasons inherent in Islamic history, that it is thought to belong exclusively to the faith and culture. Yet 'Christian' was a descriptive of Arabs centuries before Islam...."*

Arab Nationalism and Arabic-speaking Christians

So Arabic-speaking Christians have every right to be considered Arabs. But do they have a sense of nationhood, a feeling of oneness with Muslim Arabs?

There comes a point in a nation's history where, whether through oppression or pride, a moment of awakening tolls, and people with a shared identity arise and build a homeland, where they can celebrate their own culture, write their own poetry, speak their own language, wear their own national costumes and eat their own food. These are the components of an identity.

What about religion? Should it be part of a people's identity? I believe religion is central to human affairs, and it should only be a component of a nation's identity if it is shared by all the people of the nation.

What about, blood? As a student of history, I have become gradually more sceptical about blood as a component of nationhood. There is not a single nation on earth who can rightly claim genetic purity. And if there is such a nation, it is only a matter of time before that claim's validity is shot to smithereens. People travel, fight, trade, invade, exchange, and in the process genes mix and we are all changed. We are changed by intermarriage, by exchanges of ideas and beliefs, and even by exchange of material goods.

In the last section we surveyed the affairs of Arabic-speaking Christians up to the time of the crusaders. In the ensuing centuries Arabic-speaking Christians had a varied existence, alternating between persecution and prosperity. At times they were elevated, and at others they were brought down. There were times when they were embraced by the Muslim majority, yet there were times when they were rejected and banished.

What fuelled Arab nationalism? Shockwaves of the French revolution and the American civil war reverberated throughout the world. The church was an important vehicle of learning and intellectual exchange in the Middle East. Christian Arab families sent their children, as did some Muslim families, to church schools, and often to European universities, where they were exposed to Western philosophy either directly or through literature. The weakening Ottoman Empire was less feared by the ruled Arabs than it had been previously. Demanding independence from the sick man of Europe was no longer a fearful prospect.

One nadir in the history of Arabic-speaking Christians under the Ottomans was the massacre of Christians in Lebanon, by the Druze, with the tacit support of the Muslim Ottomans, to be shortly followed by the Damascus Massacre of Arabic-speaking Christians in 1860, by their Muslim brothers. I quote from an original report by *The Banner of Liberty newspaper*, Middletown, NY, August 22, 1860:

"Hearing how the Government had everywhere not only sided against their co-religionists, but how it had everywhere in Lebanon actually helped to betray, if not really to murder them, the Christians of Damascus were from the very outset downhearted and frightened, as well they might be, when threatened from day to day that the Muslims would rise and exterminate them."

Just as evil words are the bitter fruit of evil thoughts, so are evil actions the bitter fruit of evil words. What ensued were actions that graduated from insult of religious sensibility to sacrilege and bloodshed:

"Matters got worse and worse, the one party becoming daily more frightened, the other hourly more insolent, until at last, on Sunday the 8th July, when the Christians came out of their various churches, a mob of Muslim lads were busy in the streets, making crosses in chalk on the ground, and then stamping and spitting on the sacred emblem. But so utterly downhearted were the Christians, that they did not even complain to the authorities of this wanton insult. On the contrary, all they did was to confine themselves still more strictly within their houses for the rest of the day....

"At two. p.m., three hundred of the lowest Muslims of Damascus, rushed armed, into the Christian quarter, crying 'Slay the dogs of Christianity' and immediately the work of plunder, burning and murder commenced. Achmet Pacha, Governor General and Commander-in-Chief of the place and field marshal in the Sultan's army, was at once informed of what had taken place. But, although he had at his disposal some eight hundred regular troops, and several field pieces, not a man nor a gun did he move. He never showed himself in the streets, nor took any steps whatever to stop the massacre...."

An account by the New York Times states that the marauding Muslims were confident that the soldiers would not interfere. They carried out their aggression, killing and looting, without any intervention, whilst their women were spurring them on to do more violence to the Christians of Damascus. The reporter stated: *"I believe firmly that 100, or at most 200 soldiers, or armed resolute men, not soldiers, could have put down the insurrection at the worst moment."* (*New York Times*, "The Syrian Outbreak.; details of the Damascus massacre. foreign intervention in Syria." Published: August 13, 1860.)

What of Arab nationalism in 1860? The entire Arab population of the Middle East had been ruled by the non-Arab Ottomans, Mongols from the East, who espoused the Muslim faith. Both Muslim and Arabic-speaking Christians were ruled by the despotic Ottomans for hundreds of years. Arabic-speaking Christians, like other minorities in the Ottoman Empire, were given a degree of autonomy under the Millet system. Millets were religious minorities endowed with the right to conduct their affairs with a degree of independence, such as having their own religious courts. However, as Non-Muslim, Millets were underprivileged and denied certain rights. Some Millets were expected to pay Jizya, a form of protection tax, but all Millets were generally considered to be second class Ottoman citizens (Barkey, Kristen (of Columbia University). Islam and Toleration: Studying the Ottoman Imperial Model. 27 Aug. 2008).

The Muslims may have fared better under the Ottomans because of their shared faith, but not much better. Whilst the Ottomans had adopted the faith of the majority of Arabs, and even the Arabic script and, in part, language, by the early 20th Century, their disdain for Arabs as inferior subjects had reached such a peak that they wanted to do away with the Arabic Alphabet. On 1 November 1928 Kemal Ataturk, widely believed to be Jewish, introduced the new Turkish alphabet and abolished the use of Arabic script.

What national awakening was there amongst the Arabs in the Middle East, and who was at the vanguard of that awakening? Here we have Muslim Ottomans despotically ruling and exploiting Muslim Arabs. Who were the early soldiers and pioneers of Arab Nationalism? History shows it to be mainly the Arabic-speaking Christians.

Nowhere was this more obvious than in Palestine, Egypt and Syria. Al Nahdah, the awakening, was spearheaded by Arabic-speaking Christians who invested in literature, the media and theatre. *"The Secretary of Saal founder of the Journal of Law and George Michael Knight founder of an Egyptian newspaper in 1888 and Alexander Shalhoub founder of the Journal of the Sultanate in 1897 and Selim Takla and his brother Bishara Takla founding Al-Ahram newspaper, and in the jurisprudence of the Arabic language The Abraham Yazigi Yazigi and Nassif and Peter Gardener"* (*History of the Eastern Churches*, p.111).

What marks these Christian Arab pioneers as unique is their inclusiveness. Many proposed that social Islam should be used as the nidus for the birth of the new Arab nation. Confessionalism, using faith to define nationhood, was not a hundred miles away from such a proposal. However, Arabic-speaking Christians have learnt to compromise in order to survive. Nationalist philosophies of these Arabic-speaking Christians were no different in their types from their European counterparts. This includes Nazi philosophy, partly espoused by the Lebanese Christian Sa'adeh.

However, others proposed secularist nationalism in order to eschew the complications of religious sentiment.

In 1918, King Faysal, himself a descendant of the prophet Muhammad, avoided the complications of a confessional Arab nationalism by stating:

"The Arabs were Arabs before Moses, Christ and Muhammad," and even that Muhammad was *"an Arab before being a prophet."* (Dawisha, Adeed. *Arab Nationalism in the Twentieth Century: From Triumph to Despair*, Princeton, NJ: Princeton University, 2003. p42). He went further and recruited many a Christian Arab into his regime.

In Palestine, the birthplace of my parents, the British Mandate, it seems, had assumed that faith played an important part of Arab identity. *"The British Government developed organisational and political structures based on the assumption that religion was the primary element of Arab identification,"* writes Noah Haiduc-Dale in his *Arab Christians In British Mandate Palestine* (Edinburgh University Press p.3). He spends a lot of time claiming that this was a mistaken view. He takes issue with Daphne Tsimhoni, who, he says, *"maintains the primacy of religious identification."*

Perhaps neither he nor the British Mandate authorities were wrong. The role of religion in national identity in the Middle East is a matter of degree. However, to deny that religion has always played a role in Arab identity would be too dismissive. Scholarly evidence aside, I have spent years listening to my elders about Muslim Arab relationships under the Ottomans and the British. Religious sentiment always simmers under the surface.

Tsimhoni was correct in depicting an alternating ebb and flow of fortune for the Arabic-speaking Christians. She states that Palestinian Christians *"accepted their marginal and secondary position to which they were doomed as a religious minority group"* (*The British Mandate*, p.338). This is a fairly accurate and timeless depiction of the lot of Arabic-speaking Christians living in a Muslim Middle East.

For Arabic-speaking Christians to survive in the shadow of a Muslim majority in the Middle East, has been akin to living in the vicinity of a volcano which erupts every now and again. These eruptions may last for a long time, during which Christians have had to lie low and simply survive in the hope of better times to come. When the volcano has lain dormant, Christians have flourished and felt free to express themselves fully, both as Arabs and as Christians.

Notwithstanding, during the British Mandate, Palestine did not witness the same degree of religious intolerance as had been witnessed elsewhere in the Middle East, and therefore initially did not play a major role in Arab Nationalism. Indeed, Muslim Arab nationalists such as Rashid Khalidi and Muhammad Muslih promoted secular nationalism, despite leading Christian Arab nationalists proposing that Muslims should be guaranteed leadership, perhaps due to their majority status. Besides, a voluntary minority status is better worn than an imposed one.

If Arabic-speaking Christians had any confidence in their ability to lead and contribute to the growth of Arab

Nationalism, it was to some extent due not just to tolerance by their Muslim Arab brethren, but also to the intervention of Christian European nations through their ambassadors in Istanbul. Arab Nationalism in Palestine was partly fuelled by the rising influx of Jews who were acquiring a large amount of land and building new communities. Although this financially benefitted the indigenous Arab population, and provided work and facilities, and although it caused an influx of Arabs from Syria and other neighbouring countries, it was viewed as a foreign invasion none-the-less.

In Palestine, for better or for worse, the British Mandate sought to work with Mufti Haj Amin Husseini, who came from a family of Muftis, a wealthy Muslim family from Jerusalem. He was appointed in 1921, against the wishes of the majority of Muslims in Palestine. The significance of Husseini goes beyond his interesting persona. His appearance on the scene of Arab nationalism marks the beginning of the end to the mutual co-operation between Christian and Muslim Arabs. His appointment as grand Mufti of Jerusalem constituted the first step in the Islamisation of Arab nationalism and the concomitant marginalisation of Christians.

The choice of Husseini was somewhat mysterious, as not only did he rank fourth in the vote, but he was a Muslim fundamentalist whose aim was to revive a Muslim super state. He preached intense hatred of anything non-Muslim. He naturally made the right noises to appease Christians, particularly the British. His appointment was made all the more surprising by the Jewish background of Sir Herbert Samuel as Palestine High Commissioner. Sir Herbert Samuel arrived in Palestine on July 1, 1920, and he may have felt compelled to appoint Husseini in order to forestall any accusations of bias towards his fellow Jews.

Predictably, Husseini proved to be a thorn in the flesh of the British Mandate as he organised three revolts against the British Mandate and had to flee Palestine. Husseini did not spare his fellow Muslims, especially those who did not share his type of firebrand Islam, and pursued them without mercy.

In 1922 Amin Al-Husseini was appointed Head of the Supreme Muslim Council, a position he held until 1937. One of his first acts was to restore the Dome of the Dome of the Rock Mosque in 1922, and have the dome gilded for the first time ever. In 1928 Husseini joined the Muslim Brotherhood in Egypt and became a central figure in the organisation. The organisation promoted the Wahhabi creed, which is a creed of violence against non-Muslims. In 1931 he founded the World Islamic Congress.

It is obvious that Husseini was gradually becoming more of a Muslim activist than an Arab nationalist. By his allegiances, actions and utterances, he managed to alienate and marginalise the Arabic-speaking Christians. At best he created a crisis of identity for Arabic-speaking Christians, especially the practicing Arabic-speaking Christians as opposed to nominal Arabic-speaking Christians. Husseini's conduct and Islamic activities made Arabic-speaking Christians question their own belonging to the nationalist movement.

In 1936 Husseini organised suicide bombings and preached extermination of anyone opposing his pan-Islamic ideology. He ensured the murder of several powerful "opponents" from all three communities – Muslim, Christian and Jewish.

Husseini's hatred of Jewish ingress into Palestine led him to espouse Nazism. In 1937 he met with the German Consul in Jerusalem, amongst other key players, and received funds and support for his idea of a Pan-Arab state and the removal of Jews from Palestine. In 1942 Husseini met Mussolini, who also promised to support his idea of resistance to Jewish influx into Palestine. He also issued a Fatwa against the British.

He met Hitler personally in 1941 and expressed zeal for the final solution, presumably in order to reduce the number of European Jews entering Palestine. Husseini's involvement with the Nazis developed further. In 1942, he ensured the annihilation of Jews in Bosnia. He called himself the protector of Islam, and outlawed the Cyrillic Christian alphabet. These activities have little to do with Arab nationalism, but all to do with Islamic fundamentalism. He further proposed the Pejani

Plan, which involved the extermination of Serbians in Bosnia. Fortunately this was not approved by the Nazis.

Husseini, still in exile, remained active in Bosnia. In addition to ensuring the death of hundreds of thousands of Christians and Jews, he formed the Hanzar unit (meaning dagger in Arabic) which consisted of 24,000 Muslim Bosnian soldiers, who had sworn allegiance to Hitler and the Nazi cause. Husseini proudly called them "the cream of Islam". In 1943, as a reward for his support of the Nazi regime, the latter entitled Husseini "Prime Minister of the Pan Arab Government".

Having much earlier in his Nazi career visited Auschwitz, he later met Himmler, with whom he struck up a friendship. He was also introduced to the Nazi's Swiss banker, who financed many of Husseini's activities, including the opening of the Islamic Centre in Dresden. On March 1st 1944 Husseini addressed the Bosnian Muslim troops from Berlin, and instructed them to: *"Kill the Jews wherever you find them. This pleases God, history and religion. This saves your honour. God is with you."* Whilst no man should condone the dishonest acquisition of land in Palestine, Arabic-speaking Christians cannot identify with such brutality as was preached by Husseini.

In 1944, Husseini became the cofounder of the Arab league. As his influence in the Arab/Muslim world increased, the British allowed him amnesty and he returned to Palestine in 1946.

Not surprisingly, Rahman Abdul Rauf al-Qudwa al-Husseini, otherwise known as Yasser Arafat, head of the PLO, was a nephew and great admirer of Uncle Haj Amin al-Husseini. Blood was not the only link between the two men. Arafat was quoted as saying: *"We are not Afghanistan... We are the Mighty People. Were they able to replace our hero Hajj Amin al-Husseini?... There were a number of attempts to get rid of Hajj Amin, whom they considered an ally of the Nazis. But even so, he lived in Cairo, and participated in the 1948 war, and I was one of his troops."* (*Al Sharq al Awsat*, a

London Arabic daily, reprinted in the Palestinian daily *Al Quds*, Aug, 2, 2002.)

To his credit, Yasser Arafat was not a Muslim fundamentalist like Husseini. He actually married a Christian Palestinian, and ensured the participation of Christians in the political echelons of Ramallah. However, by this stage, too many Christians had left Palestine to safer lands as the result of pressure and marginalisation by Islamisers of the Palestinian cause.

Although the Arabic-speaking Christians were at the vanguard of Arab nationalism of the 19th and 20th centuries in the Middle East, over the last century and a half, there has been a gradual marginalisation of the Arabic-speaking Christians and a concomitant emigration out of the Middle East. According to Daphne Tsimhoni, this has resulted in part from combination of harsh treatment by the Ottomans:

"Further, the proportion of Christians in the Palestinian population has steadily decreased since World War I as the result of constant Christian emigration and a higher Muslim birth-rate. Christians began migrating from Palestine during the late nineteenth century, both in search of better economic opportunities, and to escape harsh Ottoman treatment and conscription on the eve of World War I."("Israel and the Territories – Disappearance, Disappearing Christians of the Middle East", by Daphne Tsimhoni, *Middle East Quarterly*, Winter 2001, pp. 31-43.)

As for Arab Christians in Israel today, their representation has declined from being the majority in the Israeli Knesset in early days (due to their being more educated that their Muslim brethren), to only one out of twelve today. ("Arab Christians in Israeli Politics" by Daphne Tsimhoni, *Diwaniyya*, January 1, 2012)

This trend is again due to the rise in the number of Muslims, owing to their high birth-rate, and the Islamisation of national and political issues, which has alienated Christians.

The outcry of the heart is not just about marginalisation of Arabic-speaking Christians by their Arab Muslim brethren, but also about the world community being, perhaps becoming, blind and deaf to their plight.

"Arabic-speaking Christians have been one of the main casualties of the destabilizing events of the twentieth century, and especially of the Western-created system of modern Arab states. This religious community found itself deeply immersed in a series of global changes that it could not influence, let alone shape." ("Middle East Forum, Arab Christians as Symbol, Disappearing Christians of the Middle East", by Hilal Khashan, *Middle East Quarterly*, Winter 2001, pp.5-12.)

Consequently, Arabic-speaking Christians are left to feel like intelligent students with incredible creative potential in a country that neither wants them nor can utilise their skills. They are left between the rock of Zionism and the hard place of Muslim fundamentalism, with a half-hearted onlooker in the now nominally Christian West.

From a Christian Arab point of view, Arab nationalism is as confused as ever. But whatever becomes of it, however it is eventually defined, what is exceedingly clear is that Arabic-speaking Christians are increasingly excluded from that entity, by their Muslim brethren. More than ever, Muslim Arabs are openly hostile to Arabic-speaking Christians, accusing them of being Zionists, non-Arabs, traitors etc.

Notwithstanding, the descendants of Banu Taghlib, the Lakhmids and Ghassanids, are as Arab as can be. They happen to be Christian too, which if history has any influence on Arab thinking, is a positive attribute. The Arabic-speaking Christians are "The people of the book", followers of Jesus of Nazareth, inventors of the Arabic script, translators of Greek literature, poets, scientists, nationalists, and Arab descendants of Eber and Qahtan. They are true Arabs. If Muslim Arabs choose to exclude Arabic-speaking Christians, it is their loss as much as it is the Arabic-speaking Christians'. Unfortunately, the growth of Muslim fundamentalism has blinded many Muslim Arabs to the benefits of inclusiveness.

Chapter III

Anti-Arab Anti-Semitism

"During Tubi's time on the floor, it was not uncommon for his fellow deputies—many of whom were immigrants from Eastern Europe—to shout him down. In the 1950s and 1960s, most Knesset members treated any political opposition from "an Arab" as a sign of impudence toward a nation that had been magnanimous enough not to deport him" (Citizen Strangers, Shira Robinson)

Jews are often painted as victims of their Arab cousins. Arabs are usually depicted as violent, ignorant, dishonest, and almost subhuman. It is also true that Arabs are confused with Muslims, and the two terms have wrongly been interchanged.

The Zionists have played the victim role deftly for many years. As early as 1922, *The Dearborn Independent* dealt with this issue, thus: *"Many so-called 'Gentiles' are somewhat affected by the Jews' wails of "persecution."*

It may shock some naïve souls to realise that the Jews are capable of as much bigotry and evil as the Arabs. Why? Because they are equally human. The Jews have not always been the victims. They have always, like all human beings, been capable of committing some of the worst atrocities, including verbal abuse, apartheid, discrimination, assaults, killings, mass murders and ethnic cleansing.

Massacres of Christians by Jews

Beginning in Yemen in the sixth century AD, the Jews of Yemen committed a crime of genocide against Arabic-speaking Christians of Nejran, in South Yemen, which was home to a significant Jewish community who had lived there since the destruction of the second temple in 70 AD. In 519-23 AD the Jewish King of Himyar, Yusuf As'ar Dhu Nuwas orchestrated, and carried out a massacre against the Christians of Yemen. He had an ambition to establish a Jewish Davidic kingdom and saw the Byzantines as an obstacle. The Christians of South Yemen were naturally allied to Christian Byzantium.

Dhu Nuwas began with the Christian Aksumites in Zafran, destroying their homes and churches and killing indiscriminately. He then moved on to Najran, in south modern Saudi Arabia, where despite the Najranite surrender, he proceeded to kill any Christian Arab who refused to convert to Judaism. Dhu Nuwas killed 20,000 Arabic-speaking Christians.

The existence of a Christian community in Zafar is confirmed by a German archaeologist, Paul Yule, from Heidelberg, Germany, whose significant find of a stone figure 1.7 m long was reported by *Der Spiegel*: *"It depicts a man with chains of jewelry, curls and spherical eyes. Yule dates the image to the time around 530 AD. ... He is barefoot, which is typical of Coptic saints. He is holding a bundle of twigs, a symbol of peace, in his left hand. There is a crossbar on his staff, giving it the appearance of a cross. In addition, he is wearing a crown on his head like the ones worn by the Christian rulers of ancient Ethiopia."* (*Spiegel* online, 21.12.2012.)

Dhu Nuwas smelt blood and was foolish enough to write a letter to Al-Mundhir, the leader of the largely Christian Lakhmids, at Hira in January 519, where he was entertaining people from Constantinople. The letter boasted about what Dhu Nuwas had done to the Christians of Yemen and encouraged Al- Mundhir to do the same to his Christian subjects. A similar letter was sent by Dhu Nuwas to the King of Persia, encouraging him to decimate Christians. The letter was shared with Al-Mundhir's Roman guests, who were incensed.

Dhu Nuwas received his comeuppance when the Romans and Byzantines, with help from their Ethiopian Christian allies, invaded Yemen and defeated Dhu Nuwas.

The Jews in Persia had a checkered existence. But under Khosrau II (591 -628) they had a relatively care-free existence, finding ways to enter the Sassanid court and exert influence. Khosrau attacked Byzantium and had a measure of success, with Jews as full participants in his army. Jews rose up against Christians in Antioch, Calcedon and Yemen, and massacred Christians where they could. Next, King Khosrau II turned his attention to Jerusalem. Success there would give him valuable access to the Mediterranean, and would enable him to challenge Byzantium by sea as well as on land. To ensure success, the Sassanid king struck a deal with Persian Jewry. In return for the provision of 20,000 Jewish soldiers, Persian Jews would be able to participate in the capture of Jerusalem and a Jewish governor would be appointed to rule over Jerusalem and Palestina Prima, on behalf of Persia.

The Jews and Persians took Christian Jerusalem by surprise and conquered it in 614 AD. A monk rejoicing by the name Antiochus Strategos gave an eye-witness account of the destruction brought about by the Jews and Persians: *"unprecedented looting and sacrilege... Church after church was burned down alongside the innumerable Christian artefacts, which were stolen or damaged by the ensuing arson".*

Churches, including the one built by the mother of Emperor Constantine, were destroyed, and Christians were massacred. And when a few months after the fall of Jerusalem, Christians assassinated the Jewish governor and took control of the city for 19 days, the Jewish-Persian alliance responded with more vehemence. According to Antiochus, the Persian Shahrbaraz ordered a swift razing and looting of Jerusalem, giving the Jews the right to retaliate and an opportunity to personally massacre their Christian enemies. (Antiochus Strategos, "The Capture of Jerusalem by the Persians in 614 AD", *English Historical Review* 25 (1910), pp.502-517.)

Interestingly, the *Encyclopaedia Judaica* only dedicates three lines to the whole affair. However, Prof. Frank Lowenberg concludes a more detailed account thus: *"With hindsight it becomes evident that this was a major turning point in the history of the Near East. The brutalities of the invading armies, involving large scale damage to churches and a mass killing of the local Christian population, was undoubtedly one of the causes for the rapid Muslim conquests, twenty years later."* (January 2012 edition of the *Jewish Magazine*.)

The significance of the extensive destruction to Christian Palestina Prima is summarized by Gideon Avni, Director of Excavations and Surveys Department Israel Antiquities Authority thus: *"it was believed that the devastating effects of the conquest changed the urban and rural landscape of the country for many years to come."*
(www.bibleinterp.com/articles/pers357904.shtml)

The weakening of the Christian presence in the Holy Lands, thanks to Jewish persecution of Christians, is largely responsible for the military success of Islam. This would prove to be one of the worst mistakes of world Jewry, for today, almost everywhere, Muslims are the Jews' worst nightmare.

Disrespect of Arabs

The Jewish state was built by European Zionists. As Europeans, they had inherited the sense of superiority that their Europeans fellow citizens harboured towards Middle Eastern nations This has even been noted by Arabic-speaking Christians who had worked closely with European Christians.

This sense of superiority has often been expressed in words and actions. A perfect verbal example of this sense of superiority is expressed in this excerpt from a Bernard Shapiro.

(Bernard J. Shapiro is the executive director of the Freeman Centre for Strategic Studies.)

"The Arabs have always been adept at psychological-propaganda warfare due to their culture of lies and verbal skills. Students of Islamic practices have long recognized that in Arab society it is the norm to prevaricate and deceive. An Arab who tells the truth about serious events affecting ideology, history, and 'disputed' matters is considered foolish and naive."

This generalisation about Arabs illustrates a basic disdain for a whole race whose members number hundreds of millions of souls. This Jewish man has spoken out of malice and ignorance, a very dangerous blend. He has assumed that all Arabs are liars. He has also mistakenly equated Arabs with Muslims. There are a few million Arabic-speaking Christians in Egypt alone. He also mistakenly assumes that Iranians are Arabs. Ignorance often goes hand in hand with bigotry.

Whilst it would be wrong to assume that all Jews are of this ilk, it would equally be wrong to wish that this ranting is an isolated example of Jewish anti-Arab anti-Semitism. These negative images of Arabs are rife amongst Zionists, be they Evangelicals or Jews.

Zionist disdain for Arabs is so intense that if one wanted to reproach a Jew, one would tell him to *"stop behaving like an Arab"*. This is the perception that I grew up with. The hatred of Arabs is so strong that Zionists do not want to be associated with Arabs in any shape or form.

I recall many years ago Israeli Port workers in Eilat went on strike. This lead to clashes with the Israeli Police. I recall how offended I was to hear strikers protest that the police treated them as if they were Arabs. In other words, Israeli Police treat Arabs badly; it is acceptable to treat Arabs badly; and Jews deserve to be treated better than Arabs!

This sense of superiority by Jews is to be found at every level. The infamous David Ben-Gurion will always be remembered for his racism again Israeli Arabs, due to his refusal to hold an Israeli ID card, unless a special card was issued for him which bore no Arabic script. According to

Telegraph JTA archives, his objection to carrying an ID card *"was based on the fact that the card carried instructions in both Hebrew and Arabic, while he insisted that it should carry Hebrew only, as the nation's official language"* ("Israel Identity Card Evokes Protest; Ben Gurion Refuses to Accept It", *Telegraph*, JTA archive, May 1, 1958).

Whilst such disrespect for Israeli Arabs by their own President is reprehensible, it should not come as a surprise, as he belonged to a Zionist leadership born in Europe, who possessed a huge sense of imperialist entitlement and a bigger sense of superiority over their primitive cousins, and who showed no respect for their cousins' rights to land or life. The brutal way in which they pursued their goal included the killing of innocent Palestinian Arabs, theft of land, deceitful means of taking land away from its rightful owners, and evacuating Israeli Arabs under pretext of security with the clandestine intention of never returning them to their homes. With this backdrop in mind, the refusal of Ben-Gurion to accept an Israeli ID card that bore Arabic script seems relatively insignificant.

Ben-Gurion, so adored by Evangelical Zionists, was instrumental in developing the policy of shoot-to-kill of any Palestinian returning home after the so called Israeli war of independence, otherwise known by Palestinians as al-Nakbah, the catastrophe. Though such brutality dwarfs refusal to carry the same ID as an Arab, the two misdeeds share the same basic disrespect for other human beings and the same sense of superiority and arrogant entitlement.

It is, however, self-condemnation when one's more evil works dwarf one's own less shocking works.

Mr Tubi, an Israeli Arab member of the Knesset, recalls how he was treated by his Jewish counterparts, Jewish members of the Israeli Parliament. *"During Tubi's time on the floor, it was not uncommon for his fellow deputies—many of whom were immigrants from Eastern Europe—to shout him down. In the 1950s and 1960s, most Knesset members treated any political opposition from "an Arab" as a sign of impudence toward a nation that had been magnanimous enough not to deport him"* (*Citizen Strangers*, Shira Robinson).

Ben-Gurion was not the only Israeli leader to express disdain towards Arabs. He may have been the first. The terrorist-come Israeli Prime Minister Menachem Begin called Palestinians *"beasts walking on two legs".* Mr Yitzhak Shamir called them *"grasshoppers".* Another prime minister, Ehud Barak, called them *"crocodiles"*, whilst Rafael Eitan referred to Palestinians as *"cockroaches".* ("Origins of Israel's Anti-Arab Racism", by Prof. Lawrence Davidson, *Global Research*, November 28, 2012.)

My nephew and niece grew up amongst Jews and attended a Jewish kindergarten. I was astounded to hear that they pretended to shoot some Arabs during their play time. This is what they were taught in the Jewish nursery.

Anastasia Michaeli, a popular television presenter and Candidate for Kadima party, urged the Israeli Eurovision committee not to choose someone *"with an Arab look".* She was severely reprimanded in the press for her racist remarks. (*ADL Jerusalem*, January 8, 2007.)

At the other end of the scale, there are Zionist fundamentalists, the worst of whom live in Hebron, who make no secret of their intentions to massacre the Palestinians. They walk the streets of Hebron armed with machine guns and threaten Palestinians that they must either leave Hebron or face death sooner or later. When a Palestinian asked, *"So you want to do to us what Hitler and the Gestapo did to you many years ago?"* the Fundamentalist Zionist settlers replied, *"This is exactly what we will do to you. Call us Nazis, call us Gestapo, we don't care. And the world won't help you. Because we control America".* The Israeli army moved in and beat up the Palestinians and dispersed them. These are not a few crazed fanatical Zionists expressing maverick opinions. Their views are not marginal. *"Every time we do something you tell me America will do this and will do that... I want to tell you something very clear: Don't worry about American pressure on Israel. We, the Jewish people, control America, and the Americans know it."* (Israeli Prime Minister, Ariel Sharon,

October 3, 2001, to Shimon Peres, as reported on Kol Yisrael radio.)

At best, the claim that Zionists control America bears a resemblance of truth, at worst, and in reality it bears a large element of truth. The associated Press published a conversation between President Nixon and Billy Graham, which apparently went like this:

Billy Graham, the Southern Baptist evangelist, expressed disdain for what he saw as Jewish domination of the media.

"This stranglehold has got to be broken or this country's going down the drain," Graham said, agreeing with Nixon's comments earlier in the conversation.

"You believe that?" Nixon says in response.

"Yes, sir," says Graham.

"Oh boy. So do I," Nixon agrees, then says: *"I can't ever say that, but I believe it."*

"No, but if you get elected a second time, then we might be able to do something," Graham replies.

Later, Graham mentions that he has friends in the media who are Jewish, saying they *"swarm around me and are friendly to me."* But, he confides to Nixon, *"They don't know how I really feel about what they're doing to this country."*

("Nixon And Billy Graham, Anti-Semitism Caught On Tape", by James Warren, Chicago Tribune staff reporter, 3-1-02.)

There is no doubt that Zionists have a significant influence on American policy. This can be surmised from America's doting on Israel and her reluctance to rebuke Israel when Israel is in the wrong. American tolerance of Zionist misdemeanour is so great, one sometimes wonders who needs the other more, Israel or America! It is as if America is afraid to upset her golden child, Israel.

What is fascinating is the claim by Israeli soldiers that they control America, juxtaposed with the accusation of anti-Semitism levelled against Billy Graham for simply expressing concern about the Jewish influence over the USA. This is a brilliant shining example of Jewish overuse of the anti-Semitic card. Perhaps Jews have come to take for granted Christian American support of their Zionist cause.

A Harvard study of the unswerving Pro-Israeli American stance posed the question thus: *"This situation has no equal in American political history. Why has the United States been willing to set aside its own security in order to advance the interests of another state?"* Why does America continue to give Israel at least three billion dollars per year in direct aid? Israel has its aid paid at the beginning of each financial year, whereas others have their aid quarterly. Israel does not have to use its aid to purchase American goods; it can invest 25% of that aid in its own industry. Unlike other recipients of American aid, Israel does not have to account for how she uses American aid. Israel has access to the most advanced American weaponry. In addition, America has virtually always supported Israel against the Arab States in the United Nations, and has often used her veto to block decisions that may be injurious to Israel. Why so? Is it because Israel and America have common goals or interests? That is at least what the Evangelical Zionist pro-Israel lobby wants us to believe. They also want Americans to believe that this small vulnerable state needs American aid. Is Israel really so weak and vulnerable?! Does it not have the most advanced military capability in the Middle East, some of which is locally produced?!

The other argument used to justify America's unflinching support for the Zionist State is that Israel is the only democracy in the Middle East. In truth, however, though Israel may appear more democratic than its neighbours, Israel fails the basic tests of Western democracy. Its discrimination against its own Arab citizens is a living testimony to its far distance from democracy.

The following shows how far Israel is from being a democracy:

"The Official Summation of the Or Commission Report", published in *Haaretz*, September 2, 2003. For evidence of how hostile many Israelis were to the report's findings and recommendations, see "No Avoiding the Commission Recommendations", *Haaretz*, September 4, 2003; Molly

Moore. "Israeli Report Is Welcomed, Dismissed", *Washington Post*, September 3, 2003. Also see Bernard Avishai, "Saving Israel from Itself: A Secular Future for the Jewish State", *Harper's Magazine*, January 2005.

It is also worth noting that the Israel Democracy Institute reported in May 2003 that: *"53 percent of Israeli Jews are against full equality for the Arabs.; 77 percent of Israeli Jews believe that there should be a Jewish majority on crucial political decisions; only 31 percent support having Arab political parties in the government; 57 percent think that the Arabs should be encouraged to emigrate."* See *The Democracy Index: Major Findings*, 2003.

Imagine the outcry that would occur if a majority of white Americans declared that blacks, Hispanics, and Asians should be encouraged to leave the United States. For more recent surveys, which show little change in Israeli attitudes, see Yulie Khromchenko, "Survey: Most Jewish Israelis Support Transfer of Arabs", *Haaretz*, June 22, 2004; Yoav Stern, "Poll: Most Israeli Jews Say Israeli Arabs Should Emigrate", *Haaretz*, April 4, 2005.

The foregoing simply reflects disregard for the basic human rights and feelings of a section of the Israeli population. Why aren't the Americans shocked by it? Is it not the underlying negative stereotyping of Arabs? Do Americans really support all the above racism?! Moreover, one wonders how democratic all the above is!

Many readers will have seen one if not numerous films about the Holocaust. One of the most poignant scenes that sticks in mind is Jewish musicians, violinists and pianists being asked to entertain German officers with their favourite tunes before the Jewish musicians were sent to the gas chambers by their own Nazi captive audience.

In March 2006 *Haaretz* (Israel's leading Hebrew newspaper) reported that an Israeli human rights organization monitoring a military roadblock near Nablus had successfully videotaped Israeli soldiers forcing a Palestinian to play the violin for them. This was apparently not an isolated incident.

Israeli officers dismissed criticism by claiming that Israeli soldiers were dealing with a very difficult situation! However, the real reason for such treatment is that Zionists have little regard for Palestinians.

"One million Arabs are not worth a Jewish fingernail." (Rabbi Yaacov Perrin, Feb. 27, 1994.)

There are many Israeli Arabs, amongst whom there are Christians, who have found life-long partners from the West Bank or Gaza. The most they can hope for is that Israel will tolerate their partner's presence. I have a friend who is engaged to a Christian girl from Bethlehem. When they marry, she will come to live in Israel with her husband. She will never be entitled to Israeli nationality, citizenship, health care or national insurance. She will not be entitled to vote. Yet Israeli Jews can marry a Jewess from any country in the world, and their full citizenship is guaranteed.

For the last 39 years I have lived in Britain, and have for most part been a proud British citizen. We have laws now which bring to justice any person uttering words that can incite racial or religious hatred or violence. One infamous Muslim cleric by the name of Abu Hamzah has been brought to justice under these laws. He has been rightly vilified internationally, and his case has been publicised worldwide. Yet many such Jewish clerics exist in Israel and utter equal if not worse obscenities against the Arabs. Are they ever brought to justice?! *"During a sermon preceding the 2001 Passover holiday, the influential Israeli Rabbi Ovadia Yosef exclaimed: 'May the Holy Name visit retribution on the Arab heads, and cause their seed to be lost, and annihilate them.' He added: 'It is forbidden to have pity on them. We must give them missiles with relish, annihilate them. Evil ones, damnable ones.'"* (Source: *Haaretz*, April 12, 2001.)

One of my nephews has had first-hand experience of Zionist disdain for Arab human rights. He was once on a bus travelling to his digs in Jerusalem, accompanied by two cousins. The bus was stopped by soldiers at a check post. My nephew greeted the soldiers politely in Hebrew and handed them his ID. To his shock and horror, he was arrested without explanation, dragged out of the bus, and beaten in public. He was interrogated, only to be released due to mistaken identity. The blood-thirst of Zionists, their eagerness to inflict pain and suffering, makes them blind to basics, such as establishing the identity of a man before they execute punishment.

Israel is often depicted as a vulnerable small country surrounded by Arab villains. Yet the truth is that the Arabs have for many years tried to play the diplomatic game in order to secure the return of the Palestinians to their pre-1948 lands. And what has Israel's attitude been? *"We declare openly that the Arabs have no right to settle on even one centimetre of Eretz Israel... Force is all they do or ever will understand. We shall use the ultimate force until the Palestinians come crawling to us on all fours."* – Rafael Eitan, chief of staff of the Israel Defence Forces, quoted in *Yediot Ahronot*, April 13, 1983, and *The New York Times*, April 14, 1983.

Indeed, Ben-Gurion was much more explicit about the Zionist view of Palestinians: *"We must do everything to ensure they [the Palestinian refugees] never do return."* (David Ben-Gurion in his diary, July 18, 1948, quoted in Michael Bar Zohar's *Ben-Gurion: the Armed Prophet*, Prentice-Hall, 1967, p.157.)

The Balfour Declaration states *"Nothing shall be done that may prejudice the civil and religious rights of the existing non-Jewish communities in Palestine or the rights and political status enjoyed by Jews in any other country."* Zionists have breached this a hundred times. Israeli Arabs do not enjoy the same rights to ownership of land as the Jews do. This book will show in detail that many things have been either done or undone to curb the civil and religious rights of the existing non-Jews in Palestine.

How can anti-Arab views and sentiments prevail in Israel? What undergirds such views? The once anti-British terrorist, later Israeli Prime Minister Menachem Begin, provides an answer. *"[The Palestinians] are beasts walking on two legs."* (Israeli Prime Minister Menachem Begin, speech to the

Knesset, quoted in Amnon Kapeliouk, "Begin and the 'Beasts'", *New Statesman*, June 25, 1982.)

Such base views of the Palestinians abound at the highest echelons of Zionism, and have been proudly expressed down the years in diverse ways and manners. *"We must use terror, assassination, intimidation, land confiscation, and the cutting of all social services to rid the Galilee of its Arab population."* (Israel Koenig, *The Koenig Memorandum*.)

"We shall reduce the Arab population to a community of woodcutters and waiters." (Uri Lubrani, Israeli Prime Minister Ben-Gurion's special adviser on Arab Affairs. Source: *The Arabs in Israel* by Sabri Jiryas.)

Zionists are Jews who have long espoused extreme and negative views of Gentiles. Zionists have lived amongst Gentiles for centuries, and have sometimes chosen to live in their own ghettos because of their abjectly negative views of Gentiles or goyim. These views furnish a much greater motive force for a state of their own. Security is a spurious justification for the State of Israel, as the land of Israel simply makes Zionists a sitting duck for any aggressor to deal just one blow with which to annihilate millions of Jews in one instance. The real motive force for a national homeland for the Jews is that Zionists feel superior to Gentiles, who are likened to dogs and pigs and other filthy animals, who are fit for slaughter and killing with impunity. Therefore, they prefer to live on their own and not amongst Gentiles. The Talmud is peppered with such thinking:

"The Jews are called human beings, but the non-Jews are not humans. They are beasts."
– Talmud: Baba mezia, 114b

"Everything a Jew needs for his church ritual no goy is permitted to manufacture, but only a Jew, because this must be manufactured by human beings and the Jew is not permitted to consider the goyim as human beings."
– Schulchan Oruch, Orach Chaiw 14, 20, 32, 33, 39. TalDud Jebamoth 61

"The Akum (non-Jew) is like a dog. Yes, the scripture teaches to honour the dog more than the non-Jew."
— Ereget Raschi Erod. 22 30

"Even though God created the non-Jew, they are still animals in human form. It is not becoming for a Jew to be served by an animal. Therefore he will be served by animals in human form."
— Midrasch Talpioth, p.255, Warsaw 1855

"A pregnant non-Jew is no better than a pregnant animal."
— Coschen hamischpat 405

"The souls of non-Jews come from impure sprits and are called pigs."
— Jalkut Rubeni gadol 12b

"Although the non-Jew has the same body structure as the Jew, they compare with the Jew like a monkey to a human."
— Schene luchoth haberith, p.250 b

"If you eat with a Gentile, it is the same as eating with a dog."
— Tosapoth, Jebamoth 94b

"If a Jew has a non-Jewish servant or maid who dies, one should not express sympathy to the Jew. You should tell the Jew: 'God will replace your loss', just as if one of his oxen or asses had died."
— Jore dea 377, 1

"Sexual intercourse between Gentiles is like intercourse between animals."
— Talmud Sanhedrin 74b

"It is permitted to take the body and the life of a Gentile."
— Sepher ikkarim III c 25

"It is the law to kill anyone who denies the Torah. The Christians belong to the denying ones of the Torah."
– Coschen hamischpat 425 Hagah 425. 5

"A heretic Gentile you may kill outright with your own hands."
– Talmud, Abodah Zara, 4b

"Every Jew, who spills the blood of the godless (non-Jews), is doing the same as making a sacrifice to God."
– Talmud: Bammidber raba c 21 & Jalkut 772

If one held such negative views of Gentiles, one would be naturally desperate to separate oneself from them and live in a country of one's own. One would do anything, regardless of how shameful it may seem to the outside world, in order to achieve one's goal of a totally and purely Zionist State. One would kill, deceive, mislead, pretend, insult, beg, cry wolf and do anything in the book to fulfil that dream. That is what Zionists have done, and this sordid Journey of Zionism began in the mind of Zionists, minds full of hatred of anything non-Jewish; racist minds.

Zionist aggression against Palestinians in 1947 included rape of Palestinian women. What would lead to such atrocities from a people who have just come out of the Holocaust? *"A Jew may do to a non-Jewess what he can do. He may treat her as he treats a piece of meat."* (Hadarine, 20, B; Schulchan Aruch, Choszen Hamiszpat 348.) *"A Jew may violate but not marry a non-Jewish girl."* (Gad. Shas. 2:2.)

Such atrocious acts of violation are the fruit of a mind polluted with racist ideologies against non-Jews. Only such permissive ideology or casuistry can explain the repeated acts of violation against Palestinian women. *"London, UK, 23 June 2002 – Over 80 women in Nablus were raped and beaten by Israeli troops, who also killed many of their husbands and relatives trying to intervene, according to a testimony sent to British Labour MP Lynne Jones."*

The testimony was sent by Anthony Razook by e-mail from Bethlehem [Palestine] after witnessing three Israeli soldiers taking turns to violate his four-months' pregnant sister, and shooting her husband three times in the back of the neck.

"'In Nablus, there were calls made from cell phones that tell us over 86 women were raped and beaten and there are many of the men, their husbands, that have been killed when they were trying to stop these soldiers,' he said."

The Israeli authorities denounced this as sheer propaganda, but Razook claimed, *"all of these horrible things were witnessed by her seven year old son, my nephew Michel. At the end of them beating and violating my sister, they then stole her jewellery, her monies, and some other things; at that point they went and totally destroyed different things in her apartment home."* I find this account credible for one reason only: Zionist casuistry justifies such atrocities. Whether they were committed or not is a secondary issue. The existence of such thinking lends credibility to Razook's account.

Shulamit Aloni, the former Education Minister of Israel who had been awarded both the Israel Prize and the Emil Grunzweig Human Rights Award by the Association for Civil Rights in Israel, reports on how the Israeli authorities confiscate Palestinian land in the West Bank and build settlements on it. They built excellent roads leading to the settlement, and built on confiscated Palestinian property. *"When a Palestinian drives on such a road, his vehicle is confiscated and he is sent on his way."* ("Yes, there is Apartheid in Israel", *counterpunch*, January 8, 2007.) When Aloni witnessed one such incident, she challenged the soldier by asking why he was confiscating the Palestinian man's vehicle. He replied that he was acting on orders. When Aloni pointed to the lack of signs warning such drivers not to "transgress", the soldier replied *"It is his responsibility to know it, and besides, what do you want us to do, put up a sign here and let some anti-Semitic reporter or journalist take a photo so that he can show the world that Apartheid exists here?"*

Israel claims to be democratic, and makes all the right noises and dances to the right tunes in public. Yet, when no one is looking, she is capable of the most heinous atrocities. Israel is a signatory to the International Convention on the Elimination of all Forms of Racial Discrimination, 7 March 1966. Yet she practices racial discrimination on a wide scale and gets away with it.

In defence of the Zionist State, and with some sense of justification, the *Jerusalem Post* rebuts the accusation that Israel is an apartheid state. *"Last week in* The Australian, *Muslim author Irshad Manji answers: 'Would an apartheid state award its top literary prize to an Arab?... Would an apartheid state encourage Hebrew-speaking schoolchildren to learn Arabic? Would road signs throughout the land appear in both languages? Even my country, the proudly bilingual Canada, doesn't meet that standard.'"* (*The Jerusalem Post*, Feb. 14, 2007.) The truth is that no one is totally good or evil. All humans, including criminals and thieves, can point to some virtue in their character. Israel has to be saluted for its acts of fairness towards Palestinians and Israeli Arabs. However, Israel has to be equally willing to take it on the chin when she is weighed on the scales of democracy and found wanting. Doing good on Monday does not entitle a man to do evil on Tuesday.

As Canon Naim Ateek once said: *"I am not pro- this people or that. I am pro-justice, pro-freedom. I am anti-injustice, anti-oppression."*

The object of this book is not to vilify Israel, as much as to debunk the belief often firmly held by Evangelical Zionists, that Israel is perfect. The truth has to triumph, and no man is entitled to immunity from criticism. We must call a spade a spade, and Israel must blush when she practises apartheid as willingly as she celebrates her honourable acts of equality towards the Israeli Arabs.

Not only are Evangelical Zionists misguided about the righteousness of the Zionists, but they are not bashful about their negative opinions of Arabs. There is a sample of such expressions from an American Evangelical, quoted, albeit by a critic, in Media Monitors Network by Rev Thomas Williamson, 2001: *"In his Last Call newsletter, Pastor F. M. Riley of Roswell, New Mexico denounces the Palestinians as 'lazy' and accuses them of stealing Palestine from the Jews, saying, 'The Palestinians (and other Arabs) have never been anything but "squatters" on land that never belonged to them in the first place.'"*

In this statement there are simultaneous violations of human rights. Riley denies that Arabs have ever owned land, insults Palestinians with pure prejudice as "lazy" and as thieves, and calls them "squatters". These words ooze racism, and only serve to make his cause unpopular amongst reasonable, right thinking people. One wonders whether he includes the few million Christians amongst those Arabs he so easily writes off. Or is he so besotted with his Zeal for Zion that he has cut off his nose to spite his face?

Denial, The Most Effective Tool of Racism

Tawfiq Tubi, one of three Israeli Arabs to make it to the Knesset which consisted of 120 members, of Orthodox Christian background, recalls his meeting with the retired Ben-Gurion. It was an uncomfortable meeting which began with pleasantries of whether Tubi was the first or family name. However, Mr Tubi, who was a tireless champion of Israeli Arab rights, fired questions at the retired prime minister, which were simply met with denials or expressions of feigned surprise, such as: *"'Maltreatment of Palestinians since 1948?!' The Polish-born settler and founding father of the Jewish state feigned incredulity: 'We expelled people?' he asked. 'From which village did we expropriate land?' 'Is it true that our universities reject Arab applications en masse?'"* (*Citizen Strangers*, Shira Robinson.)

Ben-Gurion was simply denying the accusations levelled against his state of inequality and prejudice against the Arab citizens of Israel. Worse still, the denial of the existence of the Palestinian people is a tack used by Zionists to bypass the human-right issue, which they dare not confront. Violations against Palestinians! *"Who are these Palestinians?"* they ask, not expecting an answer. *"There have never been a Palestinian people,"* they assert, hoping to thus have won the argument. Triumph by denial seems an effective tactic. However, it tends to backfire. One can ask the same question of Jews. Who are these Jews? They have been scattered all over the world and their blood has mixed with so many races. How can you be sure who is a Jew and who isn't? This is not a rhetorical question. This is a real dilemma facing the Zionist State and has for years caused deep divisions. The Jewish state cannot decide whether to accept the 80,000 Ethiopian Jews as fully Jewish or not. The hundreds of thousands of Russian Jews are of equally dubious origins. To quote H. G Wells: *"It is highly probable that the bulk of the Jew's ancestors 'never' lived in Palestine 'at all,' which witnesses the power of historical assertion over fact."*

In fact, some Russian "Jews" are open about their Christian origins. This uncertainty about the identity of the Jewish people is well expressed by Rev Williamson, who in 2001 wrote in the Media Monitors Network: *"However, in reality there is no connection between the Edomites and the Palestinians. Josephus, in his "Antiquities of the Jews," Chapter IX, (2), stated that the entire Edomite or Idumean nation was absorbed into the Jewish nation in the 2nd Century BC, and this statement is accepted by modern historians and Bible reference works. Thus, much anti-Arab prejudice is based on a totally false application of Old Testament prophecies against ancient Edom (similar to the misapplication which places the "curse of Ham" upon modern blacks."*

Kevin Alan Brook, in *The Jews of Khazaria*, explains how the people of Khazaria converted en masse to Judaism circa 740. He quotes various references, one of which is that of Ibn al-Faqih, a 10th century author who wrote *"All of the Khazars are Jews. But they have been Judaized recently."* (Second edition, Rowman and Littlefield). The genes of a significant number of

Israeli Jews have never originated from Palestine. They are of Khazari, Turcik origin.

Broadly speaking, there are five dilemmas facing the Jewish state in attempting to answer the question of who is Jewish:

1. The orthodox view is that a Jew is someone who observes the Halakha (the walk in the faith).
2. Matrilineal Descent: A Jew is someone whose mother is Jewish. This view is usually held by conservatives.
3. The liberal view is that it is enough for someone to have one Jewish parent, father or mother, for them to lay a claim to being Jewish.
4. Those who are converts from other religions, or born-Jews, who convert to another religion. Are they Jewish still? Some say they are, whilst others says they are not. One does not confront such complexities in defining who the Palestinian people are.
5. If ancestral lineage is so important, what evidence is satisfactory for the fulfilment of the pre-requisites for Jewishness?

Any genetic emphasis on the definition of Jewishness raises many questions regarding the Jewishness of the modern State of Israel. Both Zionists and Evangelical Zionists appeal to antiquity to prove the validity of the State of Israel, claiming that the Jewish residents of the State of Israel are descendants of Abraham, Isaac and Jacob, who even in the diaspora, managed to maintain their purely Jewish blood. How true is this claim?

Indeed, the Old Testament repeatedly prohibits intermarriage with non-Jews. However, beginning from the sons of Jacob, and more specifically Joseph who married an Egyptian wife, and who begat Ephraim and Manasseh, we see that this standard has already been breached. Those two princes of Israel, were clearly not fully Jewish.

Judah, one of the ancestors of Christ, married a Canaanite called Shua. Their son Er married a Canaanite, Tamar. Upon his death Tamar married her brother-in-law Onan. In order to produce children, she disguised herself as a prostitute and seduced Judah to lie with her. She produced two sons, Perez and Zerah. Perez begat Salmon, who begat Boaz, who married Ruth the Moabite.

Next we must consider Moses, the leader of the Israelites, who took them out of Egypt to preserve their Jewish purity. He had married Zipporah the Midianite. Midian was one of the Children of Abraham begat through his Arab wife, Keturah, whom he married after the death of Sarah. The Bible also mentions two rebukes by Miriam and Aaron for Moses having married an Ethiopian. Whether Zipporah is referred to as an Ethiopian because of her dark complexion, or whether Moses married another woman after Zipporah's death, we do not know. But we can safely say that, whether he had one or two wives, neither were Jewish.

Rahab, the Canaanite prostitute of Jericho (whose people originated from Arabian Peninsula) married a Jew and begat Boaz. The beautiful story of Naomi and Ruth is another case in point. During a famine, Naomi the Israelite went to live in Moab with her husband and two sons. Her husband died. Her sons married two Moabites, Ruth and Orpah. When Naomi's sons also died, she sought to return to Israel. Ruth followed her mother-in-law into Israel, and the Bible tells how she eventually married Boaz.

Bathsheba, who was taken unfairly by David, had been wife of Uriah the Hittite, not a Jew, showing that it was not unusual for Jews to intermarry with Gentiles. Another such marriage is that of Esther from the tribe of Benjamin to Xerxes the Persian king.

During the Sassanid period in Persia, the Jews enjoyed less freedom than they did under the preceding Parthians. However, we know that just as the Roman Empire had witnessed a Judaizing movement amongst women, so did the Persian Empire. We know for instance that according to rabbinical sources Shapur II's mother Ifra-Hormiz was a convert to Judaism (*The Jewish Encyclopedia* of Brockhaus and Efron (in Russian). This is a reminder of the other diluting stream affecting the Jewish genetic purity. Believing Jews were not all Jewish by blood.

Intermarriage with Iranians and other ethnic groups is evident. Shushandukht who was the daughter of Exilarch Huna b. Nathan was married to Yazdgerd I, the Sassanid king, and therefore was also the mother of Bahram V.

When the Persian Kings Cyrus and Darius allowed the Jews to return to their land and rebuild the temple, it transpired that many of the common Jews who had been left behind had been intermarrying with the Gentiles brought into the land by the Assyrians. Ezra was extremely perturbed by this:

"The people of Israel, including the priests and the Levites, have not kept themselves separate from the neighbouring peoples with their detestable practices, like those of the Canaanites, Hittites, Perizzites, Jebusites, Ammonites, Moabites, Egyptians and Amorites. 2 They have taken some of their daughters as wives for themselves and their sons, and have mingled the holy race with the peoples around them. And the leaders and officials have led the way in this unfaithfulness. When I heard this, I tore my tunic and cloak, pulled hair from my head and beard and sat down appalled." (Ezra 9: 1-3.)

The impact of almost seventy years of intermarriage between Jews and these various nations has further diluted the "Jewish" gene. Whilst Ezra may have attempted to cast out the women and children of Gentile origin and may have managed to avoid further dilution of the Jewish gene, he could not change the past nor do we know how long he succeeded in separating the mixed couples.

It is also worth noting that despite three opportunities for the Jews to return from Babylon – in 536 BC with Zerubbabel, the builder of the second temple; in 458 BC with Ezra, the scribe, the man who reorganised the temple; and in 444 BC with Nehemiah, the builder of the walls of Jerusalem – most Jews of Babylon chose to remain in Babylon.

Despite periods of persecution, the Jews of Babylon and Persia felt quite at home in that region, some more so than their forebears had done in Israel and Judea. This would explain the following assessment:

"Over the centuries the Jews of Iran became physically, culturally, and linguistically indistinguishable from the non-Jewish population. The overwhelming majority of Jews speak Persian as their mother language, and a tiny minority, Kurdish." (Library of Congress Country-data.com. Retrieved on 2011-05-29.)

Some Zionists seek support for the theoretical purity of the Jewish race from genetic studies which have identified some genes common to most Jewish communities. (PMID: 10801975, UI: 20300976. *Proc Natl Acad Sci* U S A 2000 Jun 6;97(12):6769-74.)

However, all such studies have proven is that "Jews" have some Middle Eastern genes, as they should. Ironically, these genes are equally present in Palestinians, which underscores the futility of such a pursuit of evidence. This is also reminiscent of the mixing of Jews and Gentiles in the pre-Christian era in the Middle East. In other words, today's Jews are the result of a mixture of nations in the Middle East, as much as in North Africa, where they mixed with the Phoenicians/Berbers, and Russia where they mixed with native Khazarians. Prof Ariella Oppenheimer, the Israeli geneticist who carried out genetic analysis on Ashkenazi, Sephardic and Kurdish Jews, in her discussion states the following about Ashkenazi Jews:

"Ashkenazi Jews consolidated into a distinct ethnicity in Germany during the Middle Ages and spread eastwards to Poland and Russia in the 13th century (Ben-Sasson 1976). Previous studies of Y chromosome polymorphisms reported a small European contribution to the Ashkenazi paternal gene pool (Santachiara-Benerecetti et al. 1993; Hammer et al. 2000). In our sample, this low-level gene flow may be reflected in the Eu 19 chromosomes, which are found at elevated frequency (12.7%) in Ashkenazi Jews and which are very

frequent in Eastern Europeans (54%–60%; Semino et al. 2000). Alternatively, it is attractive to hypothesize that Ashkenazim with Eu 19 chromosomes represent descendants of the Khazars, originally a Turkic tribe from Central Asia, who settled in southern Russia and eastern Ukraine and converted en masse to Judaism in the ninth century of the present era, as described by Yehuda Ha-Levi in 1140 a.d. (Dunlop 1954)." (Almut Nebel,1 Dvora Filon,2 Bernd Brinkmann,4 Partha P. Majumder,5 Marina Faerman,3 and Ariella Oppenheim1, "The Y Chromosome Pool of Jews as Part of the Genetic Landscape of the Middle East"; *Am J Hum Genet.* Nov 2001; 69(5): 1095–1112.) This renders the purity of the Jewish blood a mere myth.

In 2005, a study by Dr David Goldstein, Dr Mark Thomas and Dr Neil Bradman of University College London, published in the *American Journal of Human Genetics*, showed that the women in nine Jewish communities including Morocco and Georgia demonstrated significantly varying genetic histories from their male counterparts. The study showed *"that the community had just a small number of founding mothers and that after the founding event there was little, if any, interchange with the host population. The women's identities, however, are a mystery, because, unlike the case with the men, their genetic signatures are not related to one another or to those of present-day Middle Eastern populations."* Dr Goldstein, combining his findings with an earlier study showing a common Middle Eastern genetic theme in Jewish men, explained this by saying that: *"The men came from the Near East, perhaps as traders....They established local populations, probably with local women. But once the community was founded, the barriers had to go up, because otherwise mitochondrial diversity would be increased."* (Nicholas Wade, in "DNA, New Clues to Jewish Roots" by the *NY Times*, May 2, 2005.)

Further evidence against the purity of the Jewish line comes from a more recent work published by Dr Eran Elhaik, a geneticist at the Johns Hopkins School of Public Health, in the online Oxford Press journal *Genome Biology and*

Evolution (17 January 2013). In "The missing link of Jewish European ancestry: contrasting the Rhineland and the Khazarian Hypotheses", Elhaik *"examined a comprehensive dataset of 1,287 unrelated individuals of 8 Jewish and 74 non-Jewish populations genotyped over 531,315 autosomal single nucleotide polymorphisms (SNPs)."* ("New study sheds light on the origin of the European Jewish population", *Science Daily*, January 16, 2013; Oxford University Press.) He concluded: *"Almost all Eastern European Jews cluster with Armenian, Georgian and Azerbaijani Jews... The most parsimonious explanation for our findings is that Eastern European Jews are of Judeo-Khazarian ancestry forged over many centuries in the Caucasus. Jewish presence in the Caucasus and later Khazaria was recorded as early as the late centuries BCE and reinforced due to the increase in trade along the Silk Road, the decline of Judah (1st-7th centuries), and the rise of Christianity and Islam. Greco-Roman and Mesopotamian Jews gravitating toward Khazaria were also common in the early centuries and their migrations were intensified following the Khazars' conversion to Judaism... The religious conversion of the Khazars encompassed most of the empire's citizens and subordinate tribes and lasted for the next 400 years until the invasion of the Mongols. At the final collapse of their empire in the 13th century, many of the Judeo-Khazars fled to Eastern Europe and later migrated to Central Europe and admixed with the neighbouring populations."*

Naturally, this displeases many Israeli Jews whose very validity has been undermined by this scientific piece of research. A column in the *Jerusalem Post* tries to discredit Elhaik's work by stating: *"The article has been gaining some buzz in a variety of places, from neo-Nazi websites to radical left-wing blogs"*, as if Elhaik were a neo Nazi or a left winger, or as if they were his only audience. The columnist goes on to state that the "Khazar hypothesis", which Elhaik proved, *"was invented by the womanizing communist intellectual Arthur Koestler in his 1976 book* The Thirteenth Tribe*".* (*The*

Jerusalem Post, By Seth J. Frantzman. 01/02/2013.) When people have no valid response to an uncomfortable piece of evidence, they resort to character assassination.

Let the Israeli historian Shlomo Sand have the final say. In his book *The Invention of the Jewish People*, Professor Sand argues that before the Christian era and well into the Christian era, there was a Judaizing movement in the Roman Empire led by Jewish women. The Jewish religion was legal in Rome and it appealed to Gentiles because of the system of law it brought to its followers. At some stage, ten per cent of the population of the Roman Empire was Jewish. The conversion of many nations to Judaism throws the question of whether Jews are descendants of Abraham, Isaac and Jacob into chaos. The genetic presence of the father of all believers, as the New Testament calls Abraham, has been hugely diluted. Professor Sand's book illustrates, at length, how at various moments in history and in different places, Jewish blood mixed with other nations, mainly through conversion.

Professor Sand alludes to Zionist recognition of the fact that the early church of the Holy Land was mainly Jewish. The early Zionist leaders Ben-Gurion and Ben-Zvi believed the Fallahin of Palestine were racially and genetically Jewish. They should be assimilated into the proposed Jewish state. *"In 1918, when David Ben-Gurion and Itzhak Ben-Zvi were staying in New York, they wrote a sociohistorical book entitled* Eretz Israel in the Past and in the Present.*"*

In their second chapter they wrote:

"The fellahin are not descendants of the Arab conquerors, who captured Eretz Israel and Syria in the seventh century CE. The Arab victors did not destroy the agricultural population they found in the country. They expelled only the alien Byzantine rulers, and did not touch the local population. Nor did the Arabs go in for settlement. Even in their former habitations, the Arabians did not engage in farming... They did not seek new lands on which to settle their peasantry, which hardly existed. Their whole interest in the new countries was political, religious and material: to rule, to propagate

Islam and to collect taxes... To argue that after the conquest of Jerusalem by Titus and the failure of the Bar Kokhba revolt Jews altogether ceased to cultivate the land of Eretz Israel is to demonstrate complete ignorance in the history and the contemporary literature of Israel... The Jewish farmer, like any other farmer, was not easily torn from his soil, which had been watered with his sweat and the sweat of his forebears... Despite the repression and suffering, the rural population remained unchanged." (*The Invention of The Jewish People*, Shlomo Sand, Verso; p.185.)

Not only are the above assertions false, but they are expedient. Ben-Zvi and Ben-Gurion were not students of history. They were users, nay abusers, of history, twisting it to meet their end. Whilst it must be true that the current Arabs of Palestine must be partly Jewish, the above claim is a major exaggeration designed to fulfill a Zionist agenda.

It should not astonish the reader to discover that the two Zionists had to abandon their integrationist belief in the light of the Hebron massacre, in which the Arabs of Hebron killed 67 Jews due to rumors that Jews were massacring Arabs in Jerusalem and slowly seizing control of Muslim holy places. In 1929, the year of the Hebron massacre, Ben-Zvi published his own update of the same book. This time, however, the Fallahin's Jewish ethnicity was not so wholeheartedly embraced. He acknowledged that the Fallahin may have only been partly Jewish. *"Obviously it would be mistaken to say that all the fellahin are descendants of the ancient Jews, but it can be said of most of them, or their core."* (Ibid, p.187).

Sand writes: *"The modern Palestinian fellahin became, in the eyes of the authorized agents of memory, Arabian immigrants who came in the nineteenth century to an almost empty country and continued to arrive in the twentieth century as the developing Zionist economy, according to the new myth, attracted many thousands of non-Jewish laborers"* (Ibid, p.188).

The above effectively exposes Zionists' attitudes towards historical truth. Whilst they arm themselves with historical references to prove Palestine belongs to them, they are happy to bend the truth and invent new "truths" to serve their own ends. Suffice it to say that Ben-Zvi and Ben-Gurion have established the futility of "blood" in the definition of who is a Jew, and have unwittingly, made shameful every fight between a Jew and an Arab, blood brothers, many of whom carry both sets of genes – partly Arab, and partly Jewish.

Such is the lack of cohesion amongst the Jewish people that there are more external forces keeping them together than inherent commonalities. This fact has led Jean-Paul Sartre to say of the Jewish identity that *"... it is a quasi-historical community.... It is the anti-Semite who creates the Jew"* (*Anti-Semite and Jew*, 1948). In other words, if the persecution of Jews in Europe did not exist, there would have been no motive to start the movement of Zionism, which eventually led to the accrual of such a mixture of people in Palestine, who claim to be Jewish.

There is a genuine historical question mark over the definition of a Jew. The Jews, according to their own history, and according to the Old Testament, have been subjected to exiles, not least the Assyrian exile of the 6th century BC. It is also to be remembered that when exiled they were forced to mix with other peoples. The Assyrians took away the most skilled and left behind the commoners. These were forced to mix with other nations, causing the Jewish blood to be diluted, so to speak.

Then there is the Hellenization of the Jews under the Seleucid Greeks. Not only did they adopt Hellenistic ideas, but there was intermarriage.

An earlier allusion to the Edomites was made to confute the Zionist claims that the Palestinians disappeared with the Edomites. Indeed Jewish history shows that the Edomites were absorbed by the Jewish people:

Judas Maccabeus conquered their territory for a time (B.C. 163; Ant. Xii, 8 par. 1, 2). They were again subdued by John Hyrcanus (c. 125 B.C.) by whom they were forced to observe Jewish rites and laws (ib. 9, par. 1; xiv. 4, par. 4). They were then incorporated into the Jewish nation, and their country was called by the Greeks and Romans 'Idumea' (Mark iii. 8;

Ptolemy, Geography v. 16). With Antipater began the Idumean dynasty that ruled over Judea until its conquest by the Romans. Immediately before the siege of Jerusalem 20,000 Idumeans, under the leadership of John, Simeon, Phinehas, and Jacob, appeared before Jerusalem to fight on behalf of the zealots who were besieged in the Temple (Josephus, B.J. iv. 4, par. 5).

"From this time the Idumeans ceased to be a separate people, though the name 'Idumea' still existed (in) the time of Jerome."

The New Standard Jewish Encyclopedia, edited by Dr Cecil Roth and Dr Geoffrey Wigoder (1970 edition), says under "Edom," on page 587:

"The Edomites were conquered by John Hyrcanus who forcibly converted them to Judaism, and from then on they constituted a part of the Jewish people, Herod being one of their descendants. During Titus' siege of Jerusalem, they marched in to reinforce the extreme elements, killing all they suspected of peace tendencies. Thereafter, they ceased to figure in Jewish history. The name in the Talmud is a synonym for an oppressive government, especially Rome; in the middle Ages, it was applied to Christian Europe."

Hence it can be seen that today's Jews are not as pure as they claim to be, and that the yardstick of identity by which they measure Palestinians does them no favours.

Denial in medical terms is a symptom of addiction, which in itself is a state of loss of control. Racism mirrors this picture amazingly. A racist is someone who wants to gain control by pretending that his opponent does not exist. If an alcoholic is addicted to alcohol, a racist is addicted to power and possessions.

When analysing addiction, one sees many types of denial:

1. Minimizing: *"Of course we discriminate against Israeli Arabs, but we provide them with health and education". "Of course we hate Christians, but think of how much worse they would fare under Muslim rule."*

2. Suppression: *"Sabrah and Shatila... yes. How about the six million Jews?" "We are ashamed of our forefathers' treatment of Jesus, so we must suppress all knowledge of it."* Mel Gibson's *The Passion of Christ* was banned from Israeli cinemas. However, a Palestinian Christian showed it repeatedly on his premises for many weeks. He commented that *"This had to be shown. To do otherwise would dilute the biblical account. I don't think there is anything that shows anti-Semitic tendencies."* (*Scotland on Sunday*, April 25, 2004.)

3. Projection, where Zionists would say to Palestinians, *"We are not racists. You are"*, despite oodles of evidence that Zionists are extremely guilty of racism.

4. Rationalization: A Zionist might say, *"I may appear to be a racist because I am afraid of the past repeating itself. I am afraid that a Palestinian State may turn out to be another Nazi state. That is why I hate Palestinians and will not grant them independence."*

5. Intellectualization: A Zionist might say, *"Our attitude towards the Arabs is pre-determined by history; our two diametrically opposed philosophies and the recent upsurge in fundamentalism throughout Islam."*

6. Withdrawing: Just as the addict withdraws from his usual relationships, a racist withdraws and isolates himself. *"I a Jew will not ride in a taxi whose driver is a Christian displaying the cross."*

7. Geographic escapes: The Zionists of Europe decided *"We need to have our own Jewish state, at any cost."* (My life is unmanageable – but it'll get better if I move to another place.)

Evangelical Zionists often reflect a deep disdain and repugnance for anything Arabic. This has been my own experience, shared by numerous Christian Israeli Arabs. You are written off, committed to the trash bin, simply for being an Arab.

Christian Anti-Arab Anti-Semitism

I recall when I was seventeen years of age, I met a Christian girl from a Western Country. We were probably infatuated, but there was longing there and we simply had to see each other. Eventually my friend managed to come and visit me at home in Kufur Yasief, Gallilee. We sat together and she looked very sad. I asked her why she was sad now that we were together. She explained that one of her relatives, who had lived amongst Arabs as a missionary for at least twenty years, had forbidden her from seeing me. Why? She hung her head in shame as she told me quietly, *"Because you are an Arab."* As much as I tried to shrug it off, and as much as I wanted to act as if I had heard nothing, there was no denying the shock at the audacity of such racism. *"She told me that you treat your women badly and that you would make me very unhappy."* The relative in question is someone who had had fellowship and shared worship with my parents for years. She had received hospitality at my parents' home on numerous occasions. She had heard my father preach and minister in Nazareth and elsewhere. How could she conceivably have come to such a racist conclusion about Arabs, and Christian Arabs at that?!

Deep in the psyche of some Western Christians is an indelible negative image of an Arab. This includes mistreatment of women. The advice given to my friend by her relative had more to do with prejudice than with reality.

When I met my wife, who is not an Arab, she naturally took interest in the Arab nation and consequently attended a Christian conference in Switzerland which would deepen her understanding of Arab culture. On meeting the course organizer and his wife, she was excited to be able to tell them that her husband to be was a Christian Arab. At that moment there was a change in tone towards her. They spent ages with her trying to persuade her that marriage to an Arab was a wrong step to take. Reasons included that Arabs were backward people and that they treated their wives badly.

I have now lived in the West for 39 years and I can testify to how much better Christian Arab women are treated than

Western women. When such racist attitudes come from a Christian, it is disappointing. When they are found in a Christian leader, they are very disappointing. When the same racist attitude is to be found in a Christian leader, who is a missionary for Arabs, it is extremely disappointing. This man's perception of Arabs was based on preconceived ideas, and not on experience. Nor has he distinguished in his mind between Muslim culture and Christian Arab culture, which are distinctly different.

The market value of Arabic-speaking Christians is very low amongst Western Christians. There is rarely any expression of unity or camaraderie or sympathy for Arabic-speaking Christians. These may exist on a small scale or on an individual level. In my view, it all stems from a negative image of a Christian Arab, and this image is indelibly printed on the alter-ego of the Western Church.

One of my brothers, who was once a successful businessman, found God, as the expression goes, later in life. He could no longer do business in his previous fashion. He asked me if I could connect him with Christian businessmen in the West. Eventually I found an organization of Christian businessmen who were willing to help. We met in Israel, and were expecting a representative of that organization. Instead, we arrived at Tiberius, we found that we were meeting with an Israeli Jew. To cut it short, nothing came of it. The most disappointing part of this experience was that an Evangelical organization did not see it fit to deal with an Arab Christian directly. They had to deal with their own Arab brethren through an Israeli Jew. It was as if they did not trust us because we were lying thieving Arabs! Talk about a slap in the face.

The above mistrust of Arabic-speaking Christians and the reluctance to fellowship with them is in the same vein as the conduct of the famous Dr Hagee. He visits fundamentalist Jews in Israel. He hands over millions of dollars to the Zionist State. He adopts a pro-Zionist political stance. However, he will neither fellowship with Christian Arab churches in Israel, nor will he support them financially, except for the odd token here and there to relieve his guilty conscience. This amounts to a sin of commission and a sin of omission, both of which have a common root in racism.

Chapter IV

Muslim Anti-Christian Arab Anti-Semitism

"Thus the golden age was more of a candle that shone brightly for a time, then it was almost completely snuffed out when the Abbasids found it expedient to do so."

Every human being needs to take pride in something or someone. Some people take pride in their nationality, or religion, whilst others in their race, or their profession or their personal achievement. I am most proud of my parents. They were deeply committed to God and made a personal sacrifice living by faith. That is just how we lived. My parents had no salary and no affiliation to any Christian denomination. We really lived by faith, and it was not easy for my parents as providers to feel that they were letting us down when they could not provide new shoes or shirts to replace the old, torn, worn out ones.

When I finished my high school education in Israel, my parents and I agreed that I should train to be a doctor. Israel was a poor option due to racial discrimination against Arabs at Israeli universities. Ultimately I had to study abroad. To my parents' disappointment, and despite years of free hospitality offered to thousands of Evangelicals from the USA and the UK, no one seemed interested in supporting me. Most disappointingly, a British mission in the Holy Land, who had made it public knowledge that they wished to eventually replace their foreign doctors with local Christian doctors, were not interested in supporting me.

Eventually I met a wonderful family, an Evangelical Anglican vicar, Rev Owen Thomas and his wife, who took me under their wing and provided me with a home. I carefully chose the word home, not "house". Those who know anything about Anglicans would know that their vicars are kept not far above the poverty line. This made their love for me all the more precious. They became my surrogate parents, and now 39 years later, they are my mum and dad, and their children are my brothers and sister. God has poured his love upon me through this wonderful family.

But I had to work to support myself. In 1975, I sought part-time work. My father who had been a free-Evangelical pastor in Israel had no salary and no pension. He had no affiliation to any denomination, and we had always lived by faith.

As an overseas student, I had to obtain a work permit. For that purpose, I had to prove that the work I was applying for could not be done by a native. The obvious choice was to teach Arabic to native Brits or English to Arabs. Eventually a church member showed me an advertisement for a translator at the Libyan News Agency, Fleet Street, London. I made a telephone call and introduced myself as a Palestinian. An appointment was made and I ensured I was there 15 minutes early.

The agency asked me to complete an application form. The form included a section about languages I could speak/read. Do I include Hebrew? They may find this attractive, as surely not many Libyans could read Hebrew. It may just be the edge I needed. Yet on the other hand, they may hate Israel so much that any hint of association, such as a nationality, may be the death for my employment prospects. Finally the dice was thrown and Hebrew was included in that section.

The piece I was given to translate was easy. I finished in less than half the allotted time. My prospective supervisor was impressed. He picked up my application form and the translation and asked me to wait for ten minutes. In the sparsely furnished office there was very little to engage the mind except for a picture of General M Ghaddafi, hanging above my head on the wall. It was a reminder of the non-democratic nature of the regime I was just about to engage with. Soon a portly tall man walked in. He was obviously the manager. He stood in the middle of the room. *"So you know Hebrew?"* he asked, staring at my application form. *"Yes,"* I responded with a self-satisfied smile, almost bragging, wondering whether I have scored a point. *"Where did you learn it?"* he inquired. Now here is a dilemma. Israel, I almost said, but managed to bridle my tongue just in time. If I say Palestine, and I am merely 19 years of age, he would have to be much more stupid than he looked not to realise that I was an Israeli citizen. I had heard the expression "sticky-wicket", and presently I experienced its meaning, and it felt very sticky.

"I learnt it at school," I replied making full eye contact with him. *"Where, which country?"* he asked impatiently. *"Palestine, of course."* *"What passport do you hold?"* he pushed for an answer. *"I am a Palestinian."* He repeated his question twice looking more annoyed each time. *"I am a Palestinian,"* I insisted. *"You look Jewish,"* he said provokingly. *"Actually, I am a Christian,"* I replied defiantly, thinking he simply wanted to know my religion, but did not have the courage to ask. *"But you are only 19 years old. Your Palestine is called Israel nowadays. You must have an Israeli passport,"* he stated. I stared at him and said nothing. *"Goodbye,"* he said to me with his gruff unrefined dialect and turned away leaving the room with a loud slam of the door; and with that the door was shut on my hopes of gaining employment in London.

It is difficult to convey my sense of disappointment and rejection. I left the Libyan News Agency and do not recall how I managed to find my way to the vicarage. My disappointment soon gave way to anger. Here I am, a Palestinian in need of work, and I turn to the country who claims to be the closest allies of Palestinians, and what do I get? I was so furious that I wrote a letter to M Ghaddafi via the embassy in London. The gist of it was that it was idiotic to spend millions of dollars supplying Palestinians with ammunition to help them return to

Palestine, whilst persecuting those who never fled Palestine in the first place, such as my parents, by refusing to employ me.

I have subsequently often wondered whether it was my Israeli passport or Christian faith, or indeed both, that prevented the Libyan News Agency from employing me.

The Saudis were far less subtle with me. I applied for work as a translator/interpreter or private teacher. They were fooled on the phone by my relatively good English accent. My name was Thomas, I claimed, since I called Rev and Mrs Thomas Dad and Mum, and indeed we had discussed adoption.

On arrival at the Saudi consulate in London, I was asked point-blank what my religion was. *"I am a Christian and my father is a pastor,"* I boasted, now partly in defiance, as I felt it was totally inappropriate to ask such questions at the outset of a job interview. They insisted that I at least considered conversion to Islam. Unless I went to one of their conversion classes at the mosque in Regents Park I would never be considered for work. I could not help noticing the enormous number of Pakistani and Bangladeshi employees in the consulate, and was astounded at their poor English.

I went along to the mosque just to please the Saudi officials. It would have been my ticket to gainful employment as a teacher or translator. It was astounding how many European converts and enquirers were present. Talking to some of them, it was obvious that they had attended to fulfil the requirement for gainful employment at one of the Arab embassies.

The main speaker was the former Cat Stevens. Interestingly, he came from Islington and had attended a church (St Mary's, Upper Street), and had been to Sunday school under my chemistry teacher Ray Turner. I found his presentation feeble, lacking any intellectual vigour, and rather unconvincing. All he did was make claims for Islam without any historical, archaeological or comparative theological content.

The event was boring and I found myself engaging with some Western people, asking them what on earth they found fascinating about Islam. Only one had the integrity to admit that he simply needed to do business in the Saudi Arabia and had been coaxed into attending.

I returned to the consulate and re-assured them of my attendance. *"Do I get a job now?"* I asked. *"Well you have to attend a few more of these sessions at the mosque, and then we will talk."* I responded by stating that I was born into a Christian family, and I had studied Christianity, Islam and Judaism. Whilst I was happy to participate in discussions and theological exchanges with anyone of any religion, I have thrown my lot with Christ fully convinced that He is the Son of God and the Saviour of the world. And with that I ruined my chances of work with the predominantly Muslim Arab Embassies in London.

Whilst still in Israel preparing to study in London, one of my English friends sent me a manual of prospective grant-giving organisations. I wrote numerous letters requesting financial sponsorship, but all was in vain.

One particular organisation caught my attention, whose title suggested that they may be interested in someone with my profile. They were called something like "The association for the advancement of friendship between Britain and the Arabs". There was one potential snag in approaching these people: what is their stance towards Israel? Would the Israeli authorities cause me problems if I had accepted money from this organisation? What better than to ask the Israelis?

An appointment was made for me at the consulate in Knightsbridge. I was warmly received. There was a structured recorded interview, which put me rather ill at ease. The long and short of it was that the Israelis would not be pleased if I associated with such an organisation. However, they would support me on condition that I agreed to "get into them". What that meant was espionage amongst Arab students. I thanked the interviewing official politely and stated that I could not participate with such activities on principle. That was my stance at 19 years of age.

The dilemma was that I was a foreign student, from a relatively poor country (Israel), studying in one of the most expensive cities in the world. How on earth would I support myself? My father was a free Evangelical Pastor, not affiliated with any organisation. He and my mother were living on his pension which had been virtually frozen at the same value of 1948, when the Jewish state took over. My parents could not support me. Besides, my father died in 1976, one year after my arrival in London.

When you do not know which way to turn, when all around you seem to be either enemies or faithless friends, it is hard to keep faith and not to despair. To top it all, my father died within one year of my leaving home, and with his death I lost a huge amount of confidence and moral support. He was a man of faith and he was confident that one day I would make it in England. His words kept me going and somehow, through one secular and one Christian source, and with the help of my mother and family and support of my Thomas family, I managed to meet all my basic needs throughout my years as a student in the UK.

My life story has taught me a simple lesson. Arabic-speaking Christians are an unwanted people. To Muslims we are traitors, and Muslim Arabs would give priority to a Bangladeshi over a Christian Arab. To the Jews, we are just Arabs. To some Western Evangelicals we might as well be Muslim.

Islam, under Mohammed, tolerated Christians under certain conditions. His successors turned Christians into second class citizens known as Dhimmis. The term comes from an Arabic word, which means to protect or guarantee safety. With that in mind, is it not plain that the Muslims created this term to create virtue out of villainy? Christians, who simply wished to be left alone to practise their faith, were forced to pay a fee (Jizya) in return for safety and protection. But protection from whom? Protection from Muslim violence! Protection again the "convert or die" mob. In other words, Jizya is a euphemism for protection money. Were Muslims, too, not protected by the same rulers? They were. If so, why did they not pay protection money, or Jizya? Are these early Muslim rulers not the forerunners of the Mafia? Is it not prudent to ask whether the Sicilian Mafia had not learnt this behaviour from their North African Muslim forebears?

In fact, the literal meaning of Jizya is punishment. So the punishment of a Christian in a Muslim world is a fee, a certain amount of money. This is hardly protection. It is exploitation and extortion under a religious guise. It is a form of discrimination or bigotry in official garb.

And why should Muslim Arabs consider themselves superior to Christian Arabs? Often it is stated openly that true Arabs are Muslim Arabs, and that the Christian faith is incompatible with Arab nationhood.

Yet a study of genealogy shows that the pre-Islamic Christian Arab tribes, of whom there were many, were mainly descendants of the true Arabs.

Eber is the watershed at which some Arabs and all Jews separate. He had two sons: Joktan (Qahtan) is the father of the "pure Arabs", otherwise known as the Qahtanites who dwelt in Yemen. Pheleg is Abraham's great, great, great grandfather. Abraham begat Ishmael through Hagar. Ishmael is claimed by Muslim tradition to have become the father of many Arab tribes (12 sons named in the Bible). According to Arab classification, the sons of Ishmael are known as "Arabised Arabs", as opposed to "pure Arabs". Muhammad is widely believed by Muslims to be a descendant of Ishmael. Therefore Muhammad was not a pure Arab.

By comparison, Joktan (Qahtan), through Kahlan who begat Yashub who begat Yarub (the origin of the word Arab), became the father of many of the "Pure Arabs", amongst whom are many Christians, such as the Ghassanids, Lakhmids, Banu Judham (who settled in Palestine), and Hamadan.

Some Christian Arab tribes descended from Ishmael's seed, such as Banu Taghlib who were the children of Adnan, who begat Rabiah. With the exception of Alghassanids, most of the other Christian tribes converted to Islam either during Muhammad's reign or mostly after his death, at the Battle of Yarmuk. Notwithstanding, many survive to date, living in Iraq, Syria, Jordan Lebanon and Palestine, which makes the question more relevant and less academic.

It behoves us to revisit the main question of whether Christian Arabs are true Arabs. Are they less Arabic than Muslim Arabs?

Based on the above, the Ishmaelites joined the stream seven generations from source. The Christian tribes, the children of Qahtan, are purer Arabs than most Arabs, especially more Arabic than the descendants of Ishmael, the father of Quraish (Muhammad's tribe).

Pre-Islamic Christian Arab Tribes

I have dealt with this extensively in Chapter II of this book. Suffice it to re-iterate that Arabs espoused Christianity fully in great numbers, including some of the biggest and most powerful Arab tribes. They built churches and monasteries all over Arabia, Syria and Iraq. Arabic-speaking Christians invented the Arabic script, having adapted the Syriac script. Christian Arab churches taught Arabic writing to children and adults.

It was the Arabic-speaking Christians who produced some of the most beautiful Arabic poetry. It was they who translated the works of the Greeks and the Persians into Arabic, which then was taken to Spain, from whence it was translated into European languages.

The Muslim rulers, be they Umayyads or Abbasids, simply moved into the palaces that the Christians built. Even the Qur'an is a modified version of the Bible. John of Damascus, whose father was the chief administrator of the Umayyad Caliph in Damascus, had a mixed Christian and Muslim education, though his family, the Mansurs, were known to be devout Christians. His family descended either from the Taghlib or Kalb Christian tribes (Sahas 1972, pp. 7). He was familiar with the Qur'an. He also succeeded his father as the chief administrator of the Umayyad Caliph, and gained further insights into the teachings of Islam. Eventually John was banished by the Caliph and joined a monastery.

John of Damascus, widely acclaimed as the last of the early church fathers, and the first Christian scholar, was the first Arabic speaker who challenged Islam theologically. In his book entitled *Concerning Heresy*, written in 749 AD, he expressed the view that the Ishmaelite or Hagarene religion (it was not yet known as Islam in the eighth century) was another Christian heresy. He wrote:

"Jews, Arians and Nestorians, from each one of these Muhammad acquired a particular teaching, and thus he formed his own heresy: from the Jews, absolute monotheism; from the Arians, the affirmation that the Word and the Spirit are creatures [and thereby not divine]; and from the Nestorians... that Christ was simply a human being." He also wrote: *"Muhammad, the founder of Islam, is a false prophet who, by chance, came across the Old and New Testament, and who... thus devised his own heresy."* The Damascene, incensed by Muhammad's adulteration of the Bible, referred to him as the fore-runner of the Antichrist, the false Christ, or the imitator of Christ.

The Syrian monk details errors in the Qur'an which unfaithfully copies Biblical narratives, such as the confusion between Mary the Mother of Christ and Mary sister of Moses.

Islam and Muslim Rulers

In modern Western countries, where people claim to be living in a post-Christian era, Muslims who have emigrated in great numbers have managed to make some ludicrous claims about how peaceful their religion is. And even in the face of mounting Islamic international violence, politicians and church leaders of Western countries either lack the courage or the knowledge to refute such claims as mere posturing and false Islamic propaganda.

Starting with Mohammed himself and the Qur'an, what did they say about Christians, and how did they say Muslims should treat Christians?

The Qur'an in:

- 5:73 denounces anyone who believes in the Holy Trinity as an infidel. *"They have certainly disbelieved who say, 'Allah is the third of three.' And there is no god except one God. And if they do not desist from what they are saying, there will surely afflict the disbelievers among them a painful punishment."*

- 5:17 denies the core Christian belief that Christ is the Son of God. *"They have certainly disbelieved who say that Allah is Christ, the son of Mary."*

- 9:29 says categorically: *"Fight those who do not believe in Allah or in the Last Day and who do not consider unlawful what Allah and His Messenger have made unlawful and who do not adopt the religion of truth from those who were given the Scripture – [fight] until they give the Jizya willingly while they are humbled."*

- 9:5 instructs Muslims to kill any Christian (polytheist, Mushrik – which is a term used for Christians who are accused of believing in three Gods). *"And when the sacred months have passed, then kill the polytheists wherever you find them and capture them and besiege them and sit in wait for them at every place of ambush. But if they should repent, establish prayer, and give zakah, let them [go] on their way. Indeed, Allah is Forgiving and Merciful."*

If this is peaceful, I would shudder to ask what belligerent is! The Qur'an denounces the original Christian doctrine held for almost six centuries before the advent of Islam, calls it infidelity (Kufr), and those who hold these core Christian doctrines are called polytheists. Worse still, the Qur'an calls Muslims to convert them or kill them. Now unless the Qur'an has changed recently, let no man claim that Islam is a religion of peace, or mercy.

Having looked at the theology of Muslims, let us look at their practices. How have they dealt with Arabic-speaking Christians down the centuries?

In a sense the die has been cast. Once you speak of a group with such derogatory terms and such aggressive intent, particularly when you claim divine authority behind your thinking, it is only a matter of time before these words of malice are translated into violence and killing.

The words of the Qur'an have given rise to the infamous conditions of Omar. These are conditions imposed by Muslims on non-Muslims, which at the beginning mainly meant Arabic-speaking Christians. The conditions are rendered in the first tense and are deliberately composed to give the impression that the prohibitive and punitive conditions were self-imposed by Christians.

According to the Conditions (Pact) of Omar, a Christian would willingly impose on himself the following restrictions, never to:

1. Build *"a monastery, church, or a sanctuary for a monk"*;
2. *"Restore any place of worship that needs restoration"*;
3. Use such places *"for the purpose of enmity against Muslims"*;
4. *"Allow a spy against Muslims into our churches and homes or hide deceit [or betrayal] against Muslims"*;
5. Imitate the Muslims' *"clothing, caps, turbans, sandals, hairstyles, speech, nicknames and title names"*;
6. *"Ride on saddles, hang swords on the shoulders, collect weapons of any kind or carry these weapons"*;
7. *"Encrypt our stamps in Arabic"*;
8. *"Sell liquor"* – Christians in Iraq in the last few years ran afoul of Muslims reasserting this rule;
9. *"Teach our children the Qur'an"*;
10. *"Publicize practices of Shirk"* – that is, associating partners with Allah, such as regarding Jesus as Son of

God. In other words, Christian and other non-Muslim religious practice will be private, if not downright furtive;

11. Build *"crosses on the outside of our churches and demonstrating them and our books in public in Muslim fairways and markets"* – again, Christian worship must not be public, where Muslims can see it and become annoyed;

12. *"Sound the bells in our churches, except discreetly, or raise our voices while reciting our holy books inside our churches in the presence of Muslims, nor raise our voices [with prayer] at our funerals, or light torches in funeral processions in the fairways of Muslims, or their markets"*;

13. *"Bury our dead next to Muslim dead"*;

14. *"Buy servants who were captured by Muslims"*;

15. *"Invite anyone to Shirk"* – that is, proselytize, although the Christians also agree not to:

16. *"Prevent any of our fellows from embracing Islam, if they choose to do so."* Thus the Christians can be the objects of proselytizing, but must not engage in it themselves;

17. *"Beat any Muslim"*.

In addition, the Christian would willingly owe the following duties to a Muslim:

1. Allow Muslims to rest *"in our churches whether they come by day or night"*;

2. *"Open the doors [of our houses of worship] for the wayfarer and passer-by"*;

3. Provide board and food for *"those Muslims who come as guests"* for three days;

4. *"Respect Muslims, move from the places we sit in if they choose to sit in them"*.

5. *"Have the front of our hair cut, wear our customary clothes wherever we are, wear belts around our waist"* – these are so that a Muslim recognizes a non-

Muslim as such and doesn't make the mistake of greeting him with As-salaamu aleikum, "Peace be upon you," which is the Muslim greeting for a fellow Muslim;

6. *"Be guides for Muslims and refrain from breaching their privacy in their homes"*.

It does not take a nuclear scientist to conclude that such conditions are made up of pure disdain for and bigotry against Christians. It violates all sorts of human rights. Not only is it not conducive to peace, but is a perfect recipe for discord and war.

Indeed, when these conditions were first enforced in Syria and Egypt, with a vast Christian majority, the Muslims could not enforce them as they feared a backlash from Christians. However as time marched and more Christians were forced to convert, eventually the Muslims exceeded the Christians in numbers and started to enforce these conditions mercilessly.

Rodney Stark believes that over a period of two years, the Muslims in Egypt and Syria demolished 30,000 Christian churches. *(God's battalions;* New York Harper Collins, 2009, p.91.)

Raymond Ibrahim gives many examples of such atrocities down the centuries (pp.37-8).

By 767 *"heavier hardships than ever fell upon the Christians, who were obliged to eat their dead; while their new churches in Egypt were destroyed."* (Taqi Ed-Din El- Maqrizi, *A Short History of the Copts and their Church*, London, D Nutt, p.7.)

In the 14th century later Islamic scholars such as Ibn Qayyim al-Jawziyya referred to churches as *"worse than brothels"* and *"houses of torment and fire"*.

The Sahfi'iyya called churches *"abodes of devils"* (Bukhari, *Sabih*, Beirut 1981, III, p.216).

Another widespread fallacy is that the world owes Islam gratitude for translating the Greek Classics. Nothing could be further from the truth. It was Arabic-speaking Christians, and not Muslims, who carried out these translations.

If it were not for the fifth-century priest Probus of Antioch, we would not have had Aristotle's works in Arabic. Hunayn Ibn Ishaq, another Christian Arab, translated Aristotle's work alongside Galen, Plato and Hippocrates into Syriac, following which his son translated these works into Arabic. Another Christian Arab, Yahya ibn A'di, also translated the classics into Arabic. His student, Abi Ali Isa ibn Zura, translated more works from Syriac into Arabic.

The contribution of Arabic-speaking Christians extended into medicine. The first Arabic medical treatise was written by a Christian physician. The first hospital to be built in Baghdad during the Abbasid era was erected by a Christian. Assyrian Christians built a medical school in Gundeshapur, Persia. (*Religion of Peace? Why Christianity is and Islam isn't*, Robert Spencer, pp.157-158.)

The Umayyad Period

The death of the fourth Caliph ushered in a new era in the history of Islam and the Arabs as a whole. The murder of Caliph Ali in 661, by members of the so called peaceful religion of Islam, and the renunciation of power by his successor and son Hasan (the grandson of Muhammad) left a power vacuum in the Muslim Arab world. Hasan was a member of Ahl al-bayt, meaning "member of the household" (of Muhammad), a rare privilege for any aspiring Muslim dynast. The shrewd governor of Syria persuaded Hasan to capitulate to him. Trading on his pedigree, Muawiyah made a bid for power and established himself as Caliph, choosing Damascus as his capital city. Muawiyah, who was a member of Prophet Muhammad's tribe of Quraysh, and a kinsman of Caliph Uthman, was revolutionary compared with his predecessors, mainly due to his relative tolerance of non-Muslims, whom he saw as useful allies and instruments of development and enhancement of his seat of power

His reign marked a paradigm shift in Muslim Arab rulership. He was the first Caliph to own a professional army, and indeed due to the ports he inherited from the Christians in Syria, he, unlike his predecessors, owned a navy too.

His reign was marked by phenomenal energy leading to both territorial expansion and impressive development in every field of life.

Caliph Mu'awiyah ibn Abi-Sufyan, who chose a Christian for a wife, saw the advantage of "tolerance" towards Christians. The Arabic-speaking Christians of Syria were the architects, the scientists, the teachers and business masters of the region. It would be to his advantage to have them on side.

Not only did Mu'awiyah choose a Christian for a wife, but he allowed his son and successor Yazid to marry a Christian Ghassanid princess, Um Ramlah. Yazid was renowned for his closeness to the Christian poet, Al Akhtal from Banu Taghlib, who was one of the greatest Arab poets who ever lived.

Thus Mu'awiyah handed over his financial affairs to a Christian family called Sarjun. He also had a Christian for a physician by the name of Ibn Athal. When the church of Ar-Raha was damaged by an earthquake, Mu'awiyah ordered it to be repaired.

Mu'awiyah recruited Christians to lead his forces. Therefore, they deserve credit for building the Umayyad Empire which extended from Kabul in the East to Tours (France) in the West.

Examples of prudent utilisation of Christian skills by the Umayyads abound. These include the appointment of the Christian scribe Istifanus in Khorosan by Abdulrahman ibn Zyad, the appointment of the Palestinian ibn Al-Batriq as the copyist of Sulaiman ibn 'Abdulmalik, and the appointment of Tadhri ibn Astin as the scribe of Hesham ibn 'Abdulmalik.

In Egypt, as in Syria, Christians formed a majority and were as learned and skilled as their Syrian Christian brethren. It made sense therefore for the Umayyad Caliphs to appoint Christians to high offices. Thus the Governor in Upper Egypt at the end of 'Abdul-'Aziz ibn Marawan's reign (685-705A.D) was a Christian Egyptian named Butrus, whilst Tadfans was the governor of Mariut. Qarah ibn Sharik ensured the governorship of Alexandria was in the hands of Tadurs.

(Hassan 'Ali Hassan, Ahlu-Dhimmah, "Non-Muslims living under the Muslim rule", p.130-131.)

'Umar ibn 'Abdul-'Aziz went further by ordering his governors to show kindness to the sick and elderly under his rule. He is also renowned for downgrading the taxes paid by the powerful Christian Arab tribe, Banu Taghlib, from Jizya to Zakat (Ibn Al-Jawzy, *Biography of 'Umar ibn 'Abdul-'Aziz*, p.79), although this has probably more to do with the power of Taghlib than the Caliph's generosity. Taghlib were powerful enough to dare to demand equality with their Muslim Arab brethren.

The beautiful Dome of the Rock Mosque, situated in the middle of mount Moriah in Jerusalem, was built by the Umayyad Caliph Abdul Malik. The mosque was built in Christian Byzantine style. Many believe it was an attempt by the Muslim dynasts to emulate Christians. The Muslim historian al-Muqaddasi asked his uncle to explain why the Umayyads had lavished so much money on the Damascus mosque. His uncle apparently answered him thus:

"O my little son, thou has no understanding. Verily al-Walid was right, and he was prompted to a worthy work. For he beheld Syria to be a country that had long been occupied by the Christians, and he noted there are beautiful churches still belonging to them, so enchantingly fair, and so renowned for their splendour, as are the Church of the Holy Sepulchre, and the Churches of Lydda and Edessa. So he sought to build for the Muslims a mosque that should be unique and a wonder to the world. And in like manner is it not evident that 'Abd al-Malik, seeing the greatness of the martyrium [Qubbah] of the Holy Sepulchre and its magnificence was moved lest it should dazzle the minds of Muslims and hence erected above the Rock the Dome which is now seen there."

Shlomo Dov Goitein believes the Dome of the Rock was built in order to compete with the many Christian churches that constituted the skyline of Jerusalem: *"The very form of a rotunda, given to the Qubbat as-Sakhra, although it was foreign to Islam, attempted to rival the many Christian domes of its time."* (Goitein, Shlomo Dov; "The Historication background of the erection of the Dome of the Rock", *Journal of American Oriental Society*, Vol. 70, No. 2, 1950.) Even the Dome of the Rock's dimensions are almost exactly the same as those of the church with which it was jostling for position. (*Encyclopædia Britannica*: "Dome of the Rock". Britannica.com. Retrieved 2012-04-04.) Thus the oldest Muslim edifice is a copy of one of the oldest churches in Christendom. Is this a form of inverted flattery?

Not only was the Dome of the Rock based on the plans of the Church of the Holy Sepulchre, it also contained a defiant message to the Arabic-speaking Christians of Jerusalem. Of all the Qur'anic verses, the Muslims saw it fit to choose a defiant excerpt from the Qur'an which has been inscribed over the inner octagonal arcade, which challenges the sonship of Christ and the Holy Trinity.

"O ye who believe! Ask blessings on him and salute him with a worthy salutation. The blessing of God be on him and peace be on him, and may God have mercy. O People of the Book! Do not exaggerate in your religion nor utter aught concerning God save the truth. The Messiah, Jesus son of Mary, was only a Messenger of God, and His Word which He conveyed unto Mary, and a spirit from Him. So believe in God and His messengers, and say not 'Three' – Cease! (it is) better for you! – God is only One God. Far be it removed from His transcendent majesty that He should have a son. His is all that is in the heavens and all that is in the earth. And God is sufficient as Defender. The Messiah will never scorn to be a servant unto God, nor will the favoured angels. Whoso scorneth His service and is proud, all such will He assemble unto Him.

"Oh God, bless Your Messenger and Your servant Jesus son of Mary. Peace be on him the day he was born, and the day he dies,and the day he shall be raised alive! Such was Jesus, son of Mary, (this is) a statement of the truth concerning which they doubt. It befitteth not (the Majesty of) God that He should take unto Himself a son. Glory be to Him!"

However, The Umayyads were not always generous. By the end of 89 years of Umayyad rule, through both financial and societal pressures, detailed above, most Syrian Arabs had converted to Islam.

In his *Historia general de España*, Juan de Mariana (1592 AD) comments on the basis of the surrender terms granted by the Umayyad conquerors which though afforded them a degree of freedom, the situation of Christians in Andalucia was described as a *"tolerable manner of servitude"*. Abd ar-Rahmân II imposed heavy taxes which made life unbearable for the Christians. He also describes the state of the Christians of Córdoba who were subjected to verbal and physical abuse by their Muslim rulers and neighbours. (Juan de Mariana, *Historia general de España* (Madrid, 1789), p.120.)

Most scholars are agreed that relatively speaking the Umayyads were tolerant of non-Muslims. They permitted non-Muslims a degree of autonomy and allowed them to have their own courts of law. This is probably attributable to the fact that the Umayyads were not particularly religious, with the exception of Umar II (717–720), who having declared all his subjects equal, paradoxically forbade Christians from wearing silk garments or turbans.

It is prudent thus to ask whether that famed Umayyad tolerance owed its virtue to the Muslim faith, or to some other ulterior motive. It must be remembered that under the Umayyads, non-Muslims had to pay land tax and Jizya unless they converted to Islam, whilst Muslim Arabs received state stipends. This disparity of status does not portray a picture of tolerance. To give someone a choice between abandoning his religion and paying tax (protection money) is hardly the epitome of tolerance.

Thus it is clear that the whole issue of Umayyad tolerance rested precariously on a fiscal pivot. This became more obvious when the far flung and remote parts of the Umayyad Empire rebelled and refused to send taxes to Damascus. A cash-strapped caliphate saw it expedient to tax converts to Islam, against the precepts of their religion, as if they were still non-Muslims. This smacks of expediency, not of genuine tolerance. The test of tolerance must be passed in times of plenty as much as in times of need. The Umayyads failed both tests. Indeed, the only religious Umayyad caliph, Umar II, was the least tolerant of them.

The Abbasid Period

Whilst the Umayyad period was marked by geographical expansion in the main, the Abbasid period was marked by development, particularly cultural, economic and intellectual development. In that respect, the Abbasids continued in the same vein as the Umayyads, less the military expansion. But the Abbasids essentially built on Umayyad foundations, and took a leaf from the Umayyads' book in how they utilized Christian and Jewish human resources.

If there was any distinction between the two dynasties, the Umayyads had ruled as privileged dynasts, an elect minority descended from the line of the prophet Muhammad. They lorded it over everyone, and exacted taxes from everyone. They ruled inequitably, imposing Zakat on Muslim subjects, and Jizya on non-Muslims. In that respect the Umayyads were xenophobes.

The Umayyads eventually imposed Jizya on converts from other religions, thus favouring money over the welfare of the Muslim kingdom of God. Many Muslim scholars believe the Umayyads had deviated from the tolerance of non-Muslims (and that is a relative term) which marked the dealings of Muhammad and the caliphs who succeeded him

Whether the Hashimites were more noble than the Umayyads, or whether they found a weakness to exploit, they called for a revolt against the Umayyads, relying mainly on the Muslims of Persia, who supported the Hashimites on the grounds that the latter descended from the uncle of the prophet Muhammad (Abbas ibn 'Abd al-Muttalib), and that they were calling for all Muslims, Arab or non-Arab, to be treated equally. The Hashimites assumed names associated with suzerainty such as al-Mhadi, al-Mansur, and al-Ma'mun. The

Persians offered the Hashimites the expertise of an old and durable empire, whilst the Hashimites offered the prestige of a pure descent and pedigree.

Hence the Abbasids, called after their first leader, Abu Abbas, were generally more lenient with their non-Arab and non-Muslim subjects. Many historians refer to their reign as the Golden Age. Whilst the founders of the Abbasid dynasty moved the court and power from Damascus to Baghdad, which was purpose built to reflect their faith and philosophy, the Abbasids still had to rely on Arabic-speaking Christians, from Christian Syria, to help them translate works of classical Greek philosophy, medicine and astronomy into Arabic. The Abbasids of the tenth century AD also needed Jewish and Christian bankers to manage their wealth and assets. No longer was access to the court based on tribal affiliations or Arabness, but rather on merit. Prove you can be of help to the dynasty and you are in with a chance.

Amongst the luminaries of the Abbasid period one finds Christians such as Yuhanna, who was the first to dissect a monkey in search of a better understanding of human anatomy.

In addition to the openness of the court to intellectuals and skilled people from non-Muslim and non-Arab backgrounds, there appeared to be an openness for religious and intellectual dialogues. Of note are two well documented dialogues. The first took place between the Patriarch Timothy I (780-823) and the Caliph al-Mahdî (775-785), in which Patriarch Timothy answered the questions and challenges posed by the Muslim dynast about Christian doctrines and practices. The second is the dialogue between the monk of Bêt Hãlê and an Arab magnate (ca. 720). The Monk Abraham openly answered questions posed by a wealthy Muslim. (Sidney H. Griffith, *Syrian Christian Writers in the World of Islam*, N.J.: The American Foundation for Syriac Studies, p.16.)

The latter dialogue may not be as impressive as the first because it lacks the scintillation of the Caliph; however it is more distinguished by the relationship between the two sides. The Muslim party came to the monk for help when he was ill and received treatment and hospitality from the Christian monk. This reflects the degree to which Muslims and Christians had learnt to be at peace with one another. The significance of this dialogue is that it is a useful yardstick by which modern Christian-Muslim relationships should be measured. It is the sort of relationship my people of Kufur Yasief have enjoyed for centuries with our Muslim neighbours; a peaceful co-existence, marked by mutual respect and trust.

In order to underscore the dexterity of Christians who lived under the Abbasids, by which they managed to be faithful to the Gospel and respect their Muslim neighbours, mention must be made of Theodore Abu Qurrah, who had a profound understanding of the Qur'an, and was a staunch defender and expounder of essential Christian doctrines such as the deity of Christ, the Holy Trinity, Christ's willingness to go to the cross, and the human existence of Christ. (Graf, "Geschichte der Christlichen Arabischen Literature", cited by N. A. Newman, *The Early Christian-Muslim Dialogue*, xxi.) His writings show that Christian theology and apologetics amongst the Arabs had developed significantly in the interval between the Umayyads and the Abbasids.

Bani Tayfouri were a famous Christian Arab family, many of whose members served the Caliphs as their private physicians. Abdallah Ben Al-Tayfouri, who had studied at Gundishapor, became physician to Al-Mahdi. Zakaria Ben Abdallah Al-Tayfouri became physician to Caliph Al-Mutasem, whilst Israel Ben Zakaria, Abdallah's grandson, was appointed physician of the Caliph's vizier Al-Mutawakel. (Shikho, pp.210-212.)

Ibn Massawayh is the author of many medical books in Arabic such as *Al-Kana'es Al-Mushajar*, another Arabic composition dealing with sciatica and renal problems, *Kitab Al-'Ain* (*The Book of the Eye*), the first of its kind, and *Al-Mahmiyat*, which dealt with conditions such as migraines, diseases of the liver and ear. (Al-Samarai, p.429.)

The translation movement of the Abbasids was largely achieved by Christians, both Assyrians and Arabs. The Assyrians are Semites, most of whom were well versed in

Arabic, having lived amongst Arabs for centuries. As mentioned earlier, during the era of the Lakhmids, their capital city Hira became a centre of learning and commerce. However the Muslims built Kufa and moved the trade and commerce out of Hira, causing its demise. However, many Christian Assyrian families (semites) preserved their traditions. Such a family is that of Hunayn ibn Ishak Al-Ibbadi, whose work involved the translation of a significant volume of works from Greek and Assyrian.

However, the Golden Age rested on unsure foundations. The Abbasids needed a secure stream of income. Indeed, they largely refrained from proselytising Christians and other non-Muslims because if such were to convert to Islam, the Muslim Abbasid dynasty would suffer loss of precious income, as these converts would pay Zakat expected of Muslims, and not Jizya which Dhimmis had to pay.

The Abbasid's true intentions towards Christians were made clear by the maltreatment of the Christians of Jerusalem under the first Abbasid Caliph. The Greek Church claims that Abdallah, head of the Arabs, the first Abbasid caliph, forbade the cross from Jerusalem. Monks were evicted from their monasteries, and the Jews were incited into destroying the Church of the Holy Sepulchre and various other scared buildings. (*A History of Palestine, 634-1099*, Moshe Gil, p.473.) This would set the general tone for the treatment of Christians by the Abbasids, with a degree of variation based on expediency.

Christians flourished at times under the Abbasids, not purely because the latter were inherently better than the Umayyads. They were, however, more shrewd. Purity is often evidenced by fire. The fire of loss and deprivation can remove façades and burn the thin outer veneer, revealing the true heart of a people. When the Christians of North Africa rebelled against the Abbasids and refused to pay tax, the Abbasid Caliph al-Mutawakkil (847–61) revived the Pact of Omar and applied it strictly, thus exacting much higher taxes on Christians and Jews, and even confiscating the property of many a wealthy Christian. He forced Christians and Jews to affix wooden images of devils to their property. Christians and Jews were expected to have flat graves. He imposed the wearing of yellow patches on external garments for Christians and Jews.

Christians were not permitted to ride on horses. They had to be contented with a donkey or a mule. They also had to use wooden saddles which were marked by two pomegranates, which gave rise to the expression "spotted" as the pomegranates looked more like circles, and helped identify Christians. (*The Arabs: A Short History*, Philip K Hitti, Gateway, p.137.) Where Christians reached a high position such as a vizir, Muslims would often refuse to treat them with the same respect they would a Muslim vizir, such as kissing a vizir's hand, as a mark of respect.

Al-Mutawakkel issued a firman against Christians and Jews which states: *"If a Christian was a servant in the house of a Muslim, he should wear a sign to show his bondage: – two straps of leather of different colour".* (*History of the Syrian Nation and the Old Evangelical-apostolic Church of the East*, George David Malech, p.279.)

Harun al-Rashid, with whom Western historians seem naively enamoured, forced Christians and Jews to wear clothes that distinguished them from Muslims. This is reminiscent of what Hitler did to the Jews in Europe, and the yellow star he forced them to wear. Harun al-Rashid also ensured the destruction of churches in his kingdom along the borders with Byzantium.

In Egypt, Abbasid governors would habitually capture a Coptic Patriarch, to whom they referred as "Abu Al-Nassara" meaning the father of the Nazarenes, and request ransom money. They would insist on money being paid even during periods of drought and locust infestation when the Copts had no means of paying the ransom. (*The Truth About Islam*, Ibn El-Neil, pp. 215-6.)

The demand for ransom money was not employed in Egypt alone. Christians all over the Muslim world were treated in the same way. Moshe Gil quotes many claims by Christians of such ilk. There is the case of the Church of the Annunciation in

Nazareth being threatened with demolition unless ransom money was paid. In Jerusalem, the Church of the Resurrection faced a similar threat by Muslims, who considered it moral and just to demand large sums of money from Christians to save their beloved sacred building from demolition. (*A History of Palestine, 634-1099*, Moshe Gil, p.473.)

According to Theophanes, in 755 the first Abbasid Caliph increased taxes due by Christians, imposed taxes on priests and monks, who were previously exempt, confiscated Christian scared articles, put his seal on them, and forced the Jews to buy them. He forbade Christians from holding midnight services or teaching the Scriptures. (*A History of Palestine, 634-1099*, Moshe Gil, p.473.)

Whilst visiting Jerusalem in 772, Caliph Abadallah al-Mansur ordered that all Christians and Jews had a special mark stamped on their hands to distinguish them from Muslims.

Thus the golden Abbasid age was more of a candle that shone brightly for a time, and then it was almost completely snuffed out when the Abbasids found it expedient to do so. Christians enjoyed most liberty during the reign of Al-Mansur (754-775) and Al-Ma'mun (813-833), during whose reigns Christians occupied many influential positions with unlimited access to the seat of power. By contrast the reign of Harun Al-Rashid (786-809) was not as kind to Christians, whilst the reign of al-Mutawakkil (847–61) was much less salubrious.

The history of Arabic-speaking Christians under the Abbasids is strewn with examples of violence, slaughter, terrorism, ransom, confiscation of property including religious items, destruction of churches, eviction of whole villages or towns, rape, and conversion at the point of the sword.

The Abbasids were succeeded by the Mongols in 1258. Non-Muslims would have hoped for a more tolerant ruler than the Abbasids. However, the Mongols adopted the religion of the dynasts they had vanquished, and as Muslims they were more hateful of Christians than ever.

The Ottomans

It is widely accepted by the Eastern Christian church that life under the Ottomans was harsher than it had been under the Muslim Arabs. No Ottoman ruler had treated the Christians so harshly as did Timur the Lame (1336–1405), who at the beginning of the 15th century targeted and slaughtered Christians throughout Syria, Mesopotamia, and Asia Minor. Those Christians he did not kill, he forced into Islam. Conversion at the point of the sword is not alien to Islam. The covenant between the Christians and Muhammad, the so-called "rightly guided Caliphs" who succeeded him, the Umayyads and the Abbasids, were completely ignored. The covenant stated that provided the Christians accepted their Muslim rulers' sovereignty, they would enjoy their protection, provided they paid Jizya. Not only did Timur fail to protect his Christian subjects, but he decimated them in the name of Islam, simply for professing the Christian faith.

The descendants of Ossman who followed on from the Caliphets invented the millets, a term deriving from an Arabic word for nation. Under this system, religious communities were awarded a degree of autonomy, in that they were allowed to be judged internally by their own religious systems. The head of a millet was an intermediary between the individual and the state. Therefore, the Patriarch of the Eastern Orthodox Church was an intermediary between his flock and the Sultan.

Christians were treated like second-class citizens. They were forced to wear black or blue whilst the Muslims wore white, so Christians were easily identified. Christians were not allowed to ride horses. Muslim apartheid was enforced. Christians and Jews could not use the same public baths as the Muslims. The conditions of the Pact of Omar were applied strictly. Christians had to always be subservient or convert. Sometimes, it was simply a matter of convert or die. (*Witnesses for Christ*, Nomikos Michael Vaporis.)
Surprisingly, despite Muslims being in the ascendancy, not a few of them converted to Christianity, preferring to be despised disciples of Christ than privileged Muslims. Such

converts struck a chord of insecurity in Ottoman Islam. Worse still were those converts to Islam, who had converted under duress for social position, money, marriage or some other privilege, many of whom repented and returned to their Christian faith. Despite the bravery of a few, the flow was mainly one-directional, draining the Coptic Church of its members. The Coptic encyclopaedia gives an idea about the effect of aggressive Ottoman proselytization of Coptic Christians in Egypt: *"It is said that their total number around the end of the eighteenth century sank to a mere 150,000 out of a total Egyptian population of 3 million. While 600,000 had paid their tithe to the Coptic patriarch immediately after the ARAB CONQUEST OF EGYPT, at this period only 15,000 are known to have done this."* ("Copts under the Ottomans", Claremont Coptic Encyclopaedia.)

In as far as the millets defined citizenship by religious criteria, that sort of development resulted in the gradual de-Arabisation and marginalisation of Arabic-speaking Christians in Muslim Arab society, where Christians are viewed mainly, if not solely, as Christians and not as Arabs; almost as aliens or misfits, not fully Arab. The irony is that this dichotomy was presided over by non-Arabs, Ottomans. Muslim Arabs were more at home with Ottomans, with whom they shared no roots, and with whom they were happy to stand against their Christian Arab brethren.

Current Muslim Injustice Against Christian Arabs

There is, nowadays, a surge of Arab Muslim anti-Christian feelings and an increase in concomitant acts of violence against Arabic-speaking Christians. The old Biblical countries are being bled dry of any Christian presence. This has been the case in Iraq and other Arab counties where Muslim extremists have flourished. In September 2004 five Christian church buildings were bombed by Muslim extremists in Iraq. This led to no fewer than 40,000 Christians fleeing the country shortly after the bombings.

No fewer than four million Lebanese Christians and one million Iraqi Christians have fled their counties in the last few years because of pressure, coercion and violence committed against them by Muslims.

"The reason is the harassment to which they are subjected by government agencies on the one hand and extremist groups on the other hand in countries they have inhabited for thousands of years," Aziza wrote.

For centuries, Christians have lived in the territory currently referred to as the Arab countries alongside other religious groups, *"particularly with Muslims who shared with them the afflictions of life,"* Aziza said.

"But the Christians have lost their partners for many reasons," Aziza added. He wrote that those reasons include *"religious extremism among some Muslims, the demographic increases out of religious reasons, and the acts of discrimination, coercion, and individual and collective expulsion of Christians, and the pressures placed upon them even when they were serving their countries. There are many examples of that in Palestine, Iraq, Sudan, Lebanon, Egypt, and other countries."*

Christians in Egypt Mauritania and Pakistan have fared no better.

"In Islamic countries like Pakistan, for example, where Christians suffer from persecution, "Islamist [spiritual leaders] have issued a fatwa [religious opinion] permitting the killing of two Christians for every Muslim killed by the American attacks in Afghanistan, as though the Americans represent Christianity in the world," wrote Aziza."("Christian Arab Faced with Continued Pressure", Iraqi columnist: "It is difficult to recall a period in which Christian Arabs were in greater danger than today", *Christian Today*, October 2, 2004.)

"Muslim Palestinian Arabs plundered a town of Christian Palestinian Arabs in southern Samaria Sunday, setting houses and cars ablaze in an apparent 'revenge' attack after a Christian man dared to date a Muslim woman." (Stan Goodenough, "Muslim 'Palestinians' firebomb Christian 'Palestinians'", *Sullivan County*, September 5, 2005.)

As their homes were being firebombed, the residents of the village of Taibe fled to neighbouring villages for safety, as Muslim vandals destroyed the homes of Christians. Though no human physical injury ensued, the Palestinian Authority's tardy response was noted.

Muslim crowds protested and the family of the girl poisoned her and buried her, an act infamously known as *"honour killing"*. Goodenough adds: *"In the Kingdom of Jordan, the law states that family members who carry out honour killings are 'totally exempt from sentence.' Between 28 and 60 such murders are estimated to take place annually in that country. The Palestinian Authority also permits these killings, with up to 22 a year reportedly taking place."*

When Coptic Christians from Egypt met in the USA to discuss discrimination by Muslim authorities against Christian Arabs, the Egyptian media reacted as if those Christians were traitors plotting a *coup d'état*, rather than look at the reasons they had travelled abroad to meet.

"The government-controlled media conveniently neglected to mention that the organizers wanted to hold the conference in Egypt, but received no response to the request they sent to Egyptian officials. There was nothing new here – we all remember that the Egyptian government prevented Saadeddin Ibrahim from convening a conference in Egypt in 1994 on minorities in the Arab world. He had to take it to Cyprus instead."

"After years of ugly anti-Christian hatred that too often emanates in mosques and government-controlled media, it was imperative that Muslims and Christians, together, said 'enough.' Many of us who attended as Muslims also share with our Christian compatriots the general lack of rights that is the plight of all Egyptians." She continued. She referred to *"the ugly riots outside an Alexandria church in October were a sad reminder of sectarianism run amok."*

She then pointed to the absence of Christians from the Egyptian echelons of power such as mayors, public university presidents or deans, *"and there are few Christians in the upper ranks of the security services and the armed forces"*. (By

Mona Eltahawy, who is a Muslim, Assyrian International News Agency 12-23-2005.)

Arabic-speaking Christians are small persecuted minorities in the largely Muslim Arab world. Indeed, on a recent visit to Tunisia, I was surprised to hear that circa 2% of the population is made up of Christians and other religions. We travelled on Easter Day from our resort in Hammamet to Sousse for an Easter service. The congregation was purely made up of ex-pats. The church was Catholic, and they permitted an Evangelical pastor from England to hold services on Sundays. The only Arabs in the church were nuns from Egypt. In vain did I look for an Arabic face in the congregation. Eventually I found one; the caretaker. I was not sure whether he was a Muslim or a Christian. Sometimes the only way forward is to be forward! I asked him directly. He stated that he was a Muslim. *"Are there no Arabic-speaking Christians in Tunisia?"* I asked in surprise. *"No. None at all,"* he replied, avoiding eye contact. Whether he was in denial or whether he was ignorant of the existence of Arabic-speaking Christians in Tunisia, was immaterial to me. Both are equally disappointing and betray a woefully negative attitude towards Christians.

We travelled to Sfax, where we were told most of the Christians and Jews of Tunisia were to be found. To our surprise, we found a huge synagogue with a large Star of David fronting it. We asked several people where we could find a church. We knew we were within one mile of a church. Most people were ignorant of the church's whereabouts. Eventually we came across a small building which was the Orthodox Church of Sfax.

Arabs, most of whom are Muslims, tend to look upon their Christian brothers with suspicion. To them, we are almost Zionists. The worst kind is, of course, the Evangelicals, because they take the Bible seriously, even when it goes against us.

Al-Aqsa's TV station, owned by the fundamentalist Islamist group Hamas, is teaching Muslim children Islamic supremacy over Christians (and Jews). Their justification is that apparently Christians and Jews lived happily under

Muslim rule in the past. (*Islamic Rule Good for Christians, Jews, Hamas 'Mickey Mouse' Creator Says*, Julie Stahl CNSNews.com Jerusalem Bureau Chief, May 16, 2007.)

There can be nothing further from the truth. Indeed, in 9th century Baghdad, under the Abbasids, a Sunni caliphate, Christians were marked by an orange badge (Jews by a yellow badge). They were the forerunners of Nazis in Germany. This is how Islam has treated Christians in the past, and the present is no less gloomy.

Muslims converted their Christian fellow Arabs by the sword. Some Christian Arab tribes, such as the Ghassanids, had to buy their freedom from the prophet Muhammad, by paying a special tax called *Jizya*.

According to al-Hadith, the prophet Muhammad would always exhort his followers before any expedition thus:

"When you meet your enemies who are polytheists, invite them to three courses of action. If they respond to any one of these, you also accept it and withhold yourself from doing them any harm. Invite them to [accept] Islam; if they respond to you, accept it from them and desist from fighting against them.... If they refuse to accept Islam, demand from them the Jizya. *If they agree to pay, accept it from them and hold off your hands. If they refuse to pay the tax, seek Allah's help and fight them."* (*Sahih Muslim*, Book 19, Number 4294.)

Apart from the *Jizya*, a kind of tribute, Christians (and other non-Muslims) were forced to:

1. Wear distinctive clothing to identify them as infidels.
2. Mark their houses.
3. Build houses no higher than their Muslim neighbours.
4. Never worship openly.
5. Never build churches (or other places of worship)
6. Pay a land tax.
7. Pay Jizya at a humiliating ceremony which involved being struck on the hcad or nape of the neck.
8. The Jizya and land tax were often obtained through torture.

9. Flee from Muslim authorities if they could not pay the tax, which was often exorbitant. History records whole villages of Christians fleeing because they were too poor to pay the hefty taxes imposed by their Muslim masters.

(*SPREAD BY THE SWORD? Is holy war against Christians and Jews – "infidels" – a perversion of Islam? Here's the evidence, from Islamic texts and history*, by Mark Hartwig, Ph.D.)

Incitement to Violence

What is surprising is that al Jizya was still being imposed in the 20th century, and one also finds hate-inspiring negative attitudes being fed to Muslim children in most Muslim countries. Not until after 9/11 did the USA exert pressure on its Saudi allies to change their school text-books which "*reflect an ideology of hatred against the other, against Christians, Jews and other Muslims, for instance, Shiites and the majority Sunni Muslims and all others who do not subscribe to the Wahhabi doctrine.*"

A report on the content of Saudi School textbooks states:

"*The centre's report cites numerous examples. It quotes a fourth-grade text as telling students to 'love for the sake of God and to hate for the sake of God.' The report says that textbooks instruct students that Christians and Jews are 'apes and pigs' and warns students not to 'greet,' 'befriend' or 'respect' non-believers.*" (NPR Middle East, "Saudi Textbooks Still Teach Hate, Group Says" by Vicky O'Hara.)

The alienation and exclusion of Christian Palestinians can only result in their being identified as the enemy. It is not an uncommon Christian Palestinian experience to have gone to school with a Muslim, who suddenly treats his Christian schoolmate as if he were a Zionist. The graffiti on the walls of Gaza sprayed by Muslim fundamentalists speaks volumes of that transformation of the Christian Palestinian from a brother to an enemy. *"When they are through with the Saturday people, they will start on the Sunday people."* (Alpert 1997: 7.)

Desecration of Christian Holy Places

In the spring of 2002, dozens of Palestinian "terrorists" were fleeing from Israeli soldiers. They adopted a cynical tactic against Israel, using the Church of the Nativity as a hiding place. They had apparently frequently fled to the vicinity of the Church of the Nativity *"with the expectation that Israel would try to avoid fighting near the shrine"*. ("Sharon Proposes Arafat's Exile While Israeli Forces Shell His Compound", *New York Times*, April 2, 2002.)

They fired at Israeli soldiers and for a short time it appeared to all and sundry that Israel was violating Holy Christian sites. However, the truth is that heavily armed Muslim Palestinians raided the Church of the Nativity, took some forty Clergy and nuns hostage, damaged the interior of the church, especially altars, stole crosses and valuables from the church, then played the victim. *"The entrance to the church is also heavily booby-trapped."* (Baruch Kra et al, "IDF Maintains Cautious Approach In Bethlehem", *Haaretz*, April 10, 2002.)

In their defence, it has been said that these men simply were seeking shelter from the Israelis. It must be asked then why they did not seek shelter in the Mosque of Omar, built in 1860, right opposite the Church of the Nativity?!

The excuse is: *"The idea was to enter the church in order to create international pressure on Israel... We knew beforehand that there was two years' worth of food for 50 monks. Oil, beans, rice, olives. Good bathrooms and the largest wells in old Bethlehem. You didn't need electricity because there were candles. In the yard they planted vegetables. Everything was there."* (Senior Tanzim commander, Abdullah Abu-Hadid, Yediot Ahronot on May 24 as reported in *Daily Alert*, Conference of Presidents of Major

American Jewish Organizations, May 30, 2002.) But it is not too difficult to have prepared a few months' worth of food and water and stored them in the mosque.

Boycott

Religious leaders in the Palestinian Authority territories have fuelled the fire of hatred for Christians amongst Muslim Palestinians. An example of this is the destruction of the YMCA in Qalqilya (netnews.com Aaron Klein, WND 09.11.06). Muslim gunmen, said to be members of Hamas and Islamic Jihad, broke into the building and set it on fire. Their motive was that apparently the YMCA had been engaged in missionary activity in a largely Muslim town. The YMCA had served the town of Qalqiliya for several years, donating money to its young people and supporting education and local clubs. There was no objective evidence of so-called missionary activity in the sense of proselytising efforts. This act of violence had been preceded by incitement to violence on the part of the Muslim leadership, who petitioned the YMCA thus: *"We the preachers of the mosques and representatives of major families in Qalqiliya ask you to close the offices of the YMCA because the population of Qalqiliya doesn't need such offices, especially since there are not many Christians in our city..."*

The presence of Christians in Qalqiliya was recognized by Muslim leaders. However, they acted as if that presence were undesirable, and irrelevant. They acted as if Christian Arabs had no right to express their culture and no need to congregate or celebrate anything holy to them. This treatment of Christians is also reflected in the draft constitution of the PA. Whilst it welcomes all monotheistic worship, it states categorically that the Sharia will be the foundation on which the constitution will be based. The primacy of the Sharia, in the genesis of the Palestinian constitution, and the exclusion of any Christian influence, just about sums up Muslim Arab attitudes towards Christian Arabs. This exclusionist attitude is the natural consequence of the Islamisation of the Palestinian issue. Islamists, desperate for a publicity vehicle, adopted the Palestinian issue, and substituted nationality for religion. The Palestinian cause, which should include Palestinian Christians, became a Muslim cause and immediately excluded Christian Palestinians. This substitution of Muslim for Palestinian nationalism has been responsible for the precipitous decline in the numbers of Christian Arabs in the PA territories.

An inevitable outcome of the Islamisation of the Palestinian cause is the consequent dismissal of Christian Palestinians as infidels. A corollary of this view of Christians is acts of violence against them, committed by their own Palestinian brethren, whose eyes have been blinkered with Islamist extremism. Vandalism of Christian graves by Muslim Palestinians in the PA controlled territories was reported in *Haaretz* (Feb. 28, 2001).

Unfair Competition

As a young child I used to look forward to trips with my eldest brother in law, who owned a truck and used to supply souvenir manufacturers with olive wood. We would leave Kufur Yasief at midnight in his Bedford truck loaded with olive timber, and would eventually reach Bethlehem by 5 am. There seemed to be an insatiable appetite for olive wood. However, now that tourism has been whittled down to a shadow of its past, the demand has slowed down.

In addition to the near-annihilation of the tourist trade, Christian souvenir sellers have had to contend with unfair competition from unlicensed Muslim traders who set up stalls outside Christian Souvenir shops and sell the same goods at cut prices. (WND, "Silent Fright: Birthplace of Jesus hijacked by Muslims", December 23, 2007.)

The aim is simply to price the Christians out of the market, starve them of business, and cause them to leave Bethlehem.

"Several local Christians, speaking on condition of anonymity, charged the Muslim vendors set up their stations

without required permits after paying what were described as 'special commissions' to the Palestinian Authority security forces that control the city. WND asked three vendors if they had obtained permits, but they refused to respond."

Alienation and Bullying

Another consequence of the Islamisation of the Palestinian cause is the alienation of Christians, who cannot identify with policies based on Islamist dogma, or participate in acts (such as suicide bombing) which are contrary to their beliefs. Whereas exclusion is what Muslim Palestinians have done to Christian Palestinians, alienation is what Christian Palestinians have been made to feel because of the imposition of Islamic extremism on Palestinians. This alienation is exemplified in Christians taking their children out of PA-run schools, because they do not want them exposed to the glorification of suicidal death and killing in the cause of the Intifada.

In Bethlehem, Christians have come under attack because their children's blood has not been shed in the cause of the intifada in the way Muslim blood was shed. (Justus Weiner, 2002.)

A Christian parent from Bethlehem told the *Telegraph* about his son's intimidation by Muslim children *"My son, Nazar, when he was just 13, used to come home from school and the Muslim boys of his age from the local refugee camp would run after him shouting 'Nazarene, Nazarene', which is a derogatory local term for Christian. Once they caught up and threatened to beat him unless he said Allah was his God and Mohammed his only prophet. We had to move house, but now my son has left university and cannot get a job, so every day he says we must leave."* (By Tim Butcher, *Telegraph* 20/12/2006.)

Misappropriation of Christian Land

A fatwa was issued by Sheikh Ekrima Sabri in July 2000 against any Palestinian selling land to non-Muslims, especially when contemplating accepting financial compensation from Israel for land taken by Zionists. *"These holy lands are the first qibla (direction of prayer), the third mosque, the destination of the isra' and the mi'raj [the Prophet Muhammad's night-time journey to the Al-Aqsa Mosque as per the Qur'an (17:1) and the story of his ascent to Heaven] of your Prophet, and the earth that is drenched with the blood of righteous Muslim warriors and the prophets, holy men, martyrs and righteous forefathers, and every step of these lands embodies all the glorified holy endowment deeds that survived over the generations, and they are what determine the Islamic nature of the Land, for there is no God but Allah and Muhammad is his Messenger."* There is no room in the Mufti's thinking for non-Muslims.

Christian Palestinians are thus regarded as alien subjects. In effect, it has meant that a Christian Palestinian cannot sell land or property to another Christian Palestinian. In 2007 another fatwah added that the whole land of Palestine was *"a holy Islamic land"* (Yitzhak Reiter 2007).

There have been many instances of Muslims in Bethlehem taking land away from Christians by deceit and force. *"It is a regular phenomenon in Bethlehem. They go to a poor Christian person with a forged power of attorney document, and then they say we have papers proving you're living on our land. If you confront them, many times the Christian is beaten. You can't do anything about it. The Christian loses and he runs away."* (WND, Aaron Klein, 23.12.2007, and 12.24.07, 15:06 / Israel Opinion.)

A case in point is Christian couple Faud and Georgette Lama, Bethlehemites who stood up to Muslims attempting to take their property away by deceit and force. When they protested to the security forces, they were simply beaten. (*Jerusalem Post*, February 2007). They lost 6 dounums (one and a half acres, which in a small country, where land is at a premium, is a considerable plot of land).

The owner of the Nativity TV station has spoken out against such acts of injustice. *"Qumsiyeh said he has documented more than 160 incidents of attacks on Christians in the area in recent years. He said a monk was recently roughed up for trying to prevent a group of Muslim men from seizing lands owned by Christians in Beit Sahur. Thieves have targeted the homes of many Christian families and a 'land mafia' has succeeded in laying its hands on vast areas of land belonging to Christians, he added."* (Khaled abu Toameh, *Jerusalem Post*, 25.01.2007)

Sexual Crimes Against Christian Women

Muslim men have violated Christian Arab women through forced marriage. In Egypt, Christian women are kidnapped by Muslim men and then raped and forced to bear children. Weinar tells of a poor Muslim Palestinian family who demanded from a wealthy Christian man that his daughter be wed to the poor Muslim's son. The Christian asked for two days to think things over. However, the following day the Muslim family turned up at the doorstep of the Christian man, this time with reinforcement in the form of fifteen men. The Palestinian Christian man had to either give in to intimidation, or stand up for his daughter's rights. He chose the latter. In the exchange, lives were lost and the Christian family had to flee the PA region. For the Christian father, the choice was between death and shame. He chose death, not for himself, but for the perpetrators of terrorism.

The Islamisation of the Palestinian issue has resulted in Christian Palestinians becoming a fair target. This extends to sexual harassment and rape of Christian women. Fairness and justice aside, these criminal and immoral acts are committed by people who claim to be close to God, against women, whose only fault is that they are Christian. More shocking than the act of violating a Christian woman is the revelation that the rapist knows that he, being a Muslim, and his victim being a Christian, grants him impunity from any legal retribution.

There is a litany of such evil acts by Muslims against Christian women, enough to fill volumes. However, I will quote a few incidents only in order to raise awareness.

Christians in Syria, the home of the Christian Ghassanids, where Christians despite their minority have enjoyed relative peace, now seem to be threatened again by the Muslim extremists, many of whom are members of the so-called opposition to Assad... *"In Syria, after the al-Qaeda linked rebel group conquered Qusair, a city of the governate of Homs, 15-year-old Mariam was kidnapped, repeatedly gang raped according to a fatwa legitimizing the rape of non-Sunni women by any Muslim waging jihad against Syria's government, and then executed."*

According to Agenzia Fides, *"The commander of the battalion 'Jabhat al-Nusra' in Qusair took Mariam, married and raped her. Then he repudiated her. The next day the young woman was forced to marry another Islamic militant. He also raped her and then repudiated her. The same trend was repeated for 15 days, and Mariam was raped by 15 different men. This psychologically destabilized her and made her insane. Mariam became mentally unstable and was eventually killed."* (WThe Degradation of Christian Women under Islam Muslim Persecution of Christians", June, 2013 by Raymond Ibrahim; September 11, 2013 at 5:00 am)

One wonders where the care for Arabic-speaking Christians in Western policy figures. The Western allies' blind support for the rebels makes no sense. The Assad regime may be evil, but have we not learnt the lessons of the other so-called Arab Springs in other countries such as Libya and Egypt? Muslim fundamentalism is the only consequence. Yes, the absence of democracy is to be bewailed, but sometimes one can only choose between two evils, and sensible people would choose the lesser evil. Muslim fundamentalist groups should never be an option, as their action has always demonstrated the abject evil of which they are capable and which they commit and justify in the name of God, whilst strangely proclaiming that Islam is a religion of peace.

We next sample the evil committed against Christian women in Egypt. A seven year old Christian girl is kidnapped in Egypt and a ransom is demanded by Muslim men from her father, equating to $100,000.00. (Raymond Ibrahim)

Demonization of Christians

During a live broadcast on official PA television on October 13, 2000, Dr. Ahmad Abu Halabiya, a member of the PA-appointed 'Fatwa Council' and former acting Rector of the Islamic University in Gaza, stated during a Friday sermon from a Gaza mosque:

"From here, Allah the almighty has called upon us not to ally with the Jews or the Christians, not to like them, not to become their partners, not to support them, and not to sign agreements with them…as Allah said: 'O you who believe, do not take the Jews and the Christians as allies, for they are allies of one another. Who from among you takes them as allies will indeed be of them.'" (Middle East Media Research Institute, 2000.)

There are times during the last 20 years, when Palestinians, particularly since the establishment of the Palestinian Authority, were near starvation. Food and clothes would often be sent from Saudi Arabia for the Palestinians. Often Christians would be denied food aid because they were not Muslim

Extortion

A story is told by international human rights lawyer Justus Weiner (2005) of a Palestinian Armenian Christian jeweller selling gold legally in Gaza. He was arrested by the Palestinian police and beaten for several hours. He was subsequently allowed to leave with only half his gold. When he protested, they beat him again took all his cash ($6000.00), his gold watch and rings, and only then was he released.

Intimidation, Vandalism and Violence

Another weapon used by the Muslims in their fight against Christian Palestinians is intimidation. Not only do Muslim Palestinians, exclude, alienate, violate, desecrate, rape, rob, and extort the Christian Palestinian Dhimmis, but they threaten those who may report such acts with violence and persecution. This is a form of bullying, though it has more far reaching consequences than what may be seen in a school yard. A Christian religious leader from Jerusalem *"compared the behaviour of Christian Dhimmis to that of battered wives and children, who continue to defend and even identify with their tormentor even as the abuse persists"* (Raab 2003). The fear inspired by the PA and Palestinian Islamists has caused Christian Palestinians and their leaders to even praise their enemies. Such is the extent of the fear inspired by the racist Muslim Palestinians.

"Christian leaders and residents, most of whom spoke to WND on condition of anonymity during recent interviews, said they face an atmosphere of regular hostility. They said Palestinian armed groups stir tension by holding militant demonstrations and marches in the streets. They spoke of instances in which Christian shopkeepers' stores were ransacked and Christian homes attacked." (WND 23.12.2007.)

When interviewed by Bridges for Peace, Weiner told Israel Mosaic Radio of phone calls received by Christian Palestinians: *"We know who you are. We know where you live, and Sharia law tells us to kill you infidels."* (December 12, 2006.) Weiner pointed out that Christian populations are in decline in virtually every Muslim state in the world. By contrast, the Christian population in Israel has increased somewhat.

"The growing influence of the Islamic movement over Arab society during the intifada has caused growing violence toward Christians and their institutions, deepening the identity crisis of many Christians and their despair over their future in the area." (Professor Tsimhoni 1993: 29.)

Acts of vandalism against Palestinian Christians have been designed to inspire fear and cause the exsanguination from Palestine of all its Christians. Muslim anti-Christian Arab racism is nothing less than an existential crisis for those Christians who are considered by Muslim fundamentalists to be infidels, fit for slaughter. Furthermore, they would happily engage in missionary activities in the Christian West, and receive grants from taxpayers in the West to build Mosques and Islamic centres. They claim benefits and obtain free health care and yet they cannot tolerate the very existence of Christians in their midst. This is brazen racism.

When some Danish cartoonists (2005) decided to make a political point about the violent characteristics of Islam, the Muslim world reacted in such a way as to render unnecessary the need for any journalist to make such a point. There were violent demonstrations all over the world. One such demonstration, which barely caught the attention of the Western media, is the setting ablaze of an Anglican church in Nablus. For me the poignancy of this atrocity is increased by the fact that my mother's cousin had once been Vicar of that church. ("MUSLIMS EXPLODE IN ANGER", *Catalyst*, November Issue 2006). Churches of other denominations were also subjected to attacks and acts of sacrilege.

Altogether, the emerging picture is of a belligerent Islam, intolerant of, resentful of, disrespectful of, hateful of and preying upon Christians as fair game. This conduct is reminiscent of the Muslim Fundamentalist Turkish party PKA, one of whose leaders said that *"the Minaret is our bayonet"*. The mosque become a military academy, Muslims become soldiers, and Islam is a war strategy against the infidel Christians and Jews, who are the object of the dark theology of Islamists.

Murder of Christians by Muslims

On a recent visit to the Holy Land, one of my childhood friends, a successful lawyer living in Jerusalem, took me to Bethlehem. I broached the subject of the persecution of Christians by Muslims. Little did I know that there was a fresh tragic example of such persecution.

It transpired that a keyworker in the Bible Society bookshop in Gaza was kidnapped by extremist Muslims and murdered in cold blood.

"At 6:30 a.m. Sunday, Ayyad's body was found, with stab wounds and bullet holes, near the bookstore where he'd devoted so much time." (CBNNews.com, October 8, 2007.)

26-year-old Rami Ayyad had served his local community in so many practical ways. His reward was to widow his pregnant wife and orphan his two young children.

The Bible society bookshop had been bombed in April 2007, following which he received death threats. (CNS news, 10/08/2007.)

"In addition to offering Bibles and Christian books, the shop, which opened in 1998, offers public computer classes and other educational opportunities to Gaza's 1.4 million people, many of whom are jobless and destitute.

"The Palestinian Bible Society's Gaza ministry includes relief work in Gaza's refugee camps and community health, educational, microenterprise, and development projects." (CNS news, 10/08/2007.)

Though Hamas condemned the murder, they have to take their share of responsibility for whipping up anti-Christian sentiments amongst the Palestinian Muslims.

A man who has served his community so well deserves to be embraced, celebrated, thanked and appreciated. Only criminal minds would even conceive of answering charity with such an atrocity. The murderers' motives were pure bigotry against Palestinian Christians. The murderers may believe that they have some great reward in heaven for committing such a heinous crime. Yet their only reward will be shame upon them and upon their people for revelling in bloodshed in the name of their religion. They have brought shame upon their religion and their people. Their act was one of cowardice. Ayyad fought openly and peacefully against hatred, injustice, poverty, violence, and all that is dark in the heart of man. He died valiantly. His murderers fought against righteousness, in the dark lest their evil deeds be seen. They hated the light because the light would have exposed their evil deeds. By murdering such a righteous man, they have put a bullet in the heart of the Palestinian nation and added a brick, nay a boulder, to the dividing wall between Christian and Muslim Arabs.

Recent events since the Arab Spring in Egypt have lifted the lid on the sort of hatred Muslim Arab fundamentalists harbour for their Christian brethren. I quote from a celebrated Christian Egyptian TV presenter, Ibrahim Eissa: *"The Christians have suffered in Egypt, over the course of 2½ years. Their churches have been burned, their children killed. The* Maspero Massacre *occurred, where several Copts were slain. Catastrophic fatwas appeared, calling them infidels and inciting against them… No one has suffered as much as they. Today, if any Christian attempts to join a protest, he does so at the risk of defying dozens of fatwas calling for his death and decapitation and the burning of churches, especially in Upper Egypt."* ("Middle East Forum, Al Qaeda Flag Flies High Above Christian Churches", Raymond Ibrahim, Gatestone Institute, August 7, 2013)

Abduction

The Muslims of Egypt have developed an appetite for abducting Christian children, demanding a handsome ransom, and sometimes despite the ransom being paid, killing the innocent children, all in the name of Islam. This was the fate of a six year old Christian boy, whose bloated body was found in the sewer of his Muslim murderer. ("Jihad on Egypt's Christian Children" by Raymond Ibrahim, June 3, 2013 at 3:30 am.)

Mr Ibrahim lists a number of similar incidents that had taken place relatively recently. A ten year old Coptic boy on his way to prayer at the Coptic Church of St Abdul Masih (Servant of Christ) in Minya, Egypt, was kidnapped by Muslim fundamentalists asking for a ransom.

A month prior to the above abduction, a twelve year old Coptic boy, by the name Abanoub Ashraf, was kidnapped by four men in front of his church, St Paul, in the Shubra al-Khayma district. Again his abductors demanded a ransom. Ibrahim believes that the motive force behind these abductions is to frighten Christian families and prevent them from sending their children to church, as some Muslim clerics openly teach that attending church is worse than attending a bar.

Ibrahim refers to a report by International Christian Concern which states: *"Abductions of Christian girls are nothing new in Egypt. Records exist of cases that were filed as early as the 1970s. However, kidnappings have increased significantly since Egypt's revolution last year. It is often the police – the very people that are trusted to uphold the law – who are responsible."* ("Egypt's Lost Daughters; the Abduction of Christian Girls", by Aidan Clay of International Christian Concern (ICC), Special to ASSIST News Service Thursday, May 10, 2012.)

"More than 500 Christian girls have been abducted in the last two years, according to the Association of Victims of Abduction and Forced Disappearance (AVAFD), which documents the disappearances. A growing number of cases involve girls between the ages of 13 and 17." (Inter press service, Tuesday, November 19, 2013.)

Ibrahim conveys the concerns of the Coptic Pope at the rise in sexual crimes and abductions and forced conversions of Christian women to Islam. Christian women are brutalised by Muslim fundamentalists. Denials by leaders of the Muslim brotherhood of such atrocities add insult to injury. He claims that in the last few years there have been at least 550 such cases. More alarming is the fact that:

"This rate only increased after the 'Arab Spring' and the Muslim Brotherhood's empowerment, which has seen a

concomitant rise in sexual harassment of all Egyptian women. When Egypt's President Morsi was in Germany last February, and asked to address the issue of victimized Coptic girls, he answered that such abductions and abuse were merely a rumour."

Religious Ethnic Cleansing

In September 2013, a Christian Egyptian man, Iskander Toss, a resident of the town of Delga in Upper Egypt, was kidnapped by Muslim fundamentalists, brutalised, then dragged through the dirt roads until he died. As if this were not barbaric enough, his Muslim fundamentalist murderers returned a few days later, exhumed his body, and dragged it through the streets again to inspire fear in the hearts of the Christian residents of the town of Delga, who number 25,000 out of a total population of 100,000.

Since the removal of Morsi from power, members of the Muslim Brotherhood have barred Christians from returning to their homes in Delga unless they are prepared to pay Jizya. (The Gatestone Institute, "The Ethnic Cleansing of Christians in Egypt", by Michael Armanious, October 1, 2013 at 3:00 am.)

Armanious reports on similar atrocities in the town of Kerdasa, which has a significant Christian community. *"The Christians of the village of Marinab in the Aswan Governorate, 700 miles south of Cairo, were also placed under siege by jihadists in October 2011. Their food supplies and contacts with the outside world were cut off until they agreed to have their church demolished because they violated the building code by displaying a cross, which the jihadists said was offensive."*

The report prefaces several such instances by pointing to the worrying escalation of violence against Christians in Egypt since the removal of Morsi from power.

Though Morsi has been removed from power, his soldiers of death are free in every town, village and hamlet in Egypt doing their evil deeds against Christians.

"Since the ouster of Mohamed Morsi, the problem has only intensified: anti-Christian violence now manifests itself in Egypt with increasing regularity... what happened to the Christians in Delga and Kerdasa, has been happening throughout Egypt. As I write these words, Egypt is in a transitory period awaiting another election. It is expected that the military leader El-Sisi will win the elections. What will that mean for the Christians of Egypt? The signs are that he is not hostile." (Ahrams online, *Nader Bakkar*, Saturday 8 Feb 2014.) However, it remains to be seen how this will translate into civil and religious freedom for the Christians of Egypt, a country in which religious intolerance has been part of the warp and weft for many centuries.

In Syria, the Christian village of Maaloula was attacked by Obama-supported rebels, who are linked to Al-Qaeda. The rebels threatened to return to the village and destroy it, once the Americans defeated President Assad. ("Al-Qaeda Vows to Slaughter Christians After U.S. 'Liberates' Syria" by Raymond Ibrahim on September 4, 2013.)

The *Telegraph* explained the feelings of Christians of Maaloula with respect to the two warring sides. *"The rebels claim they took Maaloula to punish the Christians there for supporting the Assad government, a support that is real but tepid. For most Christians in Syria the fear of what Islamists might do if they win this war outweighs any dislike they have for Assad's system."* (*The Telegraph* by Bill Neely, International Editor, ITV News, in Damascus and Maaloula, 5:00PM BST, 14 Sep 2013.)

Maaloula is home to one of the most ancient Christian communities in the Middle East, one of only three places where people still speak Aramaic. It contains two active monasteries, and the remains of numerous older churches and monasteries. For Muslim fundamentalists to threaten to kill these Christians is an affront to Christians everywhere. Yet our Western governments have been supporting these evil-doers!

Russian President Putin seems to have shown more basic common sense in this matter than leaders of the "democratic West".

The *Independent* carried a piece in which local Christians express their shock at the sight of their Muslim neighbours leading Muslim Jihadists to homes of Christians. A Christian man expressed disappointment at his betrayal by his Muslim neighbours, who had been recipients of kindness from him fairly recently.

As a result of the violence and threats against the residents, *"Not one of the 5,000 Christian residents – nor a single member of the 2,000-strong Muslim community – has returned. Maaloula is, almost literally, a ghost town."* ("Muslims and Christians had lived together in this town of churches and caves. Now it is empty", Robert Fisk, *Independent*, Wednesday 25 September 2013.)

Whether it is Egypt, Syria Palestine or anywhere else, why is so little known about the above atrocities? Why are such events not being talked about more widely in the secular media? Why do we rarely hear them mentioned in our churches in the West? Whenever I share these dreadful events with Christians in the UK, they invariably raise an eyebrow. *"A few Christians speak privately of harassment, Muslims seizing Christian land and the fear of speaking out against radical groups"* (BBC News 24 22.12. 2005). The consequence of the detailed atrocities is to inspire fear, which leads to silence. This is a common secret weapon of all aggressors.

As stated before, the effect of all the above atrocities has been to force Christians out of their homes. The Holy Land is no exception. Christians are leaving the birthplace of Christ, Bethlehem, and are being replaced with Muslims. In 2005, five of the city council seats of Bethlehem were held by Hamas (BBC News 24, 22.12.2005).

This form of ethnic cleansing cannot be attributed purely to fear of the victims. It is equally attributable to the cowardice of the West. Christians would sooner campaign against cruelty against foxes, or against globalisation, or global warming, than dirty their hands with the persecution of the citizens of the most important city in Christianity.

In December 2013, the plight of the Christians, though mainly Assyrian and Chaldeans (and Arabs), seemed to capture the imagination of the press, particularly the *Telegraph*, who ran at least three articles on the subject in one month. One of them focused on politicians being reluctant to intervene on behalf of Christian minorities. Another was about His Royal Highness Prince Charles and the heartfelt concern he expressed about the persecution of Christians in the Middle East, whom he called his *"brothers and sisters in Christ"*. I refer now to an earlier article focusing on the decline of Christians in Iraq since the capture and elimination of Saddam Hussein, under whose rule there were more than one million Christians in Iraq. By now the numbers had dwindled down to 200,000.

Whilst the words of Pope Francis, spoken a mere month previously, were still echoing – *"We will not resign ourselves to imagining a Middle East without Christians"* – it is worth remembering Al-Qaeda has killed 6000 in 2013.

The testimony of a traumatised Iraqi Christian provides a contrast between the situation before and after Saddam Hussein: *"'In Saddam's time, Christians could worship freely, and as long as you avoided politics you could survive,' said Mr Esha. 'But since the war we have been attacked, robbed, raped and forced out of both Doura and the country.*

"'Often just psychological pressure has been enough; people will drive past here and fire guns in the air, or leave bullets and threatening messages outside Christian homes. Sometimes Islamic extremism is used as an excuse, sometimes it's just blackmail for criminal purposes.'" ("Iraq's battle to save its Christian souls: 'Christians are finished here'", *The Telegraph*, Colin Freeman, Baghdad, 15 Dec 2013.)

ISIS Delivers the Last Blow to Eastern Christendom

Although ISIS had been around for almost a year before it captured media attention, no one took notice of them until they conquered parts of Syria, followed by part of Iraq. ISIS, the Islamic State of Iraq and Sham, otherwise abbreviated in Arabic as DA'ASH, led by the self-proclaimed Caliph Abu Bakr Al-Baghdadi, has been persecuting Christians in Iraq and Syria, at least since November 2013.

Their first bounty was Raqqa in north Syria. Seized in 2013, Raqqa has had a strong Christian presence in the past with the word Deir (Arabic for monastery) prefixing many of its village names. ISIS gave the tiny Christian remnant three choices: convert to Islam, pay Jizya or face the sword. Jizya in Raqqa amounted to 14 grams of pure gold. In a statement released by ISIS online, ISIS imposed restrictions on Christians in Raqqa. *"It says Christians must not make renovations to churches, display crosses or other religious symbols outside churches, ring church bells or pray in public. Christians must not carry arms, and must follow other rules imposed by ISIS (also known as ISIL) in their daily lives."* ("Syria crisis: ISIS imposes rules on Christians in Raqqa", BBC News, 27 February 2014.)

A Christian anti-Assad activist, who collaborated with the rebels, was captured and handed over to ISIS. He was to be executed until he converted to Islam and changed his name to Mohammed Nour al-Mallouhi. (Al-Akhbar Firas al-Akhbar, November 8, 2013.)

Islamist militants in Raqqa had killed a young Christian man leaving his body by the wayside, and desecrated crosses and church bells as early as November 2013.

ISIS justified the burning of churches by claiming Christians were not entitled to "protection".

"An ISIS official, who is incidentally not a Syrian national, said during a Friday sermon that burning churches is 'an action based on fatwas from Abdullah ibn Abbas, holding that churches in conquered cities must be burned and their crosses removed. As for cities taken peaceably, with its inhabitants

paying the jizya (tax payable by non-Muslims), their churches and their temples must not be harmed, and can continue practicing their rituals, albeit not publicly.'" However, Raqqa did not benefit from "protection", because its Christians did not pay Jizya. The militants have never considered why in the first instance Christians in Syria needed protecting.

In addition, Islamists have forbidden Christians from displaying crosses or Christian books in the sight of Muslims. They have forbidden Christians from ringing their church bells or making public readings of Christian books within earshot of a Muslim. No doubt, many a liberal Muslim would agree with some of the residents of Raqqa and stand up for their Christian neighbours, as did this rebel Louay Safi, a spokesman for the Syrian Coalition, who said *"ISIS's treatment of non-Muslims was un-Islamic."* ("Islamists in Syrian city offer Christians safety – at a heavy price", By Saad Abedine and Jethro Mullen, CNN, February 28, 2014.) The trouble with this denial is that, embarrassing as it is for liberal Muslims, ISIS's treatment of Christians has a strong foundation in true Islam.

Although ISIS had been operating for several months, showing the extreme face of Islam, pouring out its wrath on Eastern Christendom, and reviving the Pact of Omar, it was not until the spring of 2014 that the media's ears were cocked.

Militant members of ISIS destroyed the grave of Jonah, of "Jonah and the Whale" fame, in Nineveh. Ancient Christian communities have seen their ancient church buildings set on fire or razed to the ground. Christians have been pressurised to either convert or pay the Jizya, or simply leave their homes and possessions. This has meant that for the first time ever, Mosul has no Christian human presence.

On 21st July 2014, the *Christian Post* showed pictures of an 1800 year old Church on fire, courtesy of ISIS. (Leonard Blair, "ISIS Torches 1,800-year-old Church in Mosul: Priest says City Is Now Empty of Christians", *Christian Post*, on 21st July 2014.) Muslim militants robbed houses and took women's jewellery off them, telling Christian women that all their possessions were Muslim property.

CNN reported that ISIS militants prevented Christians from taking any possessions other than the clothes they wore. CNN showed pictures of Christian homes with the words "Property of ISIS" scrawled on their walls in black. Christian homes were marked in red with the letter N in Arabic, which is short for Nasara (Christians). The world derives from the Arabic for Nazarene, as in Jesus the Nazarene. (CNN News, Hamdi Alkhshall and Joshua Berlinger, 20th July 2014.)

The BBC, reporting on a fourth-century monastery near Mosul in Iraq, Bar Behnam Monastery, stated that monks were forced by ISIS militants to abandon their monastery, situated near the Christian town of Qaraqosh, and were only allowed to take the clothes they were wearing. (BBC News 21st July 2014.) Convert or die is the battle cry of ISIS. One man who was given the choice of converting or watching his children murdered "said the words". Racked with guilt, sought reassurance from his vicar "and said: *"'Abouna [Father], I said the words, does that mean that Yesua [Jesus] doesn't love me anymore?' I said, 'Yesua still loves you, he will always loves you.'"* ("Isis beheads 4 Christian children in Iraq for refusing to convert to Islam claims 'Vicar of Baghdad'" by Jack Moore, *International Business Times*, December 8, 2014.)

The incredibly courageous Andrew White, Canon of Baghdad, who was ordered by the Archbishop of Canterbury to leave Baghdad for his own safety, gave this shocking account to CBN, about the brutality of ISIS to the Christians of Iraq: *"Things were bad in Baghdad, there were bombs and shootings and our people were being killed, so many of our people fled back to Nineveh, their traditional home. It was safer, but then one day, ISIS – Islamic State. They came in and they hounded all of them out. They killed huge numbers, they chopped their children in half, they chopped their heads off, and they moved north and it was so terrible what happened."* (Canon Andrew White: "Christian children beheaded for refusing to convert to Islam", Mark Woods 01 December 2014.) The *Daily Mail* reported Canon Andrew White giving more harrowing details of what happened to Christian Children who refuse to convert to Islam: *"'Islamic State turned up and said to the children, "you say the words that you will follow Mohammad"', he said, his voice cracking with emotion.*

"'The children, all under 15, four of them, said "no, we love Yesua; we have always loved Yesua; we have always followed Yesua; Yesua has always been with us".They [ISIS] said, "Say the words." They [the children] said, "No, we can't." They chopped all their heads off. How do you respond to that? You just cry. They are my children. That is what we have been going through and that is what we are going through.'" (Four-young-Christians-brutally-beheaded-ISIS-Iraq-refusing-convert-Islam-says-Vicar-Baghdad-Canon-Andrew-White, *Daily Mail*, Tim Macfarlane, 12 December 2014.)

As if the dreadful events in Syria and Iraq were not shocking enough, and the lack of action from Western governments were not disheartening enough, the boldness of ISIS supporters in the West has gone unchallenged. A Cardiffian Muslim fundamentalist is calling for an Islamic state in Britain. He wants to impose the infamous Pact of Omar, according to which non-Muslims are not allowed to walk on pavements, must be marked out by having their head shaved and by wearing a red band round their necks, and riding on mules. Non-Muslims *"should give nice clothes to Muslims and wear mismatched shoes"*. He was seen at a barbeque flying ISIS flags. Interestingly, he is reported by the *Mail* Online to be claiming benefits for himself and his wife as well as his three disabled children. He also enjoys the privilege of living in a council house, paid for by the British taxpayer, whom he condemns as infidels. (Abul Taher and Nic North, *Mail* Online, 28th June 2014.)

This attitude is in keeping with a brand of Islam which preaches that benefits claimed in Europe by Muslims are their due desert and are in lieu of Jizya. Anjem Choudary, a radical Islamic cleric who lives on British benefits, preaches that Muslims are entitled to benefits as a form of Jizya. According to the *Sun*, he takes home £25,000.00 in benefits. In a video filmed by the *Sun*, he tells Muslims to "Jihad Seeker's

Allowance". According to Choudary *"The normal situation is to take money from the Kuffar."* (The *Sun*, 17th February 2013.)

Though the secular world may believe the lie that these extremists do not represent Islam, unfortunately the truth is that they do so better than liberal Muslims. Jihad, the imposition of Jizya or forced conversion of Christians to Islam, is part of Islam as discussed in details in previous chapters.

The Case of Meriam Yahia Ibrahim Ishag

Although Muslim persecution of Christians goes largely unreported and unchallenged, this is one occasion on which the free world stood up to despotic Islam.

Sudanese Meriam (sometimes spelled Mariam or Miriam) Ibrahim, who had a Muslim father and a Christian mother, chose to marry a Christian man. A relative reported her to the Muslim courts. She was arrested and imprisoned with her two year old child. On March 4th 2014 she was charged with apostasy for "converting" to Christianity and adultery for sleeping with a Christian man, her husband. In other words, Sharia law considers Christianity to be evil. *"Mariam Yahya Ibrahim, 27, was charged with adultery for marrying a Christian man and has been ordered by the courts to abandon her newly adopted Christian faith and return to Islam."* (*Daily Mail*, Jennifer Newton, 15 May 2014.)

Her punishment was 100 lashes for adultery, and a death sentence for apostasy.

Protesters outside the court held banners in Arabic stating *"It is Miriam's right to be a Christian"*.

A joint statement by embassies of the United States, Canada, the United Kingdom, and the Netherlands appealed to *"the government of Sudan to respect the right to freedom of religion, including one's right to change one's faith or beliefs"*. ("Sudan woman faces death penalty for apostasy, Court gives Mariam Yahya until Thursday to abandon her

Christian religion or face death sentence." Al-Jazeera, 15 May 2014.)

To add insult to injury, Miriam was chained in prison, as she gave birth to a baby daughter; a picture of cruelty and ignominy. (*Independent*, Heather Saul, Thursday 29 May 2014.)

A Muslim cleric tried to persuade her to recant and convert to Islam. However she told the judge *"I am a Christian and I never committed apostasy."* The judge, who throughout called her by a Muslim name, remonstrated that she had three days to change her mind. He then sentenced her. *"But you insist on not returning to Islam. I sentence you to be hanged to death."* (*Independent*: Chris Green, Senior Reporter, Thursday 15 May 2014.)

British leading politicians, David Cameron (PM), Nick Clegg and Labour leader Ed Miliband, all condemned the actions of the court and appealed. *"The way she is being treated is barbaric and has no place in today's world,"* Mr Cameron told *The Times*: *"Religious freedom is an absolute, fundamental human right. I urge the government of Sudan to overturn the sentence and immediately provide appropriate support and medical care for her and her children."* ("The Prime Minister has vowed to press the Sudanese government to act", *Independent*, Heather Saul, Saturday 31 May 2014.)

On June 6 2014 CNN aired an interview with a man said to be one of Meriam's three brothers. *"Her name isn't Miriam; her name is Abrar al-Hadi. I am al-Samani al-Hadi Mohamed Abdullah, her full – older – brother."* He simply wanted her to convert to Islam or die. When the CNN reporter asked him whether he really wanted his own sister to be hanged, he replied that this issue rises above emotions. It is a matter of obedience to God! No one asked him how a God who is supposedly merciful and compassionate would call for the killing of a woman such as Meriam.

After much pressure from the International community, there followed a period of uncertainty. Rumours of her imminent release were followed by long periods of inaction. *"Daniel Wani, whose wife Miriam gave birth to their daughter*

Maya in prison last week, said that the rumours were media speculation." (*Tablet*, 02 June 2014 14:24, by Liz Dodd.)

Meriam was sheltered in the American embassy in Sudan for one month before she was allowed to depart. On 24th July 2014 she travelled to meet the Pope in Rome. Meriam and her family enjoyed a half hour meeting with the Argentine pontiff, who expressed gratitude to Meriam for her *"courageous testament of faith"* and her *"tenacity"* ("Sudan's Mariam Ibrahim meets Pope", Al-'Arabiya 25 July 2014). The release was secured with the help of the Italian regime. CNN reported that Meriam had never been a Muslim, and her treatment in Sudan amounted to persecution. Meriam was fathered by a Muslim, but her mother was an Ethiopian Orthodox Christian. She was raised a Christian and chose as an adult to remain a Christian. To claim that she had apostatised is a complete violation of her human rights to choose. But Islam respects no choice.

A Sense of Alienation Amongst Arabic-speaking Christians

Owing mainly to the growing Islamisation of Arab affairs, not least the Palestinian Israeli struggle, Arabic-speaking Christians have felt increasingly alienated, leading to the efflux of Arabic-speaking Christians from the Holy Lands. This efflux has not been helped by the open persecution of Arabic-speaking Christians by their Muslim brothers and countrymen, which has been accelerated since the so-called Arab Spring, more akin to an Arab inferno for the Christians.

In Israel, where Arabs number no more than 1.8 million in a population of 8 million, Christians are in a tiny minority of 128,000. The Islamisation of the Israeli-Palestinian conflict and the increasing persecution of Christians in Arab countries have driven some Christians to call for closer co-operation with the Zionist State.

In 2004 *Haaretz* ran an article about Arab recruits in the Israeli Defence Force (IDF). In the 1990s the IDF saw a small number of Arab citizens join its ranks. *"The IDF does not furnish exact numbers, but it appears that the annual number of volunteers from both sectors together does not exceed 150."* However, the conduct of the Israeli army during the Intifada, during which the IDF killed 13 Israeli Arabs in the associated riots, stemmed the small tide. ("Number of Muslim Christian Arab volunteers in IDF growing", Amos Harel and *Haaretz* Correspondent, Dec 30, 2004.)

Why would Israeli Arabs wish to join an army whose aim is to fight against fellow Arabs, in which process Arabs would be called upon to kill Arabs? The answer is simply that they wish to be treated equally as Israeli citizens, enjoying full rights and opportunities; Israeli Arabs want equality with their Jewish fellow citizens. *"It is a step toward becoming more a part of Israeli society."*

Since 1984, there have always been a minority of Israeli Arabs willing to join the IDF. However, of late there has been a lot of emotion surrounding the call to serve in the IDF, led by a Christian Arab Orthodox priest and the Israeli Prime Minister Netanyahu.

On Christmas day 2013, the *Jerusalem Post* published an article reporting the highest rise in Israeli Christian Arab recruits to the Israeli Defence Force: *"'The last recruitment cycle is the largest observed in recent years,' an army source told* The Jerusalem Post *on Tuesday. A total of 140 Arabic-speaking Christians are on active service, while 400 are in the reserves."*

The *Jerusalem Post* reported a gathering in Nazareth of active and reservist IDF soldiers from the Christian Israeli Arab community. *"Prime Minister Binyamin Netanyahu sent a video greeting to the conference, which met on Sunday, vowing to stand by the soldiers and to face down threats together with it. 'I salute you, and support you,' the prime minister told the forum."*

Why would an Arab Israeli priest encourage his youth to join the IDF? *"We want young Christians to be completely integrated into Israeli society, and this means also carrying an equal share of the burden."* ("Arab pastor: Our future is with

Israel", Ryan Jones, *Israel Today*, Tuesday, July 09, 2013.) But full integration does not really explain such an unusual and ground-breaking initiative, which has brought the priest many threats from Israeli Arabs opposing his initiative. Fr Nadaf's rationale for encouraging Christian Israeli Arab youth to enlist in the IDF is clearly linked to the persecution of Christians in the Middle East. By comparison with Christians in Muslim countries, Christian Israeli Arabs *"feel secure in Israel"*. He continued: *"Our future as a Christian minority is wrapped up in the future of the State of Israel."* His spokesman spelled it out more clearly. Speaking of Muslim Fundamentalists in Iraq, Syria and Egypt, he said, *"They are burning churches, they are slaughtering them (Christians), they are raping the girls."* ("Push to recruit Arab Christians into Israeli army", by Karin Laub, Associated Press, Fri, Dec 27, 2013.)

Nor are these sheer sentiments. Fr Nadaf was not just venting. A new Christian Israeli Arab party has been founded, rejoicing in the Hebrew name "B'nei Brit Hahadasha" which when translated means "Sons of the New Testament" (SOTNT). The name has been cleverly thought out. The New Testament is the Christian holy book. By the same token, these Christian Israeli Arabs are seeking a new pact with Israel. As a rejected part of the Arab nation, they are turning their backs on militant Islamic Arabs and throwing their lot in with the Zionist State, the arch enemy of Muslims worldwide. In doing so, these Christian Israeli Arabs have become targets. They have taken a huge risk, and therefore both merit and have asked for rights in return for their commitment to the Zionist State. ("New Christian Arab party calls for IDF enlistment" by Lazar Berman and Elhanan Miller, *The Times of Israel*, July 10, 2013.)

The leader of the nascent movement justifies their risk taking thus: *"People see what's happening now in Lebanon, Egypt, and Syria,"* said Shilyan. *"They understand where we're living."*

Opposition to this movement is based on the premise that Zionist support, and it has come from the Prime Minister and members of other parties, is inspired by the desire to divide

Christian Israeli Arab society. However, in reality society is divided, perhaps not so palpably as in Iraq or Syria or Egypt. But cracks have long been appearing in the two Christian Arab towns of Nazareth and Bethlehem, where Islamic militancy has grown to such a pitch that many Christians have felt a compelling need to leave the two historic Christian towns. The building of a Mosque right next door to the biggest church in the Middle East, the Church of the Annunciation, in the centre of Nazareth, comes to mind. This was only halted by Vatican and Saudi intervention.

If it were not for the restraining hand of the Zionist State, no one knows whether the fate of Christian Israeli Arabs would not have been at least as bad as that of their Iraqi, Egyptian and Syrian brethren.

Muslim Arabs who have accused supporters of the SOTNT of treachery should pause to reflect on the reasons that gave rise to such a movement. Every Muslim Arab has had a share in the birth of this party. There has been little credible opposition from Muslim Arabs anywhere to the brutality towards and butchery of Christians in Syria, Iraq or Egypt. One must ask whether it is not more credible for the critics of this new movement to aim their rhetorical guns at the Muslim fundamentalists. Only when they show such integrity, can they earn the right to criticise or point the fingers at the Sons of The New Testament (SOTNT). Yes, Israel may have ulterior motives for wanting to integrate Christian Arabs, but at least there is a promise of equality for the Christian Arabs. No Arab Muslim state has offered Arabic-speaking Christians such terms.

The reader should expect further developments, more heat, and more fire from this issue. A young cousin of mine sent me this link on Facebook, which sheds more light on the vehemence of passion amongst Israeli Christian Arabs. (Channel One's report on the Recruitment of Christians in Israel, YouTube.)

One of my Albanian patients, who somehow figured out I was a Christian Arab, asked me, in the middle of a busy surgery, why we Christians worship the cross. Of course we do not, although some Christians may pay too much attention to the physical symbol. He then turned to why we believe Jesus is the Son of God. I answered him as concisely as I could, begging him to come back at the end of the surgery to complete the chat. But he was too much in the flow to take any notice of my predicament. Our conversation was strewn with his frequent claims that Islam was a religion of peace. Eventually, I threw caution to the wind and asked him to explain why it was necessary to use the sword to spread Islam. I asked him to explain to me why by contrast the apostles did not use a sword, other than the word of God, to spread Christianity. He was nonplussed. I then finally asked him to explain to me why Muslims throughout the world are massacring innocent Christian neighbours in cold blood. To my relief, he looked rightly ashamed and was completely silenced, and I could get on with seeing my patients.

Oh that this could be the response of all my fellow Arabs of the Muslim creed! Until such a time, no Muslim Arab should be surprised that some Christians feel safer in a Zionist State.

Chapter V

Zionist Anti-Christian-Arab Anti-Semitism

According to Shahak, the Talmud and associated traditional teachings *"inculcate an attitude of scorn and hatred toward Gentiles,"* especially Christians. One ancient prayer beseeches, *"[May] all the Christians perish instantly."*

"If racism were venom and the viper's killing powers were concentrated in its fangs, the Talmud constitutes the fangs of Jewish racism."

The world is accustomed to hearing Jews complain about the way they were treated by Christians in Europe. As a Christian, I am not proud of the cruelty with which European Christians had, at times, treated Jews. However, this is a two-sided story; a two-thousand-year long see-saw of persecution, in which today's persecutor is tomorrow's persecuted. The Jews have not always been the victims. Indeed, the two-thousand year old saga began with the Jews persecuting the Christians.

By the end of the fourth century AD, Christianity had become the main religion in Palestine. Ethnically, Palestinian Christians were a mixture of Jews, Arabs, Armenians, Assyrians and other minorities.

The Muslim conquest of Palestine had been facilitated by the Persian war against Byzantium. Therefore Muslim forces were fighting against weakened, if not exhausted Byzantium, thanks to Jewish efforts. The Muslim conquest of Palestine was uneventful, except in the case of walled Christian cities, such as Hebron, Caesarea, Jerusalem and Lod.

To conquer these cities the Muslim Arab armies had to rely on Jewish co-operation. But why would Jews co-operate with the Muslims who massacred their brethren in Arabia?

Only shortly before the Muslim Conquest of Palestine, Muhammad had declared the Jews of Medina to be *"asses who carry books"* (sura lxii). All the Jews had done was to challenge the way in which Muhammad had distorted Old Testament accounts. Worse still, in 627, the Jewish Medinan tribe of Banu Qurayza were accused of deception and betrayal of their Muslim allies. They were judged and punished according to their Jewish Law, which resulted in the beheading of 600-900 Jewish men, and the enslavement of all their women and children and the confiscation of all their property.

Why would Jews, a mere ten years later, change their view of Muhammad and Islam? It is all about time and place. The Jews of Palestine were forbidden by the Christians from entering Jerusalem, although there is evidence of exceptions. The early church had suffered a great deal at the hands of the Jews, and so mistrust of the Jews persisted into the seventh century, leading to the extreme act of Jewish exclusion from Jerusalem. This may have been frowned upon by the Jews of Medina. But Medina is hundreds of miles away from Jerusalem, and the Jews of Medina, who were very wealthy, were not directly affected by such an act of discrimination by the Christians.

At the time of the Muslim conquest of Palestine, Jewish theologians in Palestine were teaching that the Messiah was at hand. Rabbis were talking about a saviour arising from the house of Ishmael, or the Kingdom of Ishmael. The advent of the Kingdom of Ishmael was the last stage before the salvation of the Jews. Muhammad was seen as the King of Ishmael.

Just as the current Evangelical Zionists believe that their intervention will bring about the fulfilment of Biblical prophesies, so did the Jewry of the seventh century believe that they had to intervene in order to precipitate the fulfilment of their Messianic prophesies. This meant co-operating with the Kingdom of Ishmael. Jewish religious leaders of the seventh century believed their religion had more in common with the new religion of the Kingdom of Ishmael than it did with Christianity. It is possible that they were also given hope by the fact that Muslims were displacing Christians as the rulers of the day, and so it was expedient for the Jews to throw their lot in with their Muslim Arab cousins.

On the other hand, Jerusalem also held a special place in Islam, even whilst Muhammad was still alive. The Qibla originally indicated the direction of Jerusalem. It was several years later that the Muslim prophet chose Mecca as the direction of the Qibla .

The *Didaskalia of Jacob* confirms that the Jews were more than excited by the idea that a prophet was to come from amongst the Arabs. Arab historians go as far as stating that many Jews converted to Islam in the belief that Muhammad was the prophet of Arabia.

Thus we see the Muslim Arab conquerors striking a deal with Jews in Jericho, which was a walled Christian city under Muslim Arab siege. Jews negotiated a deal with the Muslim Arabs, in which the Jews would show the Arabian conquerors how to breach the wall of Jericho, in return for which Jews would be allowed to build a synagogue in front of the entrance to the city.

Caesarea, which was extremely well defended by Christians, was conquered with the help of a Jew named Joseph, who apparently showed the Muslim Arabs an underground trench. His reward was an "aman" (guarantee of security), for himself and his "ahl" which could means his immediate family, or even his people, all Jews.

As for Jerusalem, we have already covered the Persian conquest in 614 and the central active role the Jews played in orchestrating and executing the destruction of the Christian city, which they spared no effort in purging of Christians. The subsequent defeat of the Persians by Heraclius in 628 may have restored Christians to their former majority. However, recovery usually takes many more years than just a military victory. The massacre of Jews by Heraclius was a literal application of Jewish *"an eye for an eye and a tooth for a tooth"*, which has no place in Christianity and is to be repudiated.

The siege of Jerusalem by the Muslim Arab forces ended peacefully. Somehow, although Caliph Umar had already promised to honour the Christian wish to bar Jews from Jerusalem, Jewish co-operation with the Muslim Arab conquerors resulted in Caliph Umar breaching that agreement and allowing seventy Jewish families to settle in Jerusalem. The Jews had requested two-hundred families be allowed to settle in Jerusalem. Umar felt that seventy families was a reasonable compromise, as a reward to the Jews for their invaluable assistance, However, Umar allowed Christians to maintain their majority in Jerusalem.

Umar was invited by the Patriarch of Jerusalem to pray in the newly restored Church of the Holy Sepulchre, which had been destroyed by the Persian-Jewish alliance. He declined, apparently out of fear that Muslims might later wish to claim the church for their own and convert it to a mosque. That said, he did not decline an invitation to pray on the temple mount, the site of the Jewish Temple of Solomon. Just as he had foreseen, Muslims have built a mosque on that site, predictably called the Mosque of Umar.

Earlier in this book, I shared some of the vituperation of some Hassidic Jews against Christians. My brother, who is a taxi-driver in Israel, told me, whilst I was on a recent visit, that on several occasions his Hassidic passengers would get into his taxi, and as soon as they spot the cross hanging from his rear-view mirror, they would leave his taxi protesting: *"I refuse to travel in a car with the cross displayed inside it."*

One of my nieces had a similar experience with a Jewish university girlfriend. When my niece was a student in Jerusalem, she was living in St Joseph monastery. A Jewish classmate wanted to visit her. On noticing the cross on the gate to my niece's residence, the Jewish friend refused to enter, explaining she was not allowed to enter any building displaying the cross.

The same niece who was, unbeknown to many of her fellow students, the only Christian in her class, recalled that when studying church architecture, most of her Jewish fiends would mock aspects of church design and architecture that stood for central Christian doctrine. The lecturer, who was aware of my niece being a Christian, would often have to remind the students that there was a Christian amongst them, whose feelings should be respected. Theological differences should never be expressed through mockery, which leads to bitterness and conflict.

In the summer of 2011, whilst on a visit to one of my favourite spots in the Holy Land, Mount Tabor, I found myself sitting with my children at a long concrete table, for a lunch break. Next to us, at a distance of two yards, there was a large Jewish family, also having lunch. Whilst waiting for the gates of the Church of the Transfiguration to open, I started reading the Gospel to my children to remind them of the story associated with the site. Suddenly as if an emergency had arisen, our Jewish neighbours interrupted their lunch, packed up in haste and went away to a different spot. I asked if we had offended them in anyway. No eye contact, no verbal response, no reaction of any sort was made. They just abandoned the table as quickly as their legs would permit, as if they were escaping a bad smell. It dawned on me they could not tolerate the New Testament being read, particularly when the name of Christ is mentioned. Some religious Jews refer to Jesus Christ as *Jeshu*, which in Hebrew stands for *"may his name be cursed and blotted forever"*. Is this not a sort of bigotry?! For a moment I felt offended that they treated us like lepers, and could not get away fast enough. However, my children and I concluded that they were to be pitied. We as Christians may believe that Jesus Christ is the only way to God, but we are not offended by the sound of Jewish or Muslim prayers or their holy writ being cited. We may disagree with them, but we do not despise them, nor hate them. It is God who is the ultimate judge, and he commands that we should love even our enemies, let alone our brethren and cousins, the sons and daughters of Shem.

In July 2013, whilst a relative was showing me round the Synagogue Church in Nazareth, where Jesus read the Scriptures in public, I was struck by an unusual observation. Tourists were going in and out of the historic building in great numbers, with the exception of a couple, who were guarded. They stuck their heads round the door posts to get a glimpse, as if there were a physical barrier preventing them from entry. I asked a Christian Arab worshipper, who had just come out of the main church, what was preventing these people from going into the synagogue church. *"Can you not see their kippa?"* he answered me. *"They are Hassidic Jews." "So what?"* I enquired further. *"Can you not see the cross inside the synagogue Church?"* he continued to taunt me. At this point, the penny dropped. It is the cross again. These religious Jews hate the cross. They would not enter the Synagogue Church because of the sign of the cross inside it. I recalled St Paul's writing to the church at Corinth *"But we preach Christ crucified, unto the Jews a stumbling block, and unto the Greeks foolishness."* (1 Corinthians 1:23.)

Some Jews, especially the religious Jews, are so allergic to the cross that they take ridiculous measures to avoid it. *"The Jewish aversion to using any sign resembling a cross was so strong that in books on arithmetic or algebra written by Jews the plus sign was represented by an inverted "ḳameẓ"* (*The Jewish Encyclopaedia*).

One of my Jewish friends, a convert to Christianity, told me that members of the Lubovitch Jewish sect attempted to convert him back to Judaism by telling him that Jesus was a *"bastard, born of adultery"*. Such views are held by numerous Jews, well documented in their Talmudic tradition, and are deeply offensive to Christians.

The Talmud

This is a Hebrew word meaning learning. It is a name given to a collection of rabbinical teachings. Compared with the Torah, it represents the oral tradition of the Jewish faith. It covers

6,200 pages and was originally written in Hebrew and Aramaic. It consists of the instructions and opinions of thousands of rabbis on diverse matters pertaining to Jewish life, including ethics, law, Jewish customs, and of course religion. The Talmud, which comprises the Mishna and Gemara, was compiled in the second to third century AD, is supplementary to the Old Testament. The Mishna consists of ancient and authoritative Oral Jewish Laws compiled by Jewish scholars over a period spanning 200 years. It was given final form in the third century AD. Later annotations by Palestinian and Babylonian Jewish scholars are called the Gemara.

The Talmud is essential for Jewish spiritual life. It is widely accepted as an authoritative source by Jewish religious leaders. For some Jews it takes precedence over the written Scriptures, the Torah. *"My son, be more careful in the observance of the words of the Scribes than in the words of the Torah (Old Testament)."* (*Talmud*, Erubin 21b (Soncino edition). Reliance on the Talmud by Jews for religious guidance is so paramount that in his preface of the *Babylonian Talmud*, Michael Rodkinson wrote: *"The modern Jew is the product of the Talmud"* (page XI).

If racism were venom and the viper's killing power were concentrated in its fangs, the Talmud constitutes the fangs of Jewish racism. The venom of the Talmud is hatred, disdain, a sense of superiority, twisted morality that legalises cheating, lying, thieving, murder and all that is despised by decent human beings. Oh yes, of course it also contains a lot of innocuous material too.

Let us sample this venom; having accused Gentiles of a propensity to bestiality, the Talmud goes on to expand its shameful low opinion of non-Jews: *"when Gentile men come to their neighbours' houses to commit adultery with their wives and do not find them at home, they fornicate with the sheep in the barns instead. And sometimes even when their neighbours' wives are at home, they prefer to fornicate with the animals;*

for they love the sheep of the Israelites more than their own women." (*Talmud*, Abhodah Zarah, 22b)

The relegation of Gentiles to the low level of a beast is a strong theme in the Talmud; *"Why are the Goyim unclean? Because they were not present at Mount Sinai. For when the serpent entered into Eve he infused her with uncleanness. But the Jews were cleansed from this when they stood on Mount Sinai; the Goyim, however, who were not on Mount Sinai were not cleansed."* (*Talmud*, Abhodah Zarah, 22b.)

Even the sexual activities of Gentiles have been relegated. *"The sexual intercourse of a Goyim is like to that of a beast."* (*Talmud*, Sanhedrin (74b) Tosephoth.) More explicitly, the Gentile seed is worthless. *"The seed (ejaculation) of a Goyim is worth the same as that of a beast."* (Kethuboth (3b).)

President Carter, in his book *Palestine, Peace Not Apartheid* referred to Menachem Begin, the former Israeli Prime minister calling the Jews *"The Master race"*. This notion of Jewish supremacy comports with a Rabbi Schneerson who taught: *"The body of a Jewish person... is of a totally different quality from the body of members of all other nations of the world. Bodies of the Gentiles are in vain. An even greater difference is in regard to the soul. ... A non-Jewish soul comes from three satanic spheres, while the Jewish soul stems from holiness."*

Naturally denial has been deployed effectively as a tool to demolish any attempt at exposing the racist contents of the Talmud. Many an author quoting from it has been discredited as anti-Jewish or anti-Semitic. Professor Steven Plaut of the University of Haifa categorically denies any anti-Christian content in the Talmud and calls anyone who makes such a claim anti-Semitic. He states: *"There are no explicit references to Christianity anywhere in the Talmud, nor to Jesus or Mary, though there are references to people who have names somewhat similar to theirs. There are mentions of several people named Yeshu (the traditional Hebrew name for Jesus), but these were people who lived in different eras, either long before Jesus or long afterward."* (*The Jewish Press*, August 17th, 2011.)

Peter Schäfer, head of Princeton University Judaic Studies Program, in his book *Jesus in the Talmud*, states that the Talmud mocks Christ's birth, ministry, punishment and resurrection. He calls the Talmudic assault on Christianity *"devastating"*.

In his book *The Moderate Religion*, Abu Abdurahman Faruq states: *"In numerous places ignominious names are also given by the Jews to the beloved Jesus and his mother who both the Muslims and Christians hold in high esteem. The Talmud mentions: JESUS is ignominiously called Jeschu – which means, May his name and memory be blotted out. His proper name in Hebrew is Jeschua, which means Salvation. Mary, the mother of Jesus, is called Charia – dung, excrement (German Dreck). In Hebrew her proper name is Miriam. The Talmud and some of the Jewish Rabbis say that the Christians and non-Jews are idolaters, the worst kind of people, murderers, fornicators, impure animals, like dirt, unworthy to be called men, beasts in human form, worthy of the name of beasts, cows, asses, pigs, dogs, worse than dogs; that they propagate after the manner of beasts, that they have diabolic origin, that their souls come from the devil and return to the devil in hell after death; and that even the body of a dead Christian is nothing different from that of an animal."* (pp.28-29, 2011.)

Jewish History, Jewish Religion, by the late Israel Shahak, illuminates the influence of Talmudic Judaism on the State of Israel. According to Shahak, the Talmud and associated traditional teachings *"inculcate an attitude of scorn and hatred toward Gentiles,"* especially Christians. One ancient prayer beseeches, *"[May] all the Christians perish instantly."*

Shahak states that Christians were largely unaware of the anti-Christian content of the Talmud till the 13th century AD. He also states that Jews reacted by physically removing such references from the Talmud and altering direct references to Christians with general words such as "stranger", (Shahak p.27). However, in Israel, where religious Jews have no fear of consequences from the Gentiles, the omissions have been published and are taught in schools, inviting Jewish children to curse the mothers of the dead when passing by a non-Jewish cemetery (Shahak p.28-29). In a uniquely candid statement, Professor Shahak says: *"For centuries, our totalitarian society has employed barbaric and inhumane customs to poison the minds of its members, and is still doing so. These inhumane customs cannot be explained away as mere reactions to anti-Semitism or persecution of Jews; they are gratuitous barbarities directed against each and every human being"* (p.29).

The Maimonidean Code, which is full of aggression and bigotry against non-Jews, was published in Hebrew with an English translation on opposite pages. Shahak refers to the deception of the publishers who ensured the English translation was either mollified or missing some key invective. (Shahak p.30.)

Referring to an American translation of Maimonides' *Guide to the Perplexed*, he exposes the great Rabbi's racist utterances: *"Some of the Turks (i.e. the Mongol race). .. and the Blacks. .. their nature is like the nature of mute animals. .. they are not on the level of human beings, and their level among existing things is below that of a man and above that of a monkey, because they have the image and the resemblance of a man more than a monkey does."* (Shahak p.30.)

The Talmudic literature is more concerned with ritual and practice than with theology as Christians understand it. Still, it is imbued with what Shahak calls *"a very deep hatred towards Christianity, combined with ignorance about it. This attitude was clearly aggravated by the Christian persecutions of Jews, but is largely independent of them. In fact it dates from the time when Christianity was weak and persecuted, not least by Jews"* (Shahak p.116). This hatred is expressed in the callous lack of mercy expressed in Abhodah Zarah (26b), which says: *"Heretics, traitors and apostates are to be thrown into a well and not rescued."*

The lack of respect for historical truth, or Christian sensibilities, is stark. *"According to the Talmud,"* Shahak writes, *"Jesus was executed by a proper rabbinical court for idolatry, inciting other Jews to idolatry, and contempt for rabbinical authority."* Other Jewish sources accuse Jesus of sorcery and assert that he was damned to hell, where he suffers in boiling excrement; also that he was a *"bastard"*, his mother having *"played the harlot"* with Roman soldiers and conceived him, uncleanly, during menstruation. (Excerpted from *The War We Are In* by Joseph Sobran, December 9, 2003.)

According to Professor Shahak, former concentration camp inmate during WWII, founder of Israel's Human Rights League and author of *Jewish History, Jewish Religion*, *"Dishonouring Christian religious symbols is an old religious duty in Judaism. Spitting on the cross, and especially on the crucifix, and spitting when a Jew passes a church, has been obligatory from around 200 A.D. for pious Jews... The increasing strength of the Jewish nation has caused these customs to become more open again but there should be no mistake: the spitting on the cross for converts from Christianity to Judaism, organized in Kibbitz Sa'ad and financed by the Israeli government, is an act of traditional Jewish piety. ... Pious Jews object to the international plus sign for it is a cross, and it may, in their opinion, influence little children to convert to Christianity... It would then be difficult to 'educate' them to spit on the cross ... In all Hebrew elementary schools (and now many high schools as well) the international plus sign has been forbidden."*

The newly born State of Israel, so beloved and adored by Evangelical Zionists, wasted no time in attacking Christian sacred sites under its control. An American catholic priest, Fr Leonard Feeney of Boston, USA, in 1955 compiled a list of Christian sites desecrated by the Jewish state:

"The Jews have defiled and destroyed the following Church buildings: the Church of Saint John the Baptist at Am Karim; the Church of the Beatitudes at Capharnaum; the Church of Mensa Christi on the shores of the Sea of Galilee; the Church of Saint Peter at Tiberias; the Cenacle (the place of the Last Supper) at Jerusalem; the Convent of Mary Reparatrix at Jerusalem; the Convent and Hospice of Notre

Dame at Jerusalem; the Convent of the Sisters of Saint Ann at Haifa; the Franciscan Convent at Tiberias; the Patriarchal Seminary at Beit-Jala, the Salesian houses at Cremisan; the Sisters' Convent at Am Karim; the School of the Sisters of Notre Dame de Sion at Katamon; the Sisters' residence at Capharnaum; and the church and rectory at Ikret. Catholic authorities have estimated that the Jews have destroyed Church property in the Holy Land at the rate of more than two million dollars' worth a year.

"To enumerate only French Catholic institutions, they have demolished four hospitals, 16 dispensaries, two hospices, four seminaries, 32 schools and orphanages, and seven retreat houses. Among the countless other desecrations we might mention, none is more heart-rending than that of Jerusalem's Church of the Dormition – the magnificent Romanesque shrine to the Mother of God which was pillaged by Israeli soldiers and then turned into a Jewish dance hall for the young men and women of Haganah. It was only after a hundred such incidents that the Apostolic Delegate, Archbishop Hughes, unequivocally charged that there is now in operation a 'deliberate Jewish effort to decimate the Arabs and to destroy Christianity in Palestine'."

Though his critics accused him of anti-Semitism, and though he was excommunicated by the Catholic Church, the list speaks for itself.

With the above animus, I was not shocked to watch an Israeli talk-show host make mockery of Christ and Mary using the most vulgar language and sexual innuendo. Had anyone made half as light of Moses or Miriam there would have been an international campaign crying "anti-Semitism".

"Christians tell you that Jesus used to walk on the water of Lake Tiberius. But this is not true. Jesu was so fat that he was ashamed to go out. So how could he go to the lake in his swimming clothes? Christians show Jesu to you like that [showing a traditional picture of Jesus Christ in a white robe]. But these pictures are fake. The truth is that Jesu used to eat holy bread from the age of three, and he was a heavy weight. He would be like that, if he got to the age of 40 [showing a

picture of a burlesque obese bearded man with grotesque gynecomastia." (Uploaded onto YouTube, Jan 4, 2010.)

The host show bragged that every night the programme denied what Christians tell Jews. *"Remember we denied that Jesu walked on water?!"* Then the host showed another clip, this time mocking Mary's virginity and making rude sexual remarks about her:

"Christians tell you that Mary Mother of Jesus was a virgin. But this is not true. The proof is simple. When John the Baptist used to surprise her with two fingers in her hips [showing a female being baptised by a male], Mary would not jump! Besides, if Mary were really a virgin, then she would not show sex toys on the evening show with Josephus Flavius [showing pictures of plastic dildos." The host continued:

"The truth is that when Mary was 15 years of age, she was impregnated by her classmate. So her parents wanted to send her to a monastery. But since Jesus had not been born yet, there was no Christianity, and there was no monastery. So Mary's parents left her on a football pitch. So Mary spent a hot night with the Canaan team! Don't believe the Christian Church!"

Haaretz (Sep 4, 2012) reported the desecration of a Christian Monastery at Latrun, just outside Jerusalem. Jewish fundamentalists set the door of the monastery on fire and left graffiti on the walls consisting of sacrilege against Christ whom they called *"a monkey"*.

In that same year, offensive graffiti was found on walls of the Greek Orthodox Monastery of the Cross in Jerusalem, and the Baptist Church in Jerusalem. Such insults included *"Jesus is Dead"*, *"Death to Christians"* and *"Mary is a prostitute"*, the latter being a Talmudic teaching, which some Jewish scholars are at pains to deny. Christians in Jerusalem reacted by demonstrating through the old city, whilst singing hymns and reciting prayers. The contrast is a matter of pride for Christians and puts Jewish extremists to shame, if they are capable of such sentiments. *"It was a spontaneous demonstration to denounce the repeated attacks against holy places carried out by an irresponsible minority, that threatens the peaceful coexistence among peoples,"* said Bishop William Shomali, vicar of the Latin Patriarchate of Jerusalem (*Catholic World News*, Oct 8, 2013).

The Anglican cemetery in Jerusalem has also been a target of Jewish acts of hatred. Tomb stones were ripped out and offensive graffiti sprayed on the walls of the cemetery. (*The Holy Land Christian Ecumenical Foundation*, Oct 17, 2013 08:12.) The same piece reported that over seventeen such attacks against Christian sacred sites had been carried out by Jewish extremists in the previous three years.

According to Hana Bendcowsky of the Jerusalem Centre for Jewish-Christian Relations, Christian leaders refrain from complaining to the Israeli police out of fear that the police may hamper their journeys between Israel (where some of them reside) and the West Bank. *"There is a very strong feeling that the police are not doing enough... and not doing work to prevent the phenomenon,"* said Bendcowsky.

I have fond memories of accompanying my father to Jaffa, where he regularly ministered to the small Christian Arab community in the 1960s. That small community has not been spared either. On 12th June 2013 the Orthodox cemetery was violated by Jewish extremists who left offensive and threatening graffiti on tombstones calling for revenge against Christians. ("Jaffa, Christian cemetery and graves desecrated. Graffiti in Hebrew", *Encounter Gospel News*, Friday, Jun14, 2013.)

"'Unfortunately" adds Balha, a human rights activist, 'the government does nothing against this phenomenon, and this encourages other similar acts. According to some residents, if the incident had occurred in a Jewish cemetery the police would have found the authors within a few hours. All Israeli newspapers would have reported it.'"

This attack is reminiscent of one committed against Christians in Jaffa forty-eight hours before the official declaration of the State of Israel. On May 13, 1948, as reported by Father Deleque, a Catholic priest, *"Jewish soldiers broke down the doors of my church and robbed many precious and sacred objects. Then they threw the statues of Christ down into a nearby garden."* He added that Jewish leaders had *reassured that religious buildings would be respected, "but their deeds do not correspond to their words."* ("Christians Discriminated Against by Israel", Donald Neff, former Israel Bureau Chief for *Time Magazine*.)

A public complaint by the Christian Union of Palestine on May 31, 1948, bewailed the desecration by Jewish forces of ten Christian churches and humanitarian institutions in Jerusalem, which were turned by the Zionist forces into military bases. The CUP protested that a total of fourteen churches were damaged by Jewish shells, as a result of which three priests were killed, and a hundred innocent women and children were wounded. By comparison, Arab forces, depicted by the west as savage, showed respect for Christian places of worship.

On May 19, 23 and 24, 1948, Jewish shells landed on the Convent of Orthodox Copts causing the death of many children. Similar treatment of the Orthodox Armenian Convent caused the death of eight refugees and wounded about one hundred and twenty. On May 16, 1948, Father Pierre Somi, secretary to the Bishop, was killed and two men were wounded at the Orthodox Syrian Church of St Mark.

September 10, 1963 was marked by co-ordinated acts of violation by Jewish fundamentalists against Christian missions in three major Israeli towns: Jaffa, Haifa and Jerusalem. The attacks, committed by two hundred members of a religious vigilante group called Hever Peelei Hamahane Hatorati, the Society of Activists of the Torah Camp, were meant to intimidate Christians in these three towns and in Israel at large. The attack on the Church of Scotland school in Jaffa involved the beating of school children and physical damage was done to the school building.

Jaffa seems to have been an easy target. In 1995 St Anthony's Catholic Church in Jaffa was entered by an Israeli soldier, Daniel Koren, aged 22, who went on a shooting rampage. He fired no fewer than 100 bullets at the altar. The perpetrator admitted to having committed a similar crime at the Gethsemane Church in Jerusalem.

Neff provides a litany of such subsequent desecrations and violence against Christians by the Jewish state:

On July 21, 1967, Jewish damage to Christian churches and violence against Christians led the Reverend James L. Kelso, a former moderator of the United Presbyterian Church, who had lived in Palestine for many years, to say: *"So significant was this third Jewish war against the Arabs that one of the finest missionaries of the Near East called it 'perhaps the most serious setback that Christendom has had since the fall of Constantinople in 1453.'"*

His description of the vile acts of the conquering Israelis shows total disrespect for any religious sensibilities: *"How did Israel respect church property in the fighting...? They shot up the Episcopal Cathedral [in Jerusalem], just as they had done in 1948. They smashed down the Episcopal school for boys.... The Israelis wrecked and looted the YMCA.... They wrecked the big Lutheran hospital.... The Lutheran center for cripples also suffered...."*

The wife of a physician at the American University Hospital in Beirut, Nancy Nolan, who was visiting Jerusalem during the Six Day War, was appalled by the excessive inexplicable violation of holy Christian sites by Israeli soldiers in Jerusalem. She recorded: *"while the Israeli authorities proclaim to the world that all religions will be respected and protected, and post notices identifying the Holy Places, Israeli soldiers and youths are throwing stink bombs in the Church of the Holy Sepulchre.*

"The Church of St. Anne, whose crypt marks the birthplace of the Virgin Mary, has been severely damaged and the Church of the Nativity in Bethlehem also was damaged. The wanton killing of the Warden of the Garden Tomb followed by the shooting into the tomb itself, in an attempt to kill the warden's wife, was another instance that we knew first-hand which illustrated the utter disregard shown by the occupation

forces toward the Holy Places and the religious sensibilities of the people in Jordan and in the rest of the world.

"The desecration of churches... includes smoking in the churches, littering the churches, taking dogs inside and entering in inappropriate manner of dress. Behavior such as this cannot be construed other than as a direct insult to the whole Christian world."

Other attacks occurred at two nearby church schools, the Greek Catholic missionary school of St Joseph and a Christian Brothers school. In Jerusalem, attacks occurred at the St Joseph convent and the Finnish Lutheran mission school. In Haifa, the American-European Beth El Messianic Mission Children's Hostel and School was attacked. No serious damage occurred in any of the attacks except at the Church of Scotland school. More than one hundred Jews were convicted in the attacks, none of them receiving more than small fines and suspended sentences.

The advent of the Likud period in power seemed to give an impetus to fundamentalist Jewish attacks on Christians in Israel. On October 8, 1982, the Baptist Church in Jerusalem was burned down. The wooden chapel was doused with kerosene and set on fire. The Baptist Church Bookstore, where one of my cousins had worked, was vandalised by Jewish fundamentalists on numerous occasions. The rebuilding of the Baptist chapel was barred initially by Jewish protests and eventually in 1985, the Israeli Supreme Court advised the Baptists to abandon the area on the grounds that it was purely Jewish.

"On Christmas Day in 1983, a hotel in Tiberias where Christians held meetings was set afire, the latest in a series of attacks on a small group of about 50 Christians. Two Jews were arrested in the arson incident. Other attacks included stones thrown through windows at the hotel while the group was meeting and break-ins at the homes of members of the group. The anti-missionary group Yad Le'Achim complained that Christian missionaries were offering money, clothes, jewellery and tennis shoes to listen to Christian lectures."

("Fifty Years of Israel", January 1, 2001. Author: Donald Neff.)

To add insult to Injury, when CBS News attempted to highlight the plight of Christian Arabs in Bethlehem and Jerusalem, Oren, The Israeli Ambassador, long before the recording of the programme was completed, let alone aired, accused the network of doing a "hatchet job". Michael Oren took the unusual step of complaining to the producer before the programme was completed. ("'60 Minutes' profiles Palestinian Christians; Michael Oren falls on his face", *Mondoweiss*, Adam Horowitz on April 22, 2012.)

By sharp contrast, Christians at large, including the Roman Catholic Church, are bending over backwards to befriend the Jews and purge their vocabulary from anything remotely offensive to Jews, even at the cost of basic Christian doctrine.

"Roman Catholics vacillate. The Second Vatican Council's ecumenically path breaking Nostra Aetate (Declaration on the Relationship of the Church to Non-Christian Religions) disavows any basis in Scripture for regarding Jews as "repudiated or cursed by God," but precedes that line with the bald statement, "the church is the new people of God." And while deploring "the hatred, persecutions, and displays of anti-Semitism directed against the Jews at any time and from any source," Nostra Aetate fails to acknowledge the church as one of those sources and takes no account of the Holocaust or the papacy's inadequate performance in the face of the Nazi regime. "A unilateral pronouncement by one party which presumes to redress on its own terms a wrong that it does not admit," was how Rabbi David Polish responded to the declaration. The same combination of contrition and obtuseness has too often characterized subsequent Vatican statements and gestures." (Luke Timothy Johnson, "Christians and Jews: Starting Over – Why the Real Dialogue Has Just Begun", January 31, 2003 issue of *Commonwealth* magazine.)

Some Christians, particularly pro-Jewish Evangelicals, are willing to even eviscerate Christian theology in order to appease Jews. In the process, they are willing to excise essential Christian dogma, as if it were an undesirable malignant growth, in order to placate the Jews. Johnson continues: *"In fact, the major difficulty in many Christian-Jewish dialogues is finding any real representation of a Christian position that is not so self-denying as to be in danger of disappearing. Many Christians, such as James Carroll (Constantine's Sword) see the New Testament as so drenched in anti-Judaism that they apply the logic of the medieval church's Talmud-burning on their own Scripture."*

Christian, particularly Evangelical, sensitivity to Jewish feelings has gone too far. Now we talk about supersessionalism, as if it were an infectious disease to be avoided at all cost, in order not to offend the Jews. The New Testament teaches clearly that the Church is the New Israel. Christians cannot abandon their belief because others find it offensive. As offense goes, the belief that Christians are the new Israel is by no means as offensive as Jewish offensive language used to reference Christ, Mary or Christians. One is a doctrinal position, whilst the other is pure bigotry.

The particularly American philo-Semitic evangelical church has spared no gesture to pacify the Jews. Some Evangelicals have even refrained from evangelising Jews in order not to offend them.

"No, Christians are not partnering with Jewish groups in order to convert them. I and others who have worked with Christians in support of Israel all report that no one has ever tried to convert us. Do Christians think that Jews should accept Jesus as their saviour? Of course they do. But they also think that Hindus, Muslims, and their Christian neighbours who have yet to be born again should also accept Jesus. And Christians believe this whether or not they support Israel." ("May 30, 2006, Evangelicals and Israel: An Interview with David Brog by Ed Lasky" – *American Thinker*, May 17 2007.)

The Jewish paranoia that they may be converted by Christians begs the question of why, in an age obsessed with democracy and freedom of speech, people are repulsed by religious discourse and an exchange of religious thought. No Christian can force a Jew to believe in Christ. Christians believe they have a duty to share the Gospel with all nations. Sharing somehow, in some minds, becomes equivalent to converting. Unless conversion is volitional, it is never real, and no Christian would want a false conversion. Therefore, the fear of being converted by a Christian must stem mainly from lack of confidence in one's personal faith, one's religion, or both.

No one can rightly claim that the Jews are equally anxious to pacify Christians. On the contrary, the old aggressive hostile attitude towards Christians and the blasphemous posture towards Christianity persist today, if only in some substrata of Jewry.

I recall examining a Jewish lawyer in my consulting rooms at Harley Street, London. He was a victim of personal injury. Upon finding out I was a Christian, he somehow decided it was appropriate for him to tell me this joke: A Protestant, a Catholic and a Jew were discussing how they celebrated Christmas. The Protestant and Catholic basically went to church; home for lunch then opened their presents. The Jew, who was a shop owner, was then asked: *"Do you actually celebrate Christmas?"* *"Oh yes,"* he answered. *"And how do you do it?"* He replied, *"I work hard before Christmas, so on Christmas day I go to my shop and walk along the empty shop aisles and sing 'What a friend we have in Jesus'!.*

Now that hymn has deep spiritual meaning for Christians, and yet this man thought it was kosher material for humour? I dare say, had I told a joke about Moses, he would have been deeply offended and accused me of anti-Semitism.

The Jews are often portrayed as the victim, and some Jewish groups revel in that role. They have been victims in the past, but the truth is that they have also been aggressors. The Talmud contains an incredible record of their intellectual, spiritual and verbal aggression against Christians. I have opted to offer numerous examples from the Talmud, not only to raise awareness of anti-Christian Jewish attitudes and teachings, but also in the belief that *"Even the most blatant bigots, when made aware of their racism, can change"* (Charles R. Ridley). Perhaps some Jewish eyes may be opened to their own anti-Semitism, another anti-Semitism.

Maimonides, in *Hilkhoth Akum* (X, 1) says:

"Do not have pity for them, for it is said (Deuter. VII, 2):
Show no mercy unto them. Therefore, if you see an Akum in
difficulty or drowning, do not go to his help. And if he is in
danger of death, do not save him from death. But it is not right
to kill him by your own hand by shoving them into a well or in
some other way, since they are not at war with us."

Such thinking is totally devoid of basic humanity, fairness,
liberality, open-mindedness, or tolerance, all of which are
antonyms of bigotry. The above casuistry explains the conduct
of Zionists towards Palestinians during the last hundred years
or more. It reflects an attitude of racial superiority, a type of
racism that flaunts itself and thumbs its nose at all that is
decent in humanity. It sets one race above all others and sets
one much lower, namely Christians, legalising the practice of
all manners of evil by a Jew towards these inferior Christians,
and all G*oyim*.

Although not all Jews are religious, nor do all Jews accept
the Talmud, it is however not difficult to see the precepts of
the Talmud embodied in the essence of Zionism.

One must ask what, in the name of God, qualifies such a
people to belong to civilised society! In what societal
framework can they be considered reasonable, decent or
worthy of being friends and neighbours to any human being?
Furthermore, it must be asked what sort of human being who
condemns themselves by their arrogant racist convictions, still
believes they are superior to other human beings, especially
Christians who are the antithesis of what Jewish racism,
believing in kindness, love, and turning the other cheek.

Some readers may skip over this Talmudic section in
disbelief. Some, I have heard it said, would simply state that
this is tradition and does not therefore rank with Scripture in
terms of authority. Such thinking is woefully mistaken. The
Talmud is held by some Jews to be more holy than the
Scriptures.

"Thus the ultimate authority for Orthodoxy is the
Babylonian Talmud. The Bible itself ranks second to it in

reality, if not in theory." (*Universal Jewish Encyclopedia*, "Authority" p. 637.)

For those who claim that Talmudic writings resulted from the persecution of Jews by Christians, they have to be advised to put the horse before the cart, as Professor Shahak has reiterated:

"Judaism is imbued with a very deep hatred toward Christianity combined with ignorance about it. This attitude was clearly aggravated by the Christian persecutions of Jews, but is largely independent of them. In fact, it dates from the time when Christianity was still weak and persecuted (not least by Jews), and it was shared by Jews who had never been persecuted by Christians or who were even helped by them..."

It has to be stated, merely in the interest of truth and justice, and by no means is the author calling for retaliation, that Jews had for centuries desecrated the name of Christ and key Christian figures, long before any Christian backlash ensued. A typical example is the infamous book *Toledot Jeshu (Book of the Life of Jesus),* which mocks, insults and curses the person of Christ. It was widely circulated amongst the Jews of the middle ages both in Europe and the Middle East. (Van Voorst, Robert E (2000). *Jesus Outside the New Testament: An Introduction to the Ancient Evidence.* WmB Eerdmans Publishing. pp. 122 ff. and Schäfer, Peter (2002). *Mirror of His Beauty: Feminine Images of God from the Bible to the Early Kabbalah.* Princeton University Press. pp. 211f.) It claims that the birth of Jesus was the result of a Roman Soldier Joseph Pandera having raped Mary. His disciples apparently stole his body and falsely claimed his resurrection. The name of Jesus, which means saviour, has been changed to Jeshu which is an acronym for *"may his name be cursed and blotted out!"*

Many of the offensive pages of this book were concealed in fear of reprisals.

In 1631, a Jewish synod in Poland ordered the offending passages to be expunged, and that these teachings were to be passed on orally to young Jews by Rabbis and parents. This is documented by P.L.B Drach:

"Drach, op.cit. I.168, 169. The text of this encyclical is given in Hebrew and also in translation, thus: 'This is why we enjoin you, under the pain of excommunication major, to print nothing in future editions, whether of Mischna or of the Gemara, which relates whether for good or evil to the acts of Jesus the Nazarene, and to substitute instead a circle like this O, which will warn the Rabbis and schoolmasters to teach the young these passages only viva voce. *By means of this precaution the savants amongst the Nazarenes will have no further pretext to attack us on this subject.' Cf, Abbe'Chiarini, Le Talmud de Babylone, p.45 (1831)."*

The offending passages are said to have been reinserted since then, although such passages may not necessarily be in English translations or newer editions.

The only place where I could find something instructive on the *Toledot* is *Jesus Outside the New Testament* (pp. 122-134), by Robert E. Van Voorst, William B. Eerdmans Publishing Company, Grand Rapids, Michigan, USA / Cambridge, UK.

Even the renowned Maimonides, living in Muslim Spain, had expressed bigoted views of Christ as one who caused the destruction of the Jewish nation: *"Even Jesus the Nazarene who imagined that he would be Messiah and was killed by the court, was already prophesied by Daniel. So that it was said, "And the members of the outlaws of your nation would be carried to make a (prophetic) vision stand. And they stumbled" (Daniel 11.14). Because, is there a greater stumbling-block than this one? So that all of the prophets spoke that the Messiah redeems Israel, and saves them, and gathers their banished ones, and strengthens their commandments. And this one caused [nations] to destroy Israel by sword, and to scatter their remnant, and to humiliate them, and to exchange the Torah, and to make the majority of the world err to serve a divinity besides God."* (A. James Rudin. *Christians & Jews Faith to Faith: Tragic History, Promising Present, Fragile Future*, Jewish Lights Publishing, 2010, pp. 128–129.)

Whilst the theology of the Holy Trinity is alien to Jewish thinking, one has to lose their sense of integrity to accuse Christians of worshipping more than one God. The Bible, both

Old and New Testament, make it clear that Christians believe in one God. Christian monotheism is expressed in the widely used Nicene Creed, which has been reiterated every Sunday in churches throughout the world since the fourth century AD: *"We believe in one God, the Father, the Almighty, maker of heaven and earth"*. Christianity is a monotheistic religion. But to make such false accusations of polytheism against Christians serves only one purpose, which is to incite Jewish hatred and violence against Christians. If an enlightened man such as Maimonides is capable of such dreadful misleading utterances, what hope is there for those less enlightened?

Maimonides goes further in demolition of the character of Christ. In his Epistle to Yemen, written about 1172, addressed to the head of Yemen's Jewish community, Rabbi Jacob ben Netan'el al-Fayyumi, he states:

"Ever since the time of Revelation, every despot or slave that has attained to power, be he violent or ignoble, has made it his first aim and his final purpose to destroy our law, and to vitiate our religion. This they have apparently done by means of force, by intellect, or both. Apparently Jesus adopted both, force and intellect or clever arguments in order to destroy the Jewish nation.

"There arose a new sect which combined the two methods, namely, conquest and controversy, into one, because it believed that this procedure would be more effective in wiping out every trace of the Jewish nation and religion. It, therefore, resolved to lay claim to prophecy and to found a new faith, contrary to our Divine religion, and to contend that it was equally God-given. Thereby it hoped to raise doubts and to create confusion, since one is opposed to the other and both supposedly emanate from a Divine source, which would lead to the destruction of both religions. For such is the remarkable plan contrived by a man who is envious and querulous. He will strive to kill his enemy and to save his own life, but when he finds it impossible to attain his objective, he will devise a scheme whereby they both will be slain.

"The first one to have adopted this plan was Jesus the Nazarene, may his bones be ground to dust."

Gone is historical integrity. Religious sentiment, passed on from one generation to the next, has proven much more powerful than education. This highly educated man can put his intellect to bed and utter such historically errant words. The curse at the end is consistent with Jewish sentiment, who call Christ Yeshu, which stands for *"May his name perish and be wiped out for ever"*.

Maimonides repeats *"may his bones be ground to dust"* almost every time he mentions Jesus of Nazareth. The hatred for Jesus expressed in this mantra is almost equal in force to the respect for Muhammad expressed by Muslims in the Sal'am, repeated by Muslims every time the name of their prophet is mentioned. Indeed Muslims use a positive mantra every time Isa (Jesus) is mentioned : *"Peace be upon Him"*. By contrast, Jewish Maimonides states:

"You know that the Christians falsely ascribe marvellous powers to Jesus the Nazarene, may his bones be ground to dust, such as the resurrection of the dead and other miracles. Even if we would grant them for the sake of argument, we should not be convinced by their reasoning that Jesus is the Messiah. For we can bring a thousand proofs or so from the Scripture that it is not so even from their point of view. Indeed, will anyone arrogate this rank to himself unless he wishes to make himself a laughing stock." (Halkin, Abraham S., ed., and Cohen, Boaz, trans. *Moses Maimonides' Epistle to Yemen: The Arabic Original and the Three Hebrew Versions*, American Academy for Jewish Research, 1952, p.xvi.)

If Christ is subjected to such vituperation, why should his followers be spared?! Maimonides repeatedly accuses Christians, amongst whom he lived, of idol worship:

1. *"Know that this Christian nation, who are making the claim of a messiah, with all their many different sects, are all idol worshippers and all their holidays are forbidden, and we deal with them regarding religious issues as we would pagans... therefore one must know that in every one of the Christian nation's cities which has an altar, meaning their house of worship, it is a pagan house of idolatry without any doubt."* (Interpretation of the Mishna, tractate Avoda Zara 1:3)

2. Maimonides issued an edict: *"The Christians are idol worshipers and Sunday is their religious holiday, therefore in Eretz Israel we may not trade with them on Thursday and Friday of every week, and needless to say on Sunday, which is forbidden [for trade with Christians] everywhere."* (Uncensored version of Hayad Hachazaka (Hilchot Avoda Zara 9:4).)

3. *"The Christians are idol worshippers and their regular wine is forbidden to be consumed"* (Hilchot Maachalot Asurot 11:7).

At the beginning of this section, I expressed the belief that bigots can change. At the risk of contradicting myself, I have to qualify my earlier statement and say that some bigots can change. There is a hardened bigot with whom reason only serves to harden his heart. *"The mind of the bigot is like the pupil of the eye; the more light you pour upon it, the more it will contract."* (Oliver Wendell Holmes). I hope that none of my readers fall into this category.

"What's in a name" has become a well-worn phrase, but in this context it has a profound meaning. The name of Christ seems to be anathema to many religious Jews. During the late 1980s and early 1990s the brilliant Abba Eban, Israeli intellectual and politician, presented a series about the history of the Jews. It was at that time that I heard the expression "Before the Common Era", which I soon understood to be one way of ignoring the existence of Christ let alone his historic impact on the entire human race. Time and again, he would deliberately substitute BC to BCE. It occurred to me that the Latin *Anno Domine* means year of our Lord. Naturally the Jews generally, as we can see from the above pages, neither respect Christ, and would not call him Lord, nor own him. Therefore as one Jewish English dictionary put it: *"Before the Common Era (used in place of B.C.). Steinmetz: '... recently, a new awareness of the Christian character of these abbreviations has led many Jewish writers and editors to replace them with [C.E. And B.C.E.]'"*. (www.jewish-languages.org/jewish-english-lexicon/words/30)

If Christians were to be equally sensitive about their religion, we would change the Christian calendar and replace the names of the days of the week and the months of the year because of their heathen origin.

Ironically, an organization called religious tolerance published "A Jewish Statement About Christianity" entitled "Dabru Emet" which is Hebrew for "speak ye the truth" (Latest update: 2006-MAR-06 Author: B.A. Robinson). In the second section of the statement entitled '21 Centuries of Oppression', one is struck by the dogged determination of the authors not to use BC and AD. Instead, the statement uses BCE and CE, again denying Jesus Christ any recognition. The irony is that the sponsors of the organisation define themselves as *"Ontario Consultants on Religious Tolerance"*. The ethos of the statement, however, is that Jews do not have to tolerate Christians. They would not even acknowledge Christ's place in History. So much for tolerance!

What is also interesting is that the aim of the statement seems to craft a list of crimes committed by Christians against the Jews. No mention is made of crimes committed by Jews against Christians, particularly in the first three centuries. The statement may be entitled 'Dabru Emet', but it certainly does not contain the whole truth, nor does it contain nothing but the truth.

The statement picks some bones with Christians over "supersession" or "displacement/replacement theology" and over a fringe, non-representative belief that Jews should be punished for crucifying Christ. Try as I may to remember how key tolerance is to the statement, I am amazed that the authors saw it fit to challenge a central teaching of the New Testament, namely that the Church is the New Israel. This may not be palatable to some Jews, but religious beliefs and doctrines cannot be changed in order to please or appease people. The statement makes no reference to the offence caused by Jews to Christians by the negative, unflattering, dismissive and insulting views some Jews hold about Jesus Christ the son of God, and his followers. Any reader of the Talmud, even with a modicum of intelligence, can see how when the shoe is on the other foot, the offence caused by the Talmud is by far greater.

Christian Israeli Arabs have to live with these people and some have to deal with them on a daily basis. The attitudes, beliefs and actions of some Hassidic Jews fully qualify for "anti-Semitism" against Christian Israeli Arabs. One wonders what Evangelical Zionists think of this. Have they ever thought about these issues? It would not surprise me if they were entirely ignorant of these issues, as they are so fatally blinded by their obsession with some Biblical prophecy, that they have ignored the rest of Scripture, let alone Jewish hostility towards Christians. Pastor Hagee, a staunch Evangelical Zionist, states boldly: *"Pastor Hagee: Every anti-Semite is going to spend eternity in Hell without God."* By anti-Semite, he means anti-Jewish. (NPR: "Pro-Israel Christians Lobby in Washington"; All Things Considered: July 17, 2006.) Does that apply to Zionists, Hassidic and Evangelical Zionists who discriminate against, hate and despise Semites such as Christian Arabs and Christian Assyrians? This should be a sobering question.

Some pro-Zionists may say of the Talmudic bigotry against Christians: *"These are just words; sticks and stones may break my bones, but names will never hurt me".* Well, Zionists do not just call Christians names. They do actually commit violence against Christians and their places of worship. It is not unusual for Hassidic Jews to spit at Christian Clergy in the streets of Jerusalem.

The Baptist Church seems to have been the object of attention from Jewish arsonists. *"Baptist House in central Jerusalem as late Tuesday night the building was set ablaze causing extensive damage to the sanctuary where four local congregations meet weekly."* (CNS News October 24, 2007.)

Jewish extremists had attempted to burn it down 25 years prior. Since the building was first opened in 1992, *"'there have been a few minor incidents of vandalism but otherwise the church has "very good relations" with the community,' said a Baptist mission representative"* (CNS News October 25, 2007). Messianic Jews and Russian Christians, who use the building, have experienced persecution for years from local Jewish extremists. Moderate Jews condemned the attack.

The leader of a right-wing group rejoicing by the name of Tzfiyah ("expectation"), who campaigned for the release from prison of members of the Jewish underground who had attempted to blow up the Dome of the Rock said in the 1980s: "Thou shalt not kill" applied only to killing fellow Jews, not non-Jews. Furthermore, in the Tzfiyah's journal, he condemned all Jews who did not support the building of the Third Temple and declared that since Christians and Muslims were idolaters, they should not be allowed to live in Israel.

On March 19th 2012, Israeli Prime Minister Netanyahu was invited by the Evangelical Zionist organisation called Christians United for Israel, led by the incorrigible Pastor Hagee, to address their annual conference. He was applauded before, during, and after his audacious address, which opened by thanking and flattering the organisation. He then scored a few Brownie points by telling them that he and his family read the Bible once a week. His son reads the Bible, and, were it not for the magnanimous intervention of the Prime Minister, would have won a national Bible knowledge competition.

He then thanked the audience for standing with *"the one and only Jewish state"*. Was there an implication that there should be more than one Jewish state? Was that a hint that the Jewish State of the Khazars should be revived?! Or perhaps because there is only one Jewish State the Jews were entitled to allowances or exemptions from international law, or fairness, or from their obligation to deal with their neighbours equitably?

Apparently there is a dramatic transformation in the relationship between Christians and Jews! He then talked about *"the common values that we share."* Which, he added *"set Israel apart"* from its Middle Eastern neighbours. These *"revolutionary values"* sprang from Israel millennia ago.

Then he talked about the story of David, Uriah the Hittite and his wife Bath Sheba, whom David impregnated, whose husband he killed and whom he took to be his wife. The lesson of this story was not that greed, lust and murder are sins. Nor was it that it is wrong to take by deception what is not yours, as Israel has done with many an unsuspecting Palestinian farmer. The lesson was not that sin is powerful and ever present with us, regardless of colour, creed or calibre. It was not that sin has consequences, even after repentance. No, no! According to Netanyahu, the lesson here was that King David was so tolerant as not to kill Nathan the priest for reprimanding him regarding his adultery and murder. How some people just have the knack to manufacture virtue out of the absence of evil. He then went on to claim that the Jews invented tolerance. The reproach of King David by Nathan the priest was tolerated by magnanimous saintly King David. As such this was *"a revolutionary statement in human affairs"*. He then stated that no one is exempt from reproach: *"All men are equal under God, all men and all women, equal under God... (applause)... with inalienable rights,"* he added, plucking on the heart strings of naïve Evangelical Zionist Americans, quoting from their declaration of independence in 1776, which states, *"We hold these truths to be self-evident, that all men are created equal, that they are endowed by their Creator with certain unalienable Rights"*. The subtext is that the Jews are more equal than anyone, if there is such a thing. After all, they invented tolerance, didn't they?! Shame they do not seem to have so much use for it, though!

The applause formed a perfect incentive for even bolder claims to be made by the right-wing Israeli Prime Minister. Tongue in cheek, he claimed: *"This is a Jewish concept....it is a revolutionary Jewish concept"*. I would wish to add that concepts have to be matched by deeds.

Of course these claims are very far-fetched. But Netanyahu was safe, probably safer, in that unsuspecting assembly than in his own party, let alone in the Israeli Knesset. Mr Hagee did not challenge these claims at all. If he were not so blinkered by his monochrome theology, he would have said something like: *"Wait a minute, Mr Netanyahu. If tolerance were a Jewish concept, if equality of all men and women were a Jewish concept, why is it that the early Church was persecuted by Jews everywhere? Why is it that your Talmud is full of bigotry against and obscenities about Christ and His followers? Why is it that your people despise the cross and spit on it? Why is it that my Christian Arab brethren living in Israel do not enjoy equal rights and opportunities. Why is it that the missionary laws have not been repealed? Why is it that Christians are not even allowed to give a New Testament to a Jew without breaking the law? Why is it that no Christian radio station is allowed to broadcast in Israel? Why is it that the Christians of Bethlehem are living within a wall?! Why is it that Christian Israeli Arab Villagers are still waiting for the Jewish state to return them to their homes since 1948? Why is it that Palestinians, amongst whom are tens of thousands of Christians, who were displaced by force in 1947/48, are still waiting to be returned to their homes and families? Why is it that the State of Israel has stolen their property under fake pretexts?"* No doubt Netanyahu would reply with all sorts of excuses or brazen denials, but at least intelligent people can make up their own minds.

I imagine one of Netanyahu's pre-emptive answers would be the reference to the undemocratic neighbours surrounding Israel. This is a common defence of Israeli undemocratic and intolerant values and practices. Besides, Israel cannot have its cake and eat it. Israel cannot claim to be tolerant, much less the inventor of tolerance, and democratic, whilst it uses undemocratic countries as its yardstick. It is hardly flattering for Israel to say that it is more democratic than Saudi Arabia, or Yemen or Bahrain. They at least have the integrity to admit that they do not believe in democracy.

Mr Netanyahu claimed that *"no one is above the law... and these values are rooted in the Bible"*. Clearly, however, Israel who has stolen land from Palestinians, and who has killed innocent Christian and Muslim Palestinians trying to return home after the 1948 war, and who continues to behave as if it were above international law, clearly it behaves as if it were above the law.

And what about freedom of expression and tolerance? A few years ago, a Hebrew Christian was stabbed by extremists Jews for distributing fliers about his Messianic faith. There are many such untold stories. Damage to Christian churches and sacred sites, already alluded to above, tells a different story of an intolerant state.

As mentioned elsewhere, the Palestinian Christians were completely eliminated from the Palestinian equation when the Zionists persuaded the British Mandate to refer to all Palestinians as Muhammadans; though they knew a significant proportion of those Palestinians were Christian. The effect of this false label is to immediately alienate Palestinian Christians as Muslims, the enemies of the Gospel and therefore the West. The consequence is a boost in the acceptability of the Zionist cause amongst Western Christian countries. Though this policy was effective, it was by no means honourable or just. This amounted to blatant misinformation and propaganda. To write off the entire Christian section of the Palestinian population in order to win support for the Zionist cause may have been shrewd and typical of Zionist manoeuvres. But more so, it was unjust and amounted to violation of the Palestinian Christian basic human rights of existence. By contrast, the Zionists of today make capital from punishing anyone who denies that the Holocaust existed. Which is more immoral: to deny that a tragedy or genocide had occurred costing the lives of millions of Jews, or to deny the existence of a people, such as the Christian Palestinians, the survivors of the original church?

Photographs

Figure 1 My father Police Inspector Rev Saleem Jiryes Shehadeh, a Palestinian Evangelical minister, baptising Christians in the River Jordan.

Figure 2 Situated right opposite one of the most important holy sites in Christendom, The Mosque of Omar built in1860, is named after Omar (Umar) ibn al-Khattab (c. 581–644), the second Caliph, who allegedly prayed at that location, having travelled to Bethlehem to grant a guarantee of safety to the Christian clergy.

Figure 3 The mosaic floor of the original basilica of the Nativity in Bethlehem, built under Emperor Constantine in the 4th century AD and destroyed during the Samaritan Revolt of 529 A.D. The current structure represents a replacement erected on the same site during the reign of Justinian (527-65).

Figure 4 The silver 14-pointed star, embedded into the marble floor, in a grotto underneath Bethlehem's Church of the Nativity, generally held by Christians to signify the site where Christ was born.

Figure 5 The controversial Israeli built separation wall near Bethlehem

Figure 6 The Church of the Annunciation in the middle of the ancient town of Nazareth, was built in the 4th century AD. This is the latest replacement, but still houses the cave where Mary is believed to have received the angelic announcement of the virgin conception and birth.

Figure 7 the moat around Caesarea, a once thriving Christian city with a Bishop of the fame of Eusebius, indicating the strength of the Christian faith in that region.

Figure 8 Remains of Caesarea

Figure 9 Remains of Caesarea

Figure 10 The Capital of a column which bears the cross, a reminder of Caesarea's Christian past.

Figure 11 Archaeological remains on the Hill of Megiddo, Armageddon, with the Plain of Megiddo in the background. This bears a great significance to dispensationalists and Evangelical Zionists.

Figure 12 The Plain of Megiddo, where dispensationalists believe the battle of Armageddon will take place.

Figure 13 Remains of Kafr Bir'im, which was a Christian Palestinian Arab village in British Mandatory Palestine, located in modern-day northern Israel, whose inhabitants were removed and replaced by Jewish settlers. The Israelis razed the village to the ground and expropriated the land. Villagers are still hoping to be allowed to return to their home one day. Meantime they are permitted to hold service in their Church.

Figure 14 The Church of Kafr Bir'im

Chapter VI

The Forgotten Victims

"In the bloody and hate-fuelled battles throughout the Middle East there is a forgotten group of people. This forgotten group of people is ignored even by many of their own brethren across the world. I'm referring, of course, to Arab Christians."

Forgetfulness is an inevitable part of the human condition, so inevitable that it draws all sorts of reactions ranging from humour to tragedy. It eventually catches up with all of us. The following Jewish joke tickled me pink:

"One Friday morning, a letter dropped through Rabbi Bloom's letterbox. He opened it and took out a single sheet of paper. On it was written just one word: 'SCHMUCK'.

"Next day, at the end of his shabbos sermon, Rabbi Bloom announced to his congregation, 'I have previously come across people who have written to me but forgot to sign the letter. This week, however, I received a letter from someone who signed it but forgot to write the letter.'"

In as far as forgetfulness is unavoidable, a certain degree of it is acceptable, even humorous. However, when forgetfulness is the result of disinterest, laziness, or refusal to deal with one's responsibilities or guilt, it becomes inexcusable. Some people are more forgettable than others because they are less interesting or less important. Therefore our tendency to forgetfulness is proportional to the interest we take in the object of our forgetfulness.

Arabic-speaking Christians seem to be a forgotten part of the Church universal. Is it lack of interest? Is it ignorance?

When I first came to live in England, my surrogate father, Rev Owen Thomas, would take me with him wherever he went preaching. Before his sermon, he would ask the congregation to welcome his adopted Arab son. At the end of the service there were always comments from interested members of the congregation about how wonderful it was to meet a converted Muslim. I was astounded at their ignorance and at how they mistakenly equated Arab to Muslim. In their minds, you could not be an Arab and a Christian. They knew nothing about the ancient traditional churches which have existed in the Middle East from the inception of Christendom.

For the best part of two thousand years the majority of inhabitants of the land of Israel have been Arabs, until the Nakbah of 1947/8. The State of Israel is not purely Jewish. No matter how hard some Zionists had tried, and despite Zionist terrorism, a significant proportion of the Palestinians remained in the land which is now called Israel.

One of my nieces attended an international Christian conference in Belgium around the time I came to live in the UK in 1975. It was interesting to compare notes with her. It was marvellous to suddenly become aware that as a Christian, one was a member of a huge body, not an insignificant minority. Yet this joy was checked by sadness that almost everyone we met had assumed that we had converted from Islam, or perhaps Judaism. Very few knew about the existence of the Arab Christians in Palestine/Israel or the Middle East.

People can be ignored for three reasons: 1. Arrogance: it may be beneath the dignity of some people to acknowledge the existence of someone they despise. 2. Blissful ignorance: if you do not know that a particular person exists, you cannot possibly acknowledge them. 3. Ostrich-like ignorance: out of sight, out of mind.

I prefer to think that most Western Christians ignore the Arabic-speaking Christians, because the former are blissfully unaware of their existence. It would be too painful to contemplate ostrich-like ignorance.

A quaint story about the silent movie actor Douglas Fairbanks serves a humorous illustration of ignorance. *"As he was driving back to his mansion, Pickfair, Douglas Fairbanks saw an Englishman of aristocratic mien and familiar face trudging along the road in the heat. He stopped to offer him a ride, which the stranger accepted. Still unable to remember the man's name, Fairbanks invited him for a drink and in the course of the conversation attempted to elicit some clues as to the visitor's identity. The visitor seemed to know many of Fairbanks' friends and was evidently well-acquainted with the estate, for he made approving comments on some recent changes. Fairbanks eventually managed a whispered aside to his secretary who had just come in. 'Who is this Englishman? I know he's Lord somebody, but I can't remember his name.' 'That,' replied the secretary, 'is the English butler you fired last month for getting drunk.'"*

Assuming Fairbanks was not demented, he could have hardly cared much for his butler, or else he would have remembered him. Often forgetfulness is a symptom of carelessness, detachment or rather lack of care for the index subject.

One forgotten group in the Middle Eastern milieu is the Arabic-speaking Christians, about whom Western Christians appear to know little. The following offers a unique insight into the plight of Arabic-speaking Christians:

"In the bloody and hate-fuelled battles throughout the Middle East there is a forgotten group of people. This forgotten group of people is ignored even by many of their own brethren across the world. I'm referring, of course, to Arab Christians.

"This unfortunate group of people is caught in the middle of tensions between Jews and Muslims. While many Arabic-speaking Christians sympathize politically and culturally with their fellow Arabs over the Jewish people, they nonetheless are often targets of scorn from Arab Muslims. What is most shocking, however, is that Christians of Arab descent are non-issues in the minds of most Western Christians." ("Does Anybody Care About the Arabic-speaking Christians?" 17.04.07 Bill Barnwell.)

We are accustomed to thinking of Israel as a Jewish country. If you were to ask the average Westerner today whether Israel/Palestine has ever been a Christian country, how many, I wonder, would really remember that for the most part of the first seven centuries AD at least, Palestine was a Christian country. Palestine was once a Christian country and there has been a continuous Christian presence in the Holy Land since the time of Jesus.

It has also been forgotten that when Zionists began settling in earnest in the late 19th century, 95% of Palestine was Arab. Those citizens had lived in Palestine for at least 1800 years. *"When political Zionism began in earnest in the late 19th century, there were only about 15,000 Jews in Palestine. In 1893, for example, the Arabs comprised roughly 95 percent of the population, and though under Ottoman control, they had been in continuous possession of this territory for 1300 years. Even when Israel was founded, Jews were only about 35 percent of Palestine's population and owned 7 percent of the land."* (*The Israel Lobby and US Foreign Policy* by John J Mearsheimer, Stephen M Watt, 2007.)

On a visit to the Holy Land, Archbishop Desmond Tutu went on a tour with Canon Naim Ateek, who showed him his former family home, now occupied by Zionists. Bishop Tutu was also shown the wall Israel had erected around Palestinian communities. Tutu was moved to the point of drawing a comparison between South African Apartheid and the Partition wall. His comments drew considerable attention, both in Israel and internationally. A comment in *Le Monde* seemed to explain Tutu's analogy at its roots. Drawing a comparison between the dominance of the whites of South Africa and the dominance of the Zionists in Palestine, the journalist wrote: *"The first, perhaps most important, is the historical colonialist foundation of the two conflicts. White settlers in South Africa, like Zionist pioneers, colonised a land already inhabited. As in South Africa, the settlers in Palestine expelled the indigenous population, some two-thirds of the Palestinians in the land that became Israel in 1948, took possession of their properties and legally segregated those who remained [...] In Palestine the*

Zionist project wanted to negate the idea of a native non-Jewish population, coining the phrase 'people without a land for a land without a people'." (By Leila Farsakh, *Le Monde Diplomatique*, November 2003.)

The conduct of the Zionists in Israel over the last sixty years can only be possible because of their utter disrespect for Palestinians, Christians included, as human beings, and more so because Western Christians are either blissfully or woefully ignorant of their very existence. The "land without a people" is a land inhabited by a people, many of whom are Christian Arabs. Just because there has never been an independent Palestinian state, this does not entitle Zionists to take over from another master, such as the British Mandate. Palestine had for centuries been part of greater Syria. Why is that an argument against Palestinians having the right to independence in their own land?!

When I came to live in England in 1975, I was privileged to live in London Bible College, with one of the Lecturers and his family. One of the things I enjoyed most was that suddenly I had friends from no fewer than 27 nations. I enjoyed a lot of attention because of my origins in the Holy Land. When students found out I was Israeli, they automatically assumed that I was Jewish. When they realised I was an Arab, they assumed I had been a Muslim. I quickly learnt to predict certain reactions, and in order to save students unnecessary embarrassment, I would introduce myself as a Christian Israeli Arab. This formula may have saved some people some embarrassment, but it almost always produced a numb response. Most students were baffled by this identity as they had no idea of what an "Israeli Christian Arab" was. *"Hang on,"* they would say, *"if you are Israeli, how can you be an Arab?"* Fewer people would find being Arab and Christian hard to reconcile, but there were enough of them.

I belong to a small minority in Israel who are Arab by race, Israeli by nationality (strictly by citizenship, since only Jews can be Israeli nationals), Christian by religion and Protestant by denomination, more specifically Evangelical. In 1947, during the Jewish-Arab conflict, many Palestinians fled Palestine. Others were chased off their land and dispossessed. A small minority, approximately 110,000 (11% of Israel's population), remained in their towns and villages. When the State of Israel was formed in 1948, these Palestinians became Israeli citizens. We are often referred to as the 1948 Palestinians, Israeli-Arabs, Arab citizens of Israel or even Israeli Palestinians. My mother came from what is known as the West Bank, though her parents owned hundreds of Dounums in Affoula. Naturally they lost their land, which is now the property of the Zionist State. In the wake of the 1858 Ottoman Land Reform or Tanzimat, land which was hitherto unregistered had to be registered to facilitate tax collection. Most poor farmers either did not register their land, or allowed rich families with Ottoman citizenship to register the land in their names, so as to avoid land tax and military service. Thus the Jewish land organisations bought land from the registered Ottoman landlords, depriving the actual poor unsuspecting Palestinian farmers of their land and livelihood. This is the story of Grandma Miriam Kahaz of Affoula.

The consequences for the Israeli Arabs of 1948 were loss of land and separation from family. In my own family, my maternal grandmother lived on the West Bank under Jordanian rule. We could only visit her at Christmas under the pretext that we were seeking pilgrimage to Bethlehem and the Holy places. And this permit was not granted every year. I recall, with sadness, the day we received news of my grandmother's death. The sad news arrived a couple of weeks after the event. We had just finished eating our lunch, when the postman delivered the missive. My mother's broken-heartedness, at reading the sad news, still brings tears to my eyes. She would not be allowed to travel the fifty miles or so to see her mother for the last time. It would have been too late, all because of 1948.

Equally, two of my father's brothers, who were on holiday in Lebanon at the time of the declaration of independence, feared a return to Palestine would lead to their imprisonment by the Jewish state. They both died abroad, without my ever seeing particularly one of them. I met one uncle in Jordan very briefly when I was barely six years of age. I hardly knew some of my cousins, though the geographical distance between us was relatively small. Some I met once only in Jordan, others I have to date never met.

Therefore Israel's day of independence is known by Israeli Arabs/ Palestinians as "al-Nakbah" which means disaster. The story of Kafr Bir'im illustrates the disrespect Zionists have shown to the Christian Arab citizens of Palestine. Just before 1948, the village, situated in north Palestine, near the Lebanese borders, was predominantly Christian, with a handful of Muslims. On October 31, 1948 during Operation Hiram the village was captured by the Haganah, a Jewish paramilitary body. In November 1948 the majority of the Bir'imites were expelled from their homes with a promise to return them at the conclusion of the war of independence. They are still waiting, thanks to Israeli justice! ("Justice for Ikrit and Biram", *Haaretz*, October 10, 2001.) In 1949 the demobilized Jewish soldiers were allowed to build a Kibbutz on the village land. In 1953 the Supreme Court of Israel ruled that the authorities had a duty to give the Bir'imites a reason as to why they may not return to their homes. To make matters worse, on September 16, 1953 the village was razed to the ground and all of its 1,170 hectares were confiscated by the State of Israel (Sabri Jiryis: "Kouetz 307 (27. Aug. 1953): 1419"). No such explanation was given to the Bir'imites as to why they could not return to their homes, other than a vague derisory excuse of security reasons. During the 1977 election campaign the then leader of the right-wing Likud party, Menachem Begin, undertook to return the Bir'imites to their homes if he won the elections. He did win. He failed to deliver, with total impunity. The inhabitants are still waiting for justice. The infamous Munich massacre of Israeli athletes in 1972, which was named after Kafr Bir'im, has rightly drawn a lot of condemnation. The adage that evil begets evil springs to mind. But very few people even know about the grievance of the villagers of Kafr Bir'im.

The village of Birwah near Acre, the birthplace of one of the most celebrated Palestinian poets of the late 20th century, Mahmud Darwish, is another case in point. Its citizens fled during the 1948 war. When they returned, they found their homes had been razed to the ground. The village mosque and church disappeared. In the following two years, Israel built two Jewish settlement on land belonging to the citizens of Birwah, Kibbutz Yas'ur and Moshav Ahihud. What about the implementation of the Balfour declaration that : *"Nothing shall be done that may prejudice the civil and religious rights of the existing non-Jewish communities in Palestine".*

According to the 1931 census to the total population of Birwah was 996, 884 Muslims and 92 Christians. (Mills, 1932, p. 100). During the British Mandate the number of Christian residents had increased to 130. (Khalidi, 1992, p.9)

The BBC News told the story of a resident who was condemned by the Israelis to the infamous Shatila camp in Lebanon.(Inside a Palestinian refugee camp, By Martin Asser, 14.05.2008)

In 1950, Arab Knesset member Tawfik Toubi demanded from the Israeli Knesset the right of the internally displaced Palestinian residents of Birwah to return to their homes. Ben Gurion replied that Birwah was an abandoned village and therefore the State of Israel had every right to do what it pleased with it. Though Ben Gurion was willing to rehouse the internally displace residents elsewhere in Israel. (Charles S. Kamen (1987), After the Catastrophe I: The Arabs in Israel, 1948-51, Middle Eastern Studies 23 (4): 453–495,).

Israeli Jewish settlers have sought to desecrate Muslim and Christian cemeteries by constructing cowsheds on site.(Israeli government and settlers turn Muslim and Christian cemeteries into animal pens, aljazeerah News, August 6 2008)

Israeli Arabs lived under Israeli military rule until 1966. In the early stages there was curfew forbidding any Arabs from travelling outside their villages/towns without permission from the military governor. At the same time, the new government issued an edict dispossessing Arabs of their land if they had not tilled it for six months. This was a perfect Zionist ploy to acquire Palestinian land with a semblance of legality.

Although the situation of Israeli Arabs has improved, it is far from perfect. For we possess citizenship, but have suffered from discrimination ever since the establishment of the State of Israel. We have been largely forgotten by the world.

"But since the situation in the Occupied Territories is more acute and more dire, the situation for the Arabs within Israel is left off the front pages of the major international papers and the issues are left off the negotiating table during the peace processes." (*Scoop Independent News*, Wednesday, 24 November 2004, Article: Am Johal.)

If the Israeli Arabs at large have been forgotten, the minority of Christians have escaped Israeli consciousness and worse still the existence of the small minority of Evangelical Arabs has even never occurred to most people.

"The Arabs living in Israel today have a mix of four identities – Israeli, Palestinian, Arab, and Muslim. The surging new identity of the Arabs in Israel may be viewed in terms of four concentric circles. They are concentric because many of these identities cut across, coincide, and often overlap with each other, and therefore they are inseparable." (Jerusalem Letters of Lasting Interest VP:82 24 Tevet 5749 / 1 January 1989, THE ARABS IN ISRAEL: A SURGING NEW IDENTITY Rafi Israeli. Dr Rafi Israeli is a senior lecturer in Islamic civilization and Chinese history at the Hebrew University of Jerusalem.)

The author of this letter assumes that Arabs are Muslim. He does actually refer to Christian Arabs towards the end of his letter. His discourse, though enlightened, lacks this fundamental consciousness that some Arabs are Christian. Many Western Christians are more desperately unaware of the existence of Arabic-speaking Christians in Israel.

Western Evangelicals, with few exceptions, subscribe to the notion that Israel has the right to the land of Palestine because they once owned it as a nation and a kingdom. But so did Arabs, and for much longer. Should antiquity and history be the litmus test of land ownership, it should be remembered that Arabs had occupied Palestine as a people, though not as a state, far longer than Jews had.

"Between 3000 and 1100BC, Canaanite civilization covered what is today Israel, the West Bank, Lebanon and much of Syria and Jordan... Those would remain in the Jerusalem hills after the Romans expelled the Jews [in the second century AD] were a potpourri: farmers and vineyard growers, pagans and converts to Christianity, descendants of the Arabs, Persians, Samaritans, Greeks and old Canaanite tribes." (Marcia Kunstel and Joseph Albright, "Their Promised Land". Washington Report on Middle East Affairs.)

The present-day Palestinians' ancestral heritage:

"But all these [different peoples who had come into Canaan] were additions, sprigs grafted onto the parent tree... And that parent tree was Canaanite... [the Arab invaders of the 7th century AD] made Muslim converts of the natives, settled down as residents, and intermarried with them, with the result that all are now so completely Arabised that we cannot tell whether Canaanites leave off and the Arabs begin." (Ilene Beatty, "Arab and Jew in the land of Canaan.")

The Jewish kingdoms were only one of many periods in ancient Palestine:

"The extended kingdoms of David and Solomon, on which the Zionists base their territorial demands, endured for only about 73 years... Then it fell apart... [Even] if we allow independence to the entire life of the ancient Jewish kingdoms, from David's conquest of Canaan in 1000 BC to the wiping out of Juda in 586 BC, we arrive at [only] a 414-year Jewish rule." (Ilene Beatty, "Arab and Jew in the land of Canaan.")

Why has nobody taken note of the plight of Israeli Arabs? As President Truman put it:

"I am sorry gentlemen, but I have to answer to hundreds of thousands who are anxious for the success of Zionism. I do not have hundreds of thousands of Arabs among my constituents." (President Harry Truman, quoted in *Anti-Zionism* ed. by Tekiner, Abed-Rabbo and Mezvinsky.)

We are the people who are "over there". We are out of sight, and hence out of mind, excluded from reckoning when it comes to the Middle East.

The Zionists justify the need for a land of their own by the Holocaust they have endured in Europe. They have their need met by making homeless a people who had occupied Palestine for several hundreds of years. By 1931, the Jewish population of Palestine was 174,606 against a total of 1,033,314. (Edward Said, *The Question of Palestine*.)

In displacing their Palestinian cousins, ironically the abused becomes the abuser, the looted the looter, and the victim becomes the devourer. Worse still, they do so without any compunction, and support their rapacious acquisition of Palestinian land by a warped casuistry.

This is how Israel got away with murder at its inception. It was like a dinosaur, barely out of its shell ready to hunt down and devour. Israel, barely born, began to commit acts of cold-blooded murder against its Arabs. The Deir Yassin Massacre of Palestine by Jewish soldiers is a poignant case in point.

"For the entire day of April 9, 1948, Irgun and LEHI soldiers carried out the slaughter in a cold and premeditated fashion... The attackers 'lined men, women and children up against the walls and shot them,'... The ruthlessness of the attack on Deir Yassin shocked Jewish and world opinion alike, drove fear and panic into the Arab population, and led to the flight of unarmed civilians from their homes all over the country." (Israeli author, Simha Flapan, *The Birth of Israel*.)

"By 1948, the Jew was able not only to 'defend himself' but to commit massive atrocities as well. Indeed, according to the former director of the Israeli army archives, 'in almost every Arab village occupied by us during the War of Independence, acts were committed which are defined as war crimes, such as murders, massacres and rapes'... Uri Milstein, the authoritative Israeli military historian of the 1948 war, goes one step further, maintaining that 'every skirmish ended in a massacre of Arabs'." (Norman Finkelstein, *Image and Reality of the Israel-Palestine Conflict*.)

Such massacres took place elsewhere, including near my home town. My family had to live through these terrors. These acts of terror ensured that Palestinians fled and never returned. Two of my uncles, who were on holiday in Lebanon before the war of 1948, feared a return to Palestine. Their homes were confiscated by the new (democratic) Jewish state. One of my brothers had to purchase one of my uncle's home from the Jewish State.

Expulsion of the Arab population of Palestine

"Joseph Weitz was the director of the Jewish National Land Fund... On December 19, 1940, he wrote: 'It must be clear that there is no room for both peoples in this country... The Zionist enterprise so far... has been fine and good in its own time, and could do with 'land buying' – but this will not bring about the State of Israel; that must come all at once, in the manner of a salvation (this is the secret of the Messianic idea); and there is no way besides transferring the Arabs from here to the neighbouring countries, to transfer them all; except maybe for Bethlehem, Nazareth and Old Jerusalem, we must not leave a single village, not as single tribe'... There were literally hundreds of such statements made by Zionists." (Edward Said, *The Question of Palestine.*)

"That Ben Gurion's ultimate aim was to evacuate as much of the Arab population as possible from the Jewish state can hardly be doubted, if only from the variety of means he employed to achieve this purpose...most decisively, the destruction of whole villages and the eviction of their inhabitants...even [if] they had not participated in the war and had stayed in Israel hoping to live in peace and equality, as promised in the Declaration of Independence." (Israeli author, Simha Flapan, *The Birth of Israel.*)

Elsewhere, this would be called ethnic cleansing, and western nations would be up in arms, defending minorities from such injustices. However, remarkably, ethnic cleansing of Israeli Arabs seems to ruffle no Western feathers. Arabs are fair game. Hitler, who ranked Arabs as even inferior to Jews, seems to have found allies in the West and amongst some Americans, who view Arabs as an inferior backward race, and such a view cannot be denied as it is well reflected in their actions or rather inaction in the face of such sacrilege committed against Arabs.

The Jews suffered from anti-Semitism in Europe. This included desecration of their synagogues. One would think that decent people would not wish to inflict anything vaguely similar to their own afflictions on their worst enemies. In 1947, in my home town, mostly Christian, my family locked themselves and their precious belongings in the Anglican Church. The Jews showed no respect for holy places. The church was broken into and all property was confiscated.

The Zionists, supported by the West, and loved by Evangelical Zionists, showed unbounded brutality in the way they dealt with Palestinians during the 1948 war.

"During May [1948], ideas about how to consolidate and give permanence to the Palestinian exile began to crystallize, and the destruction of villages was immediately perceived as a primary means of achieving this aim... [Even earlier] On 10 April, Haganah units took Abu Shusha... The village was destroyed that night... Khulda was levelled by Jewish bulldozers on April 20... Abu Zureiq was completely demolished... By mid-1949, the majority of the [350 depopulated Arab villages] were either completely or partly in ruins and uninhabitable." (Benny Morris, *The Birth of the Palestinian Refugee Problem, 1947-1949.*)

Morris writes about a similar atrocity which occurred near my home town of Kufur Yasief. The ancient Arab village of al-Kabri was subjected to the "destroy and burn" policy of the Haganah, who executed residents in cold blood. They believed that by destroying Arab villages, they would prevent their inhabitants from ever returning. Zionists justify these war crimes by the allegation that on March 27, 1948 fighters from al-Kabri ambushed a Zionist Brigade and killed forty-nine Zionist fighters.

Within two months retaliatory action was executed by official command of Operation Ben-Ami to *"attack with the aim of capturing, the villages of Kabri, Umm al Faraj and Al-Nahr, to kill the men and to destroy and set fire to the villages."* (Benvenisti (2000), pp. 138-139.) Benvenisti further stated that *"the orders were carried out to the letter."*

The Zionist forces did their evil deed with complete impunity. To date there has been no war crime tribunal. No one has been held responsible. Palestinian blood has been shed with no opportunity for justice to be served against the perpetrators. I have grown up listening to this story being told time and again by a survivor, who saved himself by pretending to be dead and who subsequently escaped to my home town. He became our local Imam, and a family friend.

There is no Arab village called al-Kabri anymore. There is a Jewish settlement, however, whose settlers most probably know nothing about the bloodshed of innocent Palestinian residents, and one doubts whether they give tuppence.

Nazzal recounts the story of a Palestinian survivor widowed by the massacre, Aminah Muhammad Musa. She and her family had managed to escape the day before the massacre. They were stopped and arrested by the Zionist fighters. They were interrogated, and Musa was released whilst her husband and other men were taken away. *"The Jews took away my husband, Ibrahim Dabajah, Hussain Hassan al-Khubaizah, Khalil al-Tamlawi, Uthman Iban As'ad Mahmud, and Raja. They left the rest of us... An officer came to me and asked me not to cry. We slept in the village orchards that night. The next morning, Umm Hussain and I went to the village... I saw Umm Taha on the way to the village courtyard. She cried and said 'You had better go see your dead husband.' I found him. He was shot in the back of the head."* (Nazzal, Palestinian Exodus p.61, interviewed at Burj al-Barajnih Camp, Beirut, Lebanon, February 24, 1973.)

A Jewish source, a commander, no less, of the 21st battalion, confirmed the Palestinian account that many residents of Kabri were killed in cold blood:

"Kabri was conquered without a fight. Almost all inhabitants fled. One of the soldiers, Yehuda Reshef, who was together with his brother among the few escapees from the Yehi'am convoy, got hold of a few youngsters who did not escape, probably seven, ordered them to fill up some ditches dug as an obstacle and then lined them up and fired at them with a machine gun. A few died but some of the wounded succeeded to escape. The battalion commander did not react." (*The Palestinian Nabka: Register of Depopulated Localities in Palestine*, Compiled by SH Abu-Sitta, The Palestinian Return Centre: London, Sep 2000, p. 18.) This account comports well with the Imam's account.

As a survivor of the Yehi'am convoy ambush, Reshef was treated as a war hero, a brave man, and enjoyed a status which caused his seniors to turn a blind eye to his self-confessed "act of revenge". The vengeful spirit extended to those who had resettled elsewhere in Palestine and were later accused of having been Kabri residents. (Walid Khalidi, *All That Remains*, ISBN 0-88728-224-5. 1992. p. 21, quoting Nafez Nazzal, 'The Palestinian Exodus from Galilee, 1948'. Beirut.)

The *Guardian* provides a more exhaustive list of confessions by Zionists of atrocities committed by their own people against innocent Palestinians. (www.guardian.150m.com/palestine/israeli-massacres.htm)

Some Evangelical Zionists justify these massacres by saying that Israel was defending itself. In reality there was no war against Israel. The Arabs simply sought to protect the Palestinian portion of the partitioned land. The Arab armies were instructed simply to defend. The Jordanian army, the only Arab army of consequence, was bound by a commitment from the King not to engage in fighting with Jews. The Arab armies were virtually non-existent, and the war was an excuse for Israel to carry out ethnic cleansing. Though Israel's motives were thinly disguised, most Westerners still labour under the misconception that in 1948, Israel was fighting for its survival against an overwhelming Arab army. Israel was viewed as the victim, when it was the aggressor and perpetrator of many atrocities against innocent Palestinians, both Muslims and Christians alike.

Those who think Israel was threatened by its Arab neighbours in 1948 could not be more wrong. Nothing could have been further from the truth. The Arab Legion was disorganised, ill-equipped and had neither aggressive intentions nor potential towards Israel. Indeed, Israel's Arab neighbours only became a real military threat in the 1970s, two to three decades too late.

What is morally questionable is that Israel has refused to allow Palestinians to return to their homes, despite UN resolution 194, which has been since reiterated by the UN on numerous occasions. This refusal by Israel to implement such a resolution gives the lie away about its 1948 intentions. Israel's intentions were to cleanse Palestine of its Palestinians or simply diminish them to a minority. If Israel were to accede to the UN's demands for Palestinians to be allowed to return to Palestine, Israel would have to concede its Jewish majority and much land, both of which would threaten its existence, let alone its sense of security. Whilst that is plausible, it is neither fair nor moral.

Much has been written and said about the PLO and its acts of terrorism against Israel and the Jews. The killing of a Jewish disabled man on a cruiser and the attack on the Israeli Olympic team in Munich were given much media attention. Yet little attention has been given to Jewish atrocities against Palestinians.

"The record of Israeli terrorism goes back to the origins of the state – indeed, long before – including the massacre of 250 civilians and brutal expulsion of seventy thousand others from Lydda and Ramleh in July 1948; the massacre of hundreds of others at the undefended village of Doueimah near Hebron in October 1948;... the slaughters in Qibya, Kafr Kassem, and a string of other assassinated villages; the expulsion of thousands of Bedouins from the demilitarized zones shortly after the 1948 war and thousands more from the Northeastern Sinai in the early 1970s, their villages destroyed, to open the

region for Jewish settlement; and on, and on." (Noam Chomsky, *Blaming the Victims*, ed. Said and Hitchens.)

From a PLO viewpoint, Munich, and other acts of terrorism committed by the PLO, were payback time for the Zionists, which came some 20-30 years later because the Palestinians did not have the means to retaliate sooner. The PLO is an incarnation of the Jewish maxim of an eye for an eye and a tooth for a tooth.

So far we have mostly dealt with the Zionist Palestinian conflict. It must be remembered that some of these Palestinians are Christians too, a forgotten fact. Just as to the Jews Israeli Christian Arabs are Arabs, so they are to some Muslims just Christian. We are the other enemy of Islam. Muslim children often chant: *"We shall fight on Saturday and then on Sunday."* In other words, once they have triumphed over the Jews, the Muslims have their sights set on the Christians as their next target. Some Muslim Palestinians have been applying pressure on Christian Palestinians to leave their homeland. They have been using fear, terror, pressure isolation and direct violence to ensure the gradual seepage of any Christian presence out of Palestine.

What has been the situation for Christians in Israel/Palestine?

In the last census conducted by the British mandatory authorities in 1947, there were 28,000 Christians in Jerusalem. The census conducted by Israel in 1967 (after the Six Day War) showed just 11,000 Christians remaining in the city. This means that some 17,000 Christians (or 61%) left during the days of King Hussein's rule over Jerusalem. Their place was filled by Muslim Arabs from Hebron.

During the British Mandate period, Bethlehem had a Christian majority of 80%. Today, under Palestinian rule, it has a Muslim majority of 80%.

Few Christians remain in the Palestinian-controlled parts of the West Bank. Those who can – emigrate, and there will soon be virtually no Christians in the Palestinian Authority controlled areas. The Palestinian Authority is trying to conceal the fact of massive Christian emigration from areas under its control. (*Palestinian Authority Persecution of Christians* (Prime Minister's Office), November, 1997.)

As a result of unceasing persecution, the Christians are forced to behave like any oppressed minority, whose primary preoccupation is to ensure survival. Christians in PA-controlled areas have taken to praying in secret. The basic need to survive compels them to assess the "balance of fear", according to which they have nothing to fear from Israel but face an existential threat from the Palestinian Authority and their Muslim neighbours.

They act accordingly: they seek to *"find favour"* through unending praise and adulation for the Muslim ruler together with public denunciations of the *"Zionist entity"*. (*Middle East Digest* – Nov/Dec 1997.)

Time magazine (April 23, 1990): *"After years of relative harmony, friction between Christians and their fellow-Arabs [in the disputed territories] has intensified sharply with the rise of Muslim fundamentalism."* Time went on to cite various examples of Muslims pressuring Christian Arabs.

The Jerusalem Post (May 2, 1991) provides more evidence of the pressure exerted upon Palestinian Christians by their Muslim counterparts: *"Muslim activists have been trying to convert Bethlehem, home of some of Christianity's holiest sites and once predominantly Christian, into a Muslim town. In contrast to the world-wide fuss over the purchase of a hostel in Jerusalem's 'Christian Quarter' by Jews, this steady and often violent encroachment has met with a thunderous silence in the Christian world. The pattern of increased violence has been unmistakable. Last December 21, a school for nuns was torched. During the first week in March, there was an attempt to break through the wall of the Carmelite monastery, followed by a break-in at a Christian school. On March 3 vandals desecrated Bethlehem's Greek Orthodox cemetery, removing crosses and disinterring and mutilating corpses..."*

La Terra Sancta (A Vatican publication, dated 1991): *"The Christians are abandoning the Middle East... [although] the Jewish presence has alarmed the Arabs... more than anything else, the commercial, cultural and technological contacts of recent years have caused a confrontation between Western civilisation and Middle Eastern culture, or, as is commonly known, Islamic culture against Judeo-Christian."*

The Jerusalem Post (May 6, 1994): In April 1994, Israel's Hebrew press reported that Christian Arabs had accused activists of Arafat's Fatah faction of the PLO of harassing Franciscan nuns in the Aida convent near Bethlehem. One nun described as a *"reign of terror"* the behaviour of the activists, who allegedly regularly invaded the convent, vandalised graves, destroyed equipment and painted graffiti.

Bethlehem is fast losing its Christian stamp through predominance of Muslim life and worship in the Christian forecourt. CNN (December 20, 1995): *"Today, Bethlehem is a predominantly Muslim town. At Friday prayers, they spill into Manger Square [the traditional site of Jesus' birth], so crowded are the mosques. Christians complain they're publicly harassed and harangued for their faith. The Christian cemetery has been desecrated and vandalised... this Christian boy said the Muslims are fascists, bad people. Muslim families of 10 and 12 children leave smaller Christian families awash in an Islamic sea, afraid they will be overwhelmed by the refugee camps and Muslim villages around Bethlehem. Many of the town's Christians are afraid to talk openly now."*

Some Palestinian Christians feel so restricted by fear of Muslim acts of bullying, that they dare not celebrate Christmas. *"Life in [PA-ruled] Bethlehem has become insufferable for many members of the dwindling Christian minority. Increasing Muslim-Christian tensions have left some Christians reluctant to celebrate Christmas in the town at the heart of the story of Christ's birth."* (*The Times*, London, December 22, 1997.)

Dealing with the subject of a declining tourism in Bethlehem, politicians blame the Israeli occupation. Israel naturally blames Palestinian violence. However, it is not the Israelis that present the major obstacle for Bethlehem. *"Though Yasser Arafat is known for having been a relatively moderate politician, few remember his origins and his blood-line being linked to the Grand Mufti of Jerusalem, who was a hater of Christians. Yes Yasser Arafat married a Christian, had Christians in his cabinet, but Bethlehem succumbed to Muslim tyranny under his rule. Christian Bethlehemites suffered the following under his reign: intimidation, beatings, incidents of torture, land theft, firebombing of churches, denial of employment opportunities, kidnappings, forced marriages, and extortions."* (*The Washington Post*, "Little Palestinian town of Bethlehem wants its tourists, Christian residents to come back", December 22nd 2013.)

A local priest emphasised that though Bethlehem, with all its "holy" sites, is important to Christians worldwide: *"It's not enough to come and see the ancient stones," said Father Shomali, a parish priest. "You need the living stones."*

Vera Baboun, the first female Mayor of Bethlehem, emphasised the need for encouraging Christian Arab residents to return to Bethlehem. *" 'This is the place where the message of peace was born with Jesus Christ,' Baboun said. 'When they talk about reviving the message, you need to revive the city.'"* And that partly means returning its Christian residents who left under duress.

And what support have we had from the West, and more specifically from our Jewish-adoring conservative evangelicals? The American Administration has earmarked $100 million for road improvement in the West Bank. That is much appreciated. But compared with the billions Israel obtains from the US alone on an annual recurrent basis, Christian brothers and sisters in the Holy Lands are entitled to feel slighted.

When did Mr George Bush, an Evangelical, speak up for the Christians of the Holy Land during his presidency? Is it important for the church to have a continuing witness in the Holy Land? Is it worth a little effort, a small strain of the political throat?? I suppose it is not in the Old Testament prophesies and therefore not exciting or sensational enough.

David Brog, writing on why Christians support the Jewish State, asked the question: *"What place do Christian Arabs have in your theology?"* He answered his own question thus:

"As for Christian Arabs, they don't have any special place in Christian theology per se. Yet because they are fellow Christians, evangelicals tend to have great compassion for their plight just as they do for other oppressed Christians around the globe. Evangelicals are well aware of the persecution that confronts Christians in many Arab countries from Sudan to Iraq as well as in the West Bank. As the Christian populations of Biblical cities such as Bethlehem continue to shrink in the face of threats and harassment from radical Muslims, evangelicals are sounding the alarm. The persecuted Arab church has become one more issue that builds sympathy among Christians for the challenges facing Israel in the Middle East." (Haaretz.com, posted: May 07, 2006.)

A brief survey of real attitudes of western Christians to the Israeli Christian Arabs shows this statement to be more gong than dinner. This statement has made me question my understanding of compassion. The word compassion is made up of two parts: com (which is a Latin prefix meaning with) and passion (from the Latin word Pati, to bear or suffer). The latter gives rise to the common English words passion (as in the passion of the Christ) and patient (as in one who suffers from disease). Therefore compassion means to suffer with, to bear the burden with someone else. Compassion is about sharing in the suffering of another. It is about being in prison with your incarcerated brother, being hungry with your famished brother, being dispossessed with your brother whose possessions have been stolen from him. Compassion is about actions that move one man to participate in his brother's grief and hardship. Compassion comes to us with an expression of comradery, solidarity and even partnership. There is a practical fellowship in compassion; a fellowship that says your pain is my pain, your grief is my grief, your need is my need, your poverty is my poverty and your welfare is my responsibility. It goes beyond identifying and sympathising, and traverses into a territory of sacrificial affirmative actions.

Those who claim to have compassion need to be equipped with more than just a chattering mouth. They need to have a feeling heart, a sincere mind and the inclination to act appropriately in proportion to the need of the situation.

What practical fruit of that great compassion has there been from Evangelical Zionists, or any Western Christians towards their suffering Arabic-speaking Christian brethren?! What expression of that great compassion have we seen?! If great compassion is just a feeling of pity, it is not worth a dime in the Kingdom of God. Real compassion moves people to action. Great compassion is expressed in fruitful deeds, sacrificial feats and acts of giving. It is manifested in a deep and anxious desire to do something positive to alleviate the suffering of the object of that compassion. It is manifested in practical solidarity.

In the New Testament, the word compassion is often associated with actions. Compassion is dynamic and kinetic. It moves people. Christ was *"moved with compassion"* and took action to alleviate the suffering of fellow humans. In all of the following incidences of the word "compassion" in the Gospel, the word is associated with action.

"And when Jesus went out He saw a great multitude; and He was moved with compassion for them, and healed their sick." (Matt 14:14 NKJV)

"Then the master of that servant was moved with compassion, released him, and forgave him the debt." (Matt 18:27 NKJV)

"So Jesus had compassion and touched their eyes. And immediately their eyes received sight, and they followed Him." (Matt 20:33-34 NKJV)

"Then Jesus, moved with compassion, stretched out His hand and touched him, and said to him, 'I am willing; be cleansed.'" (Mark 1:41-42 NKJV)

Compassion and positive actions are inseparable travelling companions. One cannot exist without the other.

Few Western Christian organizations have been reported to be in distress for what their Arab brethren are going through. Rarely do Christian celebrities or people of means speak out on behalf of their suffering Arab brethren. I have seen no Western Evangelical leaders tearing their clothes or covering their heads in ashes in mourning for their suffering Arab brethren.

A dog whimpers for its ill relative or companion. Alas Western Christian leaders have failed even this minimum standard. They would do well to spend an afternoon in a kennel, where they may learn a lesson or two about compassion for their suffering brethren. It is sheer hypocrisy and lamentable dishonesty if Western Christians were to make a claim of *"great compassion"* towards their fellow Arab Christians. Tramps on the streets of London have seen more compassion from passers-by than the Christians of the Middle East have seen from Western, more specifically, Evangelical Zionists.

Now answering another question about the Roman Catholic Inquisition, Mr Brog says: *"I would agree with you that no true Christian could be an anti-Semite or racist, and that no true Christian could commit violence against innocents in the name of Jesus. I also think that most evangelicals would agree that those 'Christians' responsible for the Inquisition, the Crusades, the Easter Day pogroms and other atrocities against the Jews were not Christians at all. At an abstract level, your point is well taken."*

Is the total inaction of Western Evangelicals in the face of their suffering Arab brethren anything less than anti-Semitism? Does it not betray an attitude of indifference where massive positive reaction should be anticipated? Does it not show total disregard for the Arabic-speaking children of Shem. This is the other anti-Semitism. There is nothing to explain their lack of action other than the Arab blood that flows through the victims' veins. To use Mr Brog's own logic, are these people Western Evangelical Christians? Or are they Evangelical Zionist fanatics?

An aggrieved Palestinian Christian wrote to David Brog thus: *"All new born Christians, and all Christians that support the State of Israel should know that your actions have caused the disintegration of the world's oldest Christian community and the first followers of Jesus. There were some 350 thousand Christians in this land prior to 1948. After they were expelled, like Muslim refugees were, now the 2006 figure probably doesn't reach 120 thousand. How ironic...... shame on you."*

Indeed, such a rebuke is very fitting. Shame cover the heads of Western Evangelical Zionists for shouting from the rooftops about the Zionist cause and being totally indifferent to the plight of Palestinian Evangelicals. Shame, shame, shame...

The USA and Europe intervened with a heavy hand in Kosovo against the Serbians' ethnic cleansing. Who is going to stand up against Palestinian ethnic cleansing of Christian Palestinians? Or indeed who is going to stand up for the persecution of Christians in Egypt or Syria and Iraq?

Whilst Christians are being forced out of their homes and homeland, a large number of their fellow Christians in America are too busy worrying about Israel.

"This is the home of the Friends of Israel Gospel Ministry, a conservative evangelical Christian organization dedicated to supporting the Jewish state. With $8.5 million a year raised largely from evangelical donors, it airs pro-Israel broadcasts on 700 radio stations, publishes Israel My Glory magazine for 200,000 readers in 151 countries, and takes hundreds of American evangelicals each year to tour Israel. 'Our Christian Zionism – and we readily endorse that term – grows out of God's promise in Genesis 12:1-3,' executive director William Sutter said, flipping his Bible open to read the vow from God to Israel's patriarch Abraham: 'And I will make of thee a great nation, and I will bless thee, and make thy name great; and thou shalt be a blessing. And I will bless them that bless thee, and curse him that curseth thee.'

"'I would share the vision that we're living in messianic times,' said Yechiel Z. Eckstein, an Orthodox Jewish rabbi who is president of the International Fellowship of Christians and Jews, which raises $50 million a year from 440,000 evangelical donors. 'When the Messiah comes, we'll see if we were right or they were right.'

"'Palestinian Christians just don't figure in – they're invisible to evangelicals,' said William Martin, professor of religion and public policy at the Baker Institute for Public

Policy at Rice University. 'The attitude seems to be, "They're just going to have to leave.'" (By Paul Nussbaum: posted on Sun, Nov 13, 2005; *Inquirer* Staff Writer.)

I have personally encountered this sort of nonchalant attitude amongst some unthinking British pro-Israeli Evangelicals. I asked them how they expected someone of my background to agree with them. The answer was that all have to obey the Bible regardless of background and that if you want to follow Jesus you have to bear a cross. Surely they were confusing the Gospel with their pro-Jewish fanaticism. Whilst I would happily suffer for Christ, I have no reason to be tempted to suffer for the Zionists. *"Oh the Lord will bless you for blessing Israel"* was another typical response. This is, however, nothing but a gilded pill. The pill is bitter and no matter how well decorated it is, it will always be hard to swallow, and no fair-minded man would expect an Israeli-Christian Arab to swallow it.

At the risk of disappointing some people, sometimes one feels that some Evangelical interest in Israel does not stem from love of the Jews as much as a keen fondness for the sensational. Some American Evangelicals are so obsessed with Armageddon that they spend all their resources trying to predict when it is likely to take place. *"The Rapture Index – a popular evangelical Christian Web posting that calculates a global rise in natural disasters, war and inflation – bills itself as 'a Dow Jones industrial average of end-time activity.'*

"An index below 85 signifies a week of 'slow prophetic activity.' Anything above 145 signals the apocalypse is near.

"The Rapture Index this week: 158. The spike reflects many U.S. evangelicals' view that growing conflict in the Middle East signals the start of a global struggle leading to Christ's return." (Alexander Alter, *Miami Herald*, Aug 10, 2006.)

Is that the fulfilment of a calling by God for Evangelicals? Was that Christ's vision for his Church, to invent some outlandish method of predicting when Armageddon was going to take place? What a waste of precious time. This time should be spent on strengthening and boosting the morale of vulnerable Christians in danger zones around the world.

Some Western Evangelicals are so besotted with Zionist theology that they have totally lost sight of the core values of the Christian faith. Did Christ come to build a church that would one day sacrificially support the Zionist movement? Or did he come for some more mundane, down to earth purpose? Evangelical Zionists may not get a kick out of evangelism, but the last commission is what they should be busy fulfilling. Jesus came to the world to save sinners. Just that, plain and simple. Lose sight of that and you are on the road to heathenism and occultism. If you become too interested in any side issue, you have missed the point and your walk is not with God, not the God of the Bible. Nor are you seeking the will of God, but rather a fix or an adrenaline rush of some sort.

What is the most powerful witness the church has for the world? Love for the children of Zion? Most definitely not! All those who think that financing Russian Jews to immigrate to Israel has anything to do with the church's mission on earth, have widely missed the mark. The most powerful evangelistic tool the church possesses is this: *"That you love one another, as I have loved you".*

"A new commandment I give to you, that you love one another; as I have loved you, that you also love one another. By this all will know that you are My disciples, if you have love for one another." (John 13:34-35 NKJV)

American Evangelicals! Western Evangelicals! Where is your love for your suffering Arabic-speaking Christian brethren? Where is that love that God commanded you to have for them? Please do not be so foolish as to nervously prepare a list of some pathetic sallow occasional gestures you have made towards your Christian Arab brethren. Where is your genuine love for your Arab brethren? Don't even dream of answering this question. This is a rhetorical question. Instead, bow your heads in shame before God and ask for forgiveness, and turn around and change your ways.

Not only have you been indifferent to the suffering of your Arabic-speaking brethren; not only have you shown them no love; not only have you shown them no compassion, but you have been as generous to their enemies as you have been neglectful of them. The millions of dollars you give to the Zionists every year, you should be giving to your brethren, to help them thrive and to help build schools, hospitals, churches and businesses, to create employment for those who have no work, just because they are the wrong race or faith.

This is a wakeup call to some Western Evangelicals. Those mega bucks you have been pouring into the Zionist State are akin to you burying your talents. You should trade with your talents wisely. Invest them in your brethren, in your fellow disciples, your fellow soldiers for Christ. By doing so, you will have testified to the world of your faith: *"By this all will know that you are my disciples, if you have love for one another"*. By supporting the Christians of Israel you will have also inevitably benefited the Israeli economy anyway.

On 11th April 1981, following a football match, a Druze male was stabbed to death by a resident of Kufur Yasief, my home town in North Israel. The local council of Kufur Yasief refused to release the name of the culprit. Consequently, the Druze descended from their mountain village of Julis armed with Israeli army guns, rockets hand grenades and other light weapons and wreaked havoc on the mainly Christian town of Kufur Yasief. The town is predominantly Christian, though 40% of the population is Muslim. The mayor requested help from the Israeli Police, but his request was flatly turned down. On 13 April 1981, whilst 60 armed Israeli police officers took position in the fields separating Kufur Yasief and Julis, and while negotiations between the two sides were in progress hundreds of heavily armed Julis residents attacked Kufur Yasief, destroying 85 houses, 17 stores, a few workshops and 31 cars by fire. One church building was significantly damaged. (McGahern, 2011, p.162, and Mansour, p.275.)

The Druze targeted the Christians and killed three men. The Israeli Police simply waited on the outskirts of the town excusing their lack of action by saying they were not sufficiently armed to counter the marauding Druze youth. Further, no Druze individuals were brought to justice. Many

Druze marauders were active members of the Israeli Defense Force, which begs the question of what code of ethics the IDF holds. (Una McGahern, *Palestinian Christians in Israel: state attitudes to non-Muslims in a Jewish state*, p.163.)

The Christians were singled out for this cruelty by the Druze. The Jews stood by until the Druze had poured out their wrath. Had Kufur Yasief been a Jewish settlement under assault by Arabs, the IDF would have intervened in no time, and would have shown the aggressors and their families no mercy both on the battlefield and in the courts of justice.

What was the response of the Christian world? A small amount of aid. The Evangelicals, however, were not to be seen. No aid. No involvement in restoration and no compassion for those who lost loved ones. Indeed most compensation came from Muslim Waqf, whilst the World Council of Churches contributed a much smaller amount. (McGahern, 2011, p.164.)

Had this assault been carried out against some Zionist settlement, the whole world would have known about it and the Evangelical Zionists would have spearheaded some relief effort. By contrast the predominantly Christian town of Kufur Yasief had to rely on Muslim Waqf for compensation.

In a piece about an Evangelical American ship "Spirit of Grace" bringing aid to Israel, Haaretz remarks that *"Today, one of Israel's biggest and most accepted charities is an evangelical-funded group, the Chicago-based International Fellowship of Christians and Jews, which distributes $30 million a year to different projects in Israel. On arrival, the Ship was welcome and the port spokesman Yigal Ben-Zikry said, 'they're more Zionist than any Israelis I know.'"* (Haaretz.com. Last update – 21:20 26/10/2006.)

Don Tipton, the leader of this 42-strong group of Evangelical Zionists, told the Jews why they made this trip to Israel. *"'This is not aid, it's an expression of friendship and love,' Don Tipton said. The members of his crew, he said, like many other evangelical Christians, see supporting Israel as a divine commandment. They were further spurred on by the recent war in Lebanon, he said."*

These Evangelical Zionists are apparently in the business of obeying God's commandment. Whatever happened to the command: *"Therefore, as we have opportunity, let us do good to all, especially to those who are of the household of faith."* (Gal 6:10)

When did these Evangelicals ever cross the oceans to meet the needs of their fellow Arabic-speaking Christians in general, or Evangelicals to be particular, in the Arab world?! God commands that we should pay special attention to the needs of Christians (those who are of the household of faith), over and above non-Christians. Are God's commands only to be obeyed selectively?!

The extent of the Evangelical Zionist zeal to see their dispensationalist prophecies fulfilled has not only driven them to invest hundreds of millions of dollars in facilitating the return of Jews to Palestine, but it has led them to castigate European and American Jews for not wishing to immigrate to Israel: Hess accuses American Jews of being enslaved by the god of mammon, and tells them, *"It's time to stop saying, 'I'm an American Jew,' stop bowing down and worshipping the god of materialism in America and fulfil your end-time biblical destiny. Return to the land of your forefather..."* (Tom Hess, *Let My People Go*, 1987.)

Were it that such zeal were applied to the care of fellow Arabic-speaking Christians in the Middle East. Or are they simply to remain forgotten? How refreshing it would be to see American Christians encourage and finance the return of Arabic-speaking Christians to their homes in the Middle East, including Israel.

Chapter VII

Denial of the Existence of the Israeli Arab Church

"Occasionally I would sing familiar hymns along with these Western Christians, from a distance, with pain in my heart and tears in my eyes, and would recall the story of the Bible lepers who were eschewed." An Israeli Christian Arab.

"Denial ain't just a river in Egypt" (Mark Twain). It is a serious ploy at evading the truth. In its starkest form it is a form of prevarication.

Humour aside, although denial could stem from simple ignorance, often it is an evasive response to a situation that calls an individual to confess his wrong-doing and make amends. It is often a defence mechanism against taking responsibility, or unpalatable challenging truths which bring guilt to the culprit. Some people deny the existence of God; because He challenges the way they live. It is too much for them to face a radical change in lifestyle, and therefore it is more convenient to deny His existence. Often criminals, whose crime is as evident as broad daylight, resort to denial in their desperation to avoid dealing with their guilt or making restitution.

There are two animals that characterise two extreme responses to negative situations. The ostrich hides its head in the sand, in denial. The badger lunges at any challenger with all its teeth bare and ready to deliver a fatal bite. Denial is the ostrich approach to the truth and is one of the most ghastly components of a cowardly disposition or a guilty conscience.

When I was a teenager, growing up in Israel, I used to go fishing with my father. We would often go to the Jordan River, where it exits from the Sea of Galilee, a place called Dagania. Though my main interest was catching fish, I could not help getting excited when I saw coach loads of Western Christians alight and descend towards the river. Most would stand a matter of yards away from me. For a young Christian Arab, who belongs to a tiny minority in a non-Christian country to suddenly realise that he belongs to a huge body, the worldwide church, is an exhilarating experience. Suddenly I felt like a fish being lifted out of a tiny fish tank into a huge ocean teeming with sea life. However, sadly this exhilaration would not last long. My eagerness to make contact with my Western brethren, though checked by my shyness, was never reciprocated. It was as if I were invisible. As far as these people were concerned, I could not possibly be a Christian!

Looking back, I think the most normal behaviour for a tourist is to take interest in the natives. That is what I do when visiting other countries. The most beautiful thing I discovered about Portugal some twenty years ago was the warmth of its people. People are far more important than places or objects. This should be a given for a Christian; more so when dealing with a fellow Christian, more so when meeting a Christian native of the Holy Land.

It should be a most natural and spontaneous act for a Christian pilgrim to want to converse with a young Christian Palestinian fisherman? Fellowship aside, whatever has become of curiosity?! I stood on the banks of the river desperate to make contact, but I was met with indifference from some and total coldness from others. And when I tried to break the ice, there was absolute freezing coldness that both baffled me and disappointed me. The saying "water, water everywhere, but not a drop to drink" took on a new meaning for me, not because the river water was undrinkable, but because I was surrounded by Christians who wanted nothing to do with me. Here I was, a local Christian, one of Christ's countrymen trying to make contact with my Western brethren, without any reciprocity from them. They were more interested in the "holy water" of the Jordan River. Some filled their small bottles with water, some with sand. They stopped and prayed. Some sang, some were baptised where I fished. I just watched in amazement at their disinterest. Occasionally I would sing familiar hymns along with these Western Christians, from a distance, with pain in my heart and tears in my eyes, and would recall the story of the Bible lepers who were eschewed. At least I could sympathise with those poor lepers who may have stood on this very spot 2000 years ago.

When I complained to my father, he responded with a knowing smile. He had long resigned himself to the status quo. *"Don't be too harsh on them,"* my father responded in his typically sagacious and magnanimous way. *"They had already been instructed by their Jewish guides not to make contact with Arabs..."* *"Why not?"* asked I, feeling hard done by. *"What is wrong with us...?"* It suddenly dawned on me. Jewish guides. I know what some Jews think of us and therefore I should know what they would say about us to tourists. I recalled Jewish children regularly taunting me and my brother with insulting words "Aravee Melochlach", which is Hebrew for "dirty Arab".The Jewish guides would have painted a negative, derogatory picture of Arabs as being backwards, greedy, rude, lustful, nomadic, violent and ungodly people.

Many Western Christians know little about the existence of Arab Churches in Israel. It is assumed that Israel is a Jewish state, and as such all churches in Israel must be Jewish. This is a form of ignorance, which in this day and age is almost unforgivable. As Israel has moved ever closer to the centre of global attention over the past 60 years, Western Evangelicals cannot be excused for not knowing of the existence of sister Arab churches in Israel. The truth is that of the millions of Christians, especially Evangelicals, who have visited the Holy Land over the past few years, hardly any have made an attempt to make contact with Arab Christians. I can say that this problem has worsened over the years. When I was a child, we had almost daily fellowship with Western Evangelicals, usually Plymouth Brethren. Such contacts have diminished over the years to almost nothing at present.

The ignorance of Western Evangelicals about the existence of Evangelicals amongst Palestinians is well expressed in this account of an American Evangelical who had spent time in Bethlehem with an Evangelical pastor, whose name remains a secret for security reasons.

"Pro-Israel, anti-Arab evangelical Christians often don't realize that some of our own spiritual family consists of Arab and Palestinian believers. They are perhaps the most forgotten Christians on earth, who are sometimes tempted to think that Western Christians care more about Jews who have rejected Christ than they do about their own brothers and sisters who are in Christ."

Those are the sentiments expressed by one Palestinian pastor by the name of X with whom I spent time during my trip last month to Israel. He ministers in Bethlehem, the city where Jesus was born. His congregation consists of believing Arabs and Palestinians. Their church building has been fire-bombed fourteen times. Pastor X has been shot at three times, and on the third occasion a bullet ripped through his shoulder. All of this persecution has come because Pastor X and his congregation love Jesus, Jews, Christians and Muslims. They believe that Jesus is the only hope for peace in the Middle East.

"... His oldest brother... was living on the Mount of Olives in Jerusalem at the time, and when he began joyfully witnessing to his neighbours about Jesus they told him that he should move out. When he didn't, they murdered him with axes and knives.

"Not only do Arab and Palestinian Christians in the West Bank feel forgotten, they also feel cut off, often being unable to make any contact with the tens of thousands of Western Christians who visit Israel each year. Getting in and out of Bethlehem, just four miles from Jerusalem, is like getting in and out of a maximum-security prison. Bethlehem is within the West Bank territory and is separated from Jerusalem by a 25-foot high concrete security wall. Although Pastor X can pass through the wall because of his Israeli citizenship (he was born in Jerusalem), most of his congregation cannot. Fewer

Christian tourists come to Bethlehem to visit biblical sites as in the past, and as a result, Bethlehem's economy has taken a plunge. Unemployment runs at about 85%. Among the believers in Pastor X's church, unemployment is closer to 95% due to the fact that they are followers of Jesus. This has left people in general and especially, believers, in great hardship and struggle to meet their daily needs." (*Heaven's Family*, "The Most Forgotten Christians", July 2006.)

When one reads this, one wonders about Evangelical Zionists, and their concept of fellowship or the doctrine of the body of Christ. They donate tens of millions of dollars to Zionists in Israel, and visit the Holy Land but never make contact with Arab Evangelicals,.

I recall in 1976 being invited to visit a Christian friend in Porthcawl, South Wales. Porthcawl was a mining village and had several small churches. The chapel, as it was called, was very small. There could have been no more than 20 people in the congregation. The pastor eventually invited me to share a testimony or a word. He introduced me by saying: *"It is an honour for us to have with us a Christian from Israel. A Jew who has found Jesus. We welcome Mr Shehadeh, a member of the Jewish nation of Israel."*

At the time, I was 19 years of age. I had been accustomed to preaching in Arabic for five years. Stage fright was no issue. However, I found myself trembling. I was livid, or as my patients would say "spitting feathers". The dilemma was that if I were to disabuse the pastor and the congregation of the idea that I was a Jew, in their sense of the word, there was no "nice" way of doing it. They were going to realise how foolish and ignorant they have been. Yet I could not keep quiet. Something had to be said, if not to save these people from the consequence of their blissful ignorance. The sheer assumption that all Israelis were Jews, and worse still that any Israeli Christian was a Jew was astonishing. Do they really not know that we exist? Can people in this day and age, in Western Europe, be so dim and ignorant!?! I then recalled my love for the Welsh people. My surrogate father Rev Owen Thomas, a walking encyclopaedia, being one of them, and my best friend at the time, Lindsay Brown, being another.

Eventually I decided on some words and thanked the pastor for his genuinely gracious welcome. *"Yes I am a Jew and a member of the people of God. Not because I come from Israel, but because I am a follower of Jesus Christ."* The penny had not dropped and the congregation had to be woken up of the usual small-congregation somnolence. *"Actually I am an Arab. A Christian Arab."* I paused. Sleepy eyes were prised open by this bold revelation. If the reader could sit inside their heads I guarantee there would have been an endearing Welsh chorus of surprise: *"An Arab. You mean an Arab... I never... A Christian Arab... well, well, well, what do you know, boyo?"* I repeated: *"I am an Arab and my mother tongue is Arabic. My family descend from Alghassanids, an ancient Christian Arab Tribe who refused to convert to Islam."*

The congregation came to life. Expressions of amazement were whispered in the pews. *"We were amongst the first recipients of Christianity... remember how on the day of Pentecost Arabic was spoken because there were Jews from Arabia in Jerusalem... It is believed that they took the Gospel to Arabia... Also remember that at the beginning of his ministry Paul fled to Arabia for three years. Little is known about those years. It is believed that he evangelised the Arab tribes."*

They were nonplussed by this revelation. The pastor, partly in embarrassment, stood up and interrupted me saying *"We love Arabs too"*, and I had no reason to doubt this at all, having enjoyed hospitality in Welsh Christian homes and churches. When the service was over, he came over to tell me how much he appreciated Arab hospitality when he served in the British forces in Egypt and Palestine in the 1940s. My friend, with whom I had served in OM in Israel, laughed heartily as the *"old goats"*, as he called the church members, walked away. He was the voice of modernisation and had been kept under their conservative thumbs for years. He delighted in their self-humiliation.

I could tell numerous such stories which reflect the total ignorance of some Western Christians of the existence of Christian Arabs in Israel.

One of the greatest blessings in my life has been my unofficial adoption by an Evangelical Anglican vicar and his wife. Dad Thomas, the Rev Owen Thomas, used to travel to several churches in the South of England preaching to Evangelical congregations of all creeds and colours. He would introduce me affectionately, from the pulpit and proudly, as his Arab son from Israel. The way he enunciated *"Arab"* in a Welsh manner was heartening. At the end of the service, friendly well-wishers would engage me in conversations through which their ignorance of the existence of Christian Israeli Arabs became blatant. I felt sorry for them as they recoiled in embarrassment at the revelation of my identity. Some ended up with egg on their faces as they revealed their hardness of heart against Arabs, before discovering they had been talking to a Christian Arab. In ignorance they equated Militant Islam with Arabs.

The second most astounding revelation for me was the degree of ignorance to be found amongst Bible College Students. Often these were mature people, who were professionals, post-graduate, and had heard the call to the ministry late in life. They were streetwise and quite knowledgeable. Yet when it came to the subject of Christian Arabs, they had a huge knowledge gap.

The most appalling encounter for me as a newcomer to England was with Evangelicals who thought they knew about Christian Israeli Arabs, but actually had selective patchy knowledge and were so obviously biased and rigid with their views. One such group was Prayer Fellowship for Israel. The name would suggest that the group existed in order to pray for Israel, a laudable activity to engage in. However, the members with whom I was acquainted spent so much time drumming up political support for Israel that they had forgotten the Great Commission. As such I was not surprised by their coldness towards Arabs in general. The shocking part was their total coldness towards Christian Arabs and the abject denial of our human rights. These were secondary to God's purpose for

Israel. We, Christian Israeli Arabs, should not complain about any maltreatment, otherwise we may incur the displeasure of God who said: *"I will bless those who bless thee and curse those who curse thee"*. When I quoted the Divine instruction to *"Love ye therefore the sojourner (strangers); for ye were sojourners in the land of Egypt."* (Deut 10:19 ASV), the best response I could hope for was a mindless repetition of blind loyalty to the Zionist State. There was never any sense of brotherhood or identity with our plight as Israeli Christian Arabs. Indeed I have received more sympathy from Atheistic communists than from such Christians, who carried themselves as if they did not even acknowledge our existence.

Evangelicals are not the only Christians suffering from ignorance, or condemning their Christian Arab brethren to oblivion. A Christian Arab journalist, editor-in-chief of Arab Israeli newspaper *Kul al-Arab*, relays an experience in Italy mirroring my experiences in the United Kingdom.

"I did my academic training at the University of Rome. The Italians, pleasant and with a warm Mediterranean temperament, asked about my background. 'I am an Arab, I'm a Palestinian, and I'm a Catholic,' I said. But from their perspective, there is simply no such animal. 'Aren't all Arabs Muslim?' they asked. You try to tell them you are as Catholic as they are." (Zuhair Andraos, "Merry Minority Christmas", 12.25.05, *Israel Opinion*.)

As the wheel of history turns, history inevitably repeats itself. The recent exodus of Christians from the West Bank and Gaza has elicited little real response from Western Evangelicals or any Christians for that matter. I have spent some of the happiest days of my youth on the hills of Bethlehem, Bet-Jala and Bet-Sahoor, the birth place of our Lord. If we are to have any geographical reference for our faith communities as Christians, all Christendom should unite to ensure a vital Christian presence on these hills. Yet the opposite has happened.

"Meanwhile, more and more Christians flee. One Palestinian Christian leader told me, 'Muslims get money from the outside; Christians get nothing so they move out.' He tells

me that UNESCO, other United Nations agencies and the European Union officials are aware that the little money that does trickle down from the Palestinian Authority goes only to Muslim families. The agencies do not intervene against this religious bigotry.

"The village of Beit Jala outside of Jerusalem at one time had a Christian majority, but not anymore. It is from Beit Jala that radical Islamic gunman fire on the Israeli community of Gilo. When the Israeli tanks return fire, it is usually a Christian home that is destroyed because the terrorist gunmen use them as shields. Damaged homes stand in ruins as construction continues on the mansions of the civil servants. The Christians are forced to leave. Hundreds of Beit Jala's Christian families now live in Chile." (By William J. Murray, 2002; WorldNetDaily.com.)

American Evangelical attitudes towards Israel stand in sharp contrast to their attitudes towards Palestinians, as shown below.

One wonders how many American Evangelicals equate Palestinian to Muslim, and totally ignore the fact that there are Palestinian Evangelicals and other Christians amongst the Palestinians.

"More recently, in March-May 2004, the Pew Forum on Religion & Public Life sponsored a nationwide survey in which people were asked: 'Should the U.S. support Israel over the Palestinians?' Unlike the questions in the 2003 survey, this one specifically asked Americans what they think about U.S. policy towards Israel and the Palestinians. The complete results are provided in the table below." (The New Forum.)

	U.S. Support Israel over Palestinians		
	Agree	*No Op*	*Disagree*
ENTIRE SAMPLE	**35%**	**27**	**38**
Evangelical Protestant	**52%**	**23**	**25**
Traditionalist Evangelical	*64%*	*18*	*18*
Centrist Evangelical	*45%*	*26*	*29*
Modernist Evangelical	*28%*	*37*	*35*
Mainline Protestant	**33%**	**30**	**37**
Traditionalist Mainline	*43%*	*28*	*29*
Centrist Mainline	*34%*	*34*	*32*
Modernist Mainline	*22%*	*26*	*52*
Latino Protestants	**37%**	**30**	**33**
Black Protestants	**24%**	**32**	**44**
Catholic	**31%**	**26**	**43**
Traditionalist Catholic	*43%*	*26*	*31*
Centrist Catholic	*30%*	*24*	*46*
Modernist Catholic	*23%*	*29*	*48*
Latino Catholic	**25%**	**36**	**39**
Other Christian	**33%**	**27**	**40**
Other Faiths	**22%**	**8**	**70**
Jewish	**75%**	**13**	**12**
Unaffiliated	**20%**	**27**	**53**
Unaffiliated Believers	*19%*	*30*	*51*
Secular	*23%*	*26*	*51*
Atheist, Agnostic	*15%*	*23*	*62*

The American Religious Landscape and Politics 2004

The Survey noted that there was a 14% increase in Evangelical support for Israel between 200 and 2004. Clearly, the existence of an Evangelical Palestinian Church does not figure in American Evangelical thinking. It is all about the sensationalism of fulfilled Old Testament prophesy.

Religion Shapes Mideast Sympathies

Sympathize more with...

	Israel	Palest-inains	(Vol.) Both	(Vol.) Neither	DK
	%	%	%	%	%
Total	41	13	8	18	20=100
White	41	12	7	19	21=100
Evang	55	6	6	12	21=100
Mainline	34	17	10	19	20=100
Catholic	39	13	6	22	20=100
Black	40	17	8	16	22=100
Hispanic	40	13	7	20	20=100
Secular	24	20	11	26	19=100

American Views on Religion, Politics, and Public Policy 2003

One of the greatest signs of the inanity of the said American-Evangelical compassion for Evangelical Arabs, is the reluctance of such Evangelicals to make contact with or have fellowship with Evangelical Arabs, whilst they are extremely keen on making contact with Zionist Jews, some of whom believe that Jesus was a *"bastard"*. These *"compassionate Evangelicals"* would rather spend time, have fellowship with and donate their money to blasphemers, than fellowship with Evangelical Arabs.

"Dozens of evangelical Christians from the United States, Europe and Asia toured Jewish settlements in the West Bank in

recent days, taking time out from their organized pilgrimage to the Holy Land to show their support for the Israeli settlers.

"Many of the evangelical Christians are fervent Zionists who believe Jews are the chosen people and their return to the biblical Land of Israel will speed the Second Coming of Christ. Evangelical groups have contributed millions of dollars to Israel in recent years and gave $50,000 to the roughly 9,000 Jewish settlers displaced when Israel pulled out of the Gaza Strip last month." (Posted on 21:37:49 2005/10/24: "Evangelicals, Jews Are Kindred Spirits"; By Laurie Copans, Associated Press Writer.)

In my opinion, and from experience, the most effective way of shattering anyone's self-esteem, is to pretend that they do not exist, not to make eye contact, not to verbally engage with them, not to acknowledge them with the slightest gesture. That is precisely how these Evangelical Zionists deal with Evangelical Arabs. There is not even a trace of compassion in such behaviour. There is, however, a great deal of denigration in such eschewal of Evangelical Arabs.

Eschewal of Christian Arabs, by Evangelical Zionists, is effectively expressed in this piece:

"It is also interesting as that Christian Zionism tends to ignore the Palestinian and Arab Christians who have resided in the area for nearly two millennia. Corrine Whitlach of the Churches for Peace in the Middle East, notes:

"'U.S. Christians travel to the Holy Land as pilgrims and are a major segment of the tourism industry. They visit the holy sites but most have virtually no contact with Arab Christians themselves. Arab Christians hold strongly negative views of Christian Zionism, which is considered by some to be an instrument of Western colonialism and American imperialism. The zealous support given Israel's claim of sovereignty over all of Jerusalem and the building of settlements in "Judea and Samaria" by these Western Christians angers both Christian and Muslim Palestinians. Some evangelical churches have supportive relationships with settlements.'" (Dennis Sanders, Monday, July 24, 2006.)

Apparently, some of this Evangelical Zionist charity is fuelled by guilt for the way "Christians" have mistreated Jews in the past. *"Yaakov Koos Bouterse, 56, from Alblasserdam, Holland, said he began coordinating contributions to the community out of a feeling that Christians had to make up to the Jews for historical injustices, such as the Holocaust.*

"'The best thing we can do as Christians is clear the road of stones, because as Christians in history we have put so many stones in the way of Jews,' Bouterse said."

Firstly, if people were to be financially compensated for ill-treatment, then the Jews owe Christians a huge debt, for persecuting the early church in every corner of the Roman Empire. This is a historical fact which no amount of protestation will change.

Secondly, by doing so, these naïve Evangelicals are switching roles. They are abdicating responsibility towards their Christian Arab brethren, and taking responsibility for sins they or their Evangelical forebears did not commit. Who had persecuted the Jews in Europe? Not all Christians. It was the Roman Catholics and the Russian Orthodox Church. It is they, and not the Evangelicals, who should be rushing to make amends.

Chapter VIII

Do Not Expect the Turkey to Vote for Christmas

There are fundamentalist Christians who have made it their central doctrine that *"God's promise to Israel that the Holy Land belongs to the Jews forever had never been forfeited"* and that *"As prophesied, the Land would remain relatively 'desolate' for centuries during Israel's temporary expulsion. Finally, at God's appointed time, the Jewish people would return to their Land and this returning prosperity to the Land would attract a large influx of Arabs from surrounding nations."* ("The Israeli-Arab Peace Process and Bible Prophecy, An open letter from Christians to Christians", Bible411.com.)

What is striking in the above expression of narrow-minded dogma is the total absence of mention of Israeli (Christian) Arabs. These fundamentalists believe that God has given Palestine to the Jews and when the Jews return to claim their land, Arabs will invade Palestine!!

Ignorance is often the hallmark of fundamentalism. The obsession with one creed, dogma or principle results in such tunnel vision that anything outside that narrow field of vision is totally ignored and treated as non-existent. Fundamentalist Christians, who blindly support Zionism, are so focused on their misguided ideas that they totally miss basic facts. Before the State of Israel was formed, there had been Arabs living in Palestine for almost two thousand years, if not longer. Only an unjust and unfair mind can ignore this fact.

It is often the impression of Christian Israeli Arabs that unless they support that totally exclusive and dismissive dogma, they are ostracised by some fundamentalist Zionist

Western churches, often known as Evangelical Zionists. From their standpoint the litmus test of faith for these fundamentalist Christians is ultimately whether or not one believes that the land of Palestine exclusively belongs to the Jews. In other words, the central dogma of these fundamentalists is no longer how we are saved. This has been marginalised and condemned to the dim rim of Christian theology and supplanted by what they wrongly consider to be the more crucial a question: *"Do you support the Zionist's exclusive claim to the land of Israel?"*

A young university student, who is a relative of mine, related a telling story; she was discussing the Arab Israeli question with a Christian friend of hers at the end of a morning church service. My relative's Christian friend was aghast at the revelations of Israeli Jewish atrocities towards Palestinians in general and Christians in particular, and worse still about the Talmud's ghastly and insulting teachings regarding Christ and Christians. In response, she begged my relative to lower her voice, lest her mother heard my relative. *"Please lower your voice. My mother is a staunch supporter of Israel,"* she said. *"She does not tolerate any criticism of Israel,"* she added, fearing her mother's potential reactionary treatment of my relative. This is so typical of some Western Christians, particularly Evangelicals: blind allegiance to Israel, and an expectation that Arabic-speaking Christians have to swallow their erroneous dogma, hook, line and sinker.

Evangelical Zionists have come to evaluate the validity of the faith of other Christians, including Arabic-speaking Christians, on the basis of their attitude towards the Zionist State of Israel. If you cheer, you are in; if you jeer, you are out. It is no longer important to talk about the traditional pillars of the Christians faith (salvation by grace alone, through faith alone, in Christ alone, according to the scripture alone, for God's glory alone). It is whether you cheer or jeer the Zionist State. Arabic-speaking Christians thus find themselves stuck between a rock and a hard place. If you disagree, you are shunned by Evangelical Zionists. If you cheer, you are shunned by your own people. However, most Israeli Christian

Arabs live their lives without fear or favour. It is wrong to calculate one's beliefs based on the flavour of the day, or the latest theological fashion. *"Oh what will make us popular today? Well it is cool to support Israel. Yes why not. If that's what it takes, let's support Israel and be popular"*!!! The faith of the Israeli Arab Church is based on the unadulterated and full Word of God, nothing added and nothing taken away. If that causes offence, then offence must be caused, and no apology should be made.

The expectation of Evangelical Zionists from Arabic-speaking Christians in general is so unreasonable that by adopting the above stance, Evangelical Zionists have ranked themselves beneath Ben-Gurion, a thoroughbred Zionist, who was reported by president of the World Jewish Congress to have once said: *"Why should the Arabs make peace? If I was an Arab leader, I would never make terms with Israel. That is natural: we have taken their country. Sure, God promised it to us, but what does that matter to them? Our God is not theirs, We come from Israel, it's true, but two thousand years ago, and what is that to them? There has been anti-Semitism, the Nazis, Hitler, Auschwitz, but was that their fault? They only see one thing: we came here and stole their country. Why should they accept that?"* (*The Jewish Paradox* by Nathan Goldman, former president of the World Jewish Congress)

The tragedy of the stance of Evangelical Zionists is not only that it distorts the Gospel, which has never been about land anyway. It also places an unnecessary burden of dispossession on an already impoverished and isolated Christian community, namely the Evangelical Israeli Arab Church. This is the main part of Christendom in the Holy Land, which has the courage to want to spread the Gospel. This is the most vital part of the church in the Holy Land. This is the church whose members have to live with and be good neighbours to and evangelise Jews and Muslims alike.

To satisfy Evangelical Zionist expectations would not only render the faith of the church nonsensical, but would diminish the credibility of the church in Muslim quarters. It would shut doors of evangelism to the evangelical church in Muslim quarters. I recall, when I was a child, there was some openness to the Gospel amongst the Muslims in my country. It was quite natural to engage with Muslims in theological discussions. They would share their faith and we would share ours. I helped run summer camps under the auspices of Child Evangelism Fellowship. One particular venue that sticks in my mind is a village called "Mazraah". The host was a Muslim, who opened their home to us. We gathered 20-30 children on a daily basis in this home and shared Bible stories with them. We taught them Christian hymns and choruses. However, this came at a price; on our final day, as we were walking to the VW van we were surprised by a barrage of stones hurled at us by Muslim children, whose parents were not receptive to us, calling us Zionists.

I often wondered how likely this would have been if our team were purely made up of Arabic-speaking Christians. How much of that hostility was to the Gospel and how much was it to Americans and their pro-Zionist stance. Undoubtedly in some Muslim minds, and rightly so to some extent, American Christianity is synonymous with Zionism. Such people are no more likely to want to hear the Gospel than the Pope is likely to denounce Mary.

For me personally and for many Christian Israeli Arabs, there is an added dimension. Though mundane and material, it cannot just be dismissed lightly. To concede that the land of my forefathers is the property of the Zionists is to forfeit my right to live in the country where my forebears had lived for almost two thousand years. Without land, there is no identity, no possession, no rights and no existence. Such fundamentalist Evangelical Zionists are in essence expecting their fellow Christians to give up more than they themselves would contemplate doing. I often wonder how many such fundamentalists would be willing to forfeit their material and earthly possessions to surviving Native Americans!! Such stark hypocrisy may have escaped the notice of these zealot Evangelical Zionists.

Israeli Arabs already have significant restrictions on their right to own land in Israel. We only have access to 15% of the land of Israel. The consequence is that the average acre of building land in my region is well in excess of one million dollars. This figure well places land out of the reach of most people. For Christians, the implication is multifarious. Not only does this mean that families have to crowd into small homes, but it also means that churches can never afford to expand. The average congregation is around 100 strong. Of these, less than one-third are earners. No matter how faithfully they tithe, they can never catch up with the spiralling price of land in Galilee.

For Christian Israeli Arabs to denounce their right to land in Israel is tantamount to suicide. For fellow Christians to demand this from us is no less cruel than asking turkeys to vote for Christmas. Moreover, it amounts to the demolition of a significant part of the Church Evangelical in Israel, in one fell swoop. Where is God in all this?! All I see is the will of man, and badly misguided man at that.

The Zionists of Israel – and not all the Jews of the world are Zionist – have never made any bones about their ultimate aim of ridding themselves of all Arabs, that is my people (Israeli Arabs, often known as the Arab citizens of Israel). Such an aim has been expressed openly on numerous occasions by numerous leading Zionists.

My home town of Kufur Yasief (or Kafr Yasif), a small village in 1948, opened its doors to neighbouring villagers who escaped Zionist atrocities, receiving some 700 of them. The Zionist fighters rounded these refugees up and took them to the Lebanese borders where they were told they should never attempt to return to their villages. (Freeman, Charles. "Evacuation of Refugees from Kafr Yasif". 1949-03-25.) Am I, a Christian Arab, supposed to applaud Israel for such actions, because they are *"the people of God"*?!

Was Arab opposition to the arrival of the Zionists based on inherent anti-Semitism or a real existential concern for their community? The above deportations by foreign Zionists of Palestinians, whose lineage can claim almost two thousand years of connection with the land of Palestine, were bound to inspire Arabs in general, with fear and mistrust of Jews, and Zionists in particular.

"The aim of the [Jewish National] Fund was 'to redeem the land of Palestine as the inalienable possession of the Jewish people'...As early as 1981, Zionist leader Ahd Ha'am wrote that the Arabs 'understand very well what we are doing and what we are aiming at'... [Theodor Herzl, the founder of Zionism stated] 'we shall try to spirit the penniless [Arab] population across the border by procuring employment for it in the transit countries, while denying it any employment in our own country... Both the process of expropriation and the removal of the poor must be carried out discreetly and circumspectly'... at various locations in northern Palestine Arab farmers to move from land the Fund purchased from absentee owners, and the Turkish authorities, at the Fund's request, evicted them... The indigenous Jews of Palestine also reacted negatively to Zionism. They did not see the need for a Jewish state in Palestine and did not want to exacerbate relations with the Arabs." (*The Origin of the Palestine-Israel Conflict*, By Jews for Justice in the Middle East, Published in Berkeley, CA, 2001.)

The problem is not between Jews and Arabs, as much as between Zionists and Arabs. *"Before the 20th century, most Jews in Palestine belonged to the old Yishuv, or community, that had settled more for religious than political reasons. There was little if any conflict between them and the Arab population. Tensions began after the first Zionist settlers arrived in the 1880s... when [they] purchased land from absentee Arab owners, leading to dispossession of the peasants who cultivated it."* (Don Pertz, *The Arab-Israel Dispute*.)

"[During the Middle ages], North Africa and the Arab Middle East became places of refuge and a haven for the persecuted Jews of Spain and elsewhere... In the Holy Land... they lived together in harmony, a harmony only disrupted when the Zionists began to claim that Palestine was the 'rightful' possession of the 'Jewish People' to the exclusion of its Muslim and Christian inhabitants."

"Zionist land policy was incorporated in the Constitution of the Jewish Agency for Palestine... 'land is to be acquired as Jewish property and... the title to the lands acquired is to be taken in the name of the Jewish National Fund, to the end that the same shall be held as the inalienable property of the Jewish people.' The provision goes on to stipulate that 'the Agency shall promote agricultural colonization based on Jewish labour'... The effect of this Zionist colonization policy on the Arabs was that land acquired by Jews became extra-territorialized. It ceased to be land from which the Arabs could ever hope to gain any advantage...

"The Zionists made no secret of their intentions, for as early as 1921, Dr. Eder, a member of the Zionist Commission, boldly told the Court of Inquiry, 'there can be only one National Home in Palestine, and that a Jewish one, and no equality in the partnership between Jews and Arabs, but Jewish preponderance as soon as the numbers of the race are sufficiently increased.' He then asked that only Jews should be allowed to bear arms." (Sami Hadawi, *Bitter Harvest.*)

Given Arab opposition to them, did the Zionists support steps towards majority rule in Palestine?

"Clearly, the last thing the Zionists really wanted was that all the inhabitants of Palestine should have an equal say in running the country... [Chaim] Weizmann had impressed on Churchill that representative government would have spelled the end of the [Jewish] National Home in Palestine... [Churchill declared,] 'The present form of government will continue for many years. Step by step we shall develop representative institutions leading to full self-government, but our children's children will have passed away before that is accomplished." (David Hirst, *The Gun and the Olive Branch.*)

Arab resistance to Pre-Israeli Zionism:

"In 1936-9, the Palestinian Arabs attempted a Nationalist revolt... David Ben-Gurion, eminently a realist, recognized its nature. In internal discussion, he noted that 'in our political argument abroad, we minimize Arab opposition to us,' but he urged, 'let us not ignore the truth among ourselves.' The truth was that 'politically we are the aggressors and they defend

themselves... The country is theirs, because they inhabit it, whereas we want to come here and settle down, and in their view we want to take away from them their country, while we are still outside'... The revolt was crushed by the British, with considerable brutality." (Noam Chomsky, *The Fateful Triangle*.)

Sami Hadawi, *Bitter Harvest*:

"Serfs they (the Jews) were in the lands of the Diaspora, and suddenly they find themselves in freedom [in Palestine]; and this change has awakened in them an inclination to despotism. They treat the Arabs with hostility and cruelty, deprive them of their rights, offend them without cause, and even boast of these deeds; and nobody among us opposes this despicable and dangerous inclination."

Zionist writer Ahad Ha'am, quoted in Sami Hadawi, *BitterHarvest*:

"'Sins of the fathers' (Zionist greed) have led to the loss of goodwill by Palestinians, and a culture of hostility, which has culminated in the present sordid state we find ourselves: Israel fighting for survival and living in constant fear)."

The Zionist desire to rid Israel of its Arabs is not restricted to the political elite and aficionados of the Zionist movement.

"A University of Haifa poll released Monday reveals that a majority of the Jewish public in Israel – 63.7 percent – believes that the government should encourage Israeli Arabs to emigrate from Israel. The survey, conducted by the university's National Security Studies Center..." ("64% of Israeli Jews Support Encouraging Arabs to Leave". Israel Faxx, June, 2004. *Haaretz*.)

Whilst one cannot be disappointed by lack of support from Zionists, The American attitude, in particular, pre-determined by its lopsided view of Biblical prophecy, has always led Americans to take Israel's side despite Israel's errancy. Americans were so blindly pro-Jewish that they were totally oblivious to the unjust side of Zionism.

Were the early Zionists planning on living side-by-side with the Arabs?

In 1919, the American King-Crane Commission spent six weeks in Syria and Palestine, interviewing delegations and reading petitions. Their report stated: *"The commissioners began their study of Zionism with minds predisposed in its favour... The fact came out repeatedly in the Commission's conferences with Jewish representatives that the Zionists looked forward to practically complete dispossession of the present non- Jewish inhabitants of Palestine, by various forms of purchase...*

"If [the] principle [of self-determination] is to rule, and so the wishes of Palestine's population are to be decisive as to what is to be done with Palestine, then it is to be remembered that the non-Jewish population of Palestine – nearly nine-tenths of the whole – are emphatically against the entire Zionist program... To subject a people so minded to unlimited Jewish immigration, and to steady financial and social pressure to surrender the land, would be a gross violation of the principle just quoted... No British officers, consulted by the Commissioners, believed that the Zionist program could be carried out except by force of arms. The officers generally thought that a force of not less than fifty thousand soldiers would be required even to initiate the program. That of itself is evidence of a strong sense of the injustice of the Zionist program... The initial claim, often submitted by Zionist representatives, that they have a 'right' to Palestine based on occupation of two thousand years ago, can barely be seriously considered." (Quoted in *The Israel-Arab Reader*, ed. Laqueur and Rubin.)

Non-Christians seemed to have a more acute sense of justice, and common sense than Western Evangelicals – Gandhi on the Palestine conflict, 1938:

"Palestine belongs to the Arabs in the same sense that England belongs to the English or France to the French... What is going on in Palestine today cannot be justified by any moral code of conduct... If they [the Jews] must look to the Palestine of geography as their national home, it is wrong to enter it under the shadow of the British gun. A religious act cannot be performed with the aid of the bayonet or the bomb.

They can settle in Palestine only by the goodwill of the Arabs... As it is, they are co-sharers with the British in despoiling a people who have done no wrong to them. I am not defending the Arab excesses. I wish they had chosen the way of non-violence in resisting what they rightly regard as an unacceptable encroachment upon their country. But according to the accepted canons of right and wrong, nothing can be said against the Arab resistance in the face of overwhelming odds." (Mahatma Gandhi quoted in *A Land of Two Peoples*, Martin Buber)

Few people realize that Some Zionists have espoused the very evil that almost led to their annihilation in Europe. Nazism would have wiped out Jewry from Teutonic territory. Some Zionists have adopted a similar attitude towards Israeli Arabs or Palestinians.

"Eitam, leader of the Religious Zionism faction in the National Union party, said at a September 10 memorial ceremony in the West Bank settlement of Eli: 'The vast majority of West Bank Arabs must be deported... all these Arabs cannot stay there and that territory cannot be forsaken. Most of them would have to leave.'

"In relation to Israeli Arabs, Eitam said, 'We will have to make an additional decision, banning Israeli Arabs from the political system. Here to, it is plain and simple. We have cultivated a fifth column, a group of traitors of the first degree, and therefore we cannot afford to allow such hostile presence, so comprehensive, within Israel's political system.'" (By Yuval Yoaz and Gideon Alon, *Haaretz* Correspondents. Haaretz.com, last update – 22:41 28/12/2006.)

These violations of the basic human rights of Israeli Arabs go largely unchecked. There may be a word of rebuke from the odd corner. In the United Kingdom, any such utterances against the Jews would result in an arrest for speech inciting racial hatred. Not so in Israel, where a certain anti-Semitism is allowed to flourish.

Chapter IX

The Six Day War

"The defeat of Israel's Arab neighbours was so devastatingly convincing that one could sense Israel's confidence wax almost daily after the war."

This war will live in infamy in the history of the modern Arab nation.

The Zionist movement's aims of expelling all Arabs from Palestine had provoked *"an eye for an eye and a tooth for a tooth"* response from their Arab neighbours. History shows that Arabs have been relatively generous to their Jewish cousins. Arabs have treated Jews more generously than European Christians have, especially Catholic Europe. The Jews who suffered under the Catholic Church, had flourished under the Arabs in Spain. It would be a serious error of judgement to assume that the default Arab position towards Jews is one of hostility.

The Six Day War was the first real attempt by Arabs to retaliate against Zionist expulsion of Palestinians in 1948. Expulsion is often denied by Zionists. However, a recent survey shows that a significant proportion of Israeli Jews believe that expulsion of Palestinians from their native Palestine in 1948 actually took place.

"NEW YORK, NY April 6, 2009 – A new public opinion survey finds surprising attitudes on the part of Israeli Jews regarding Israel's ongoing conflict with Arabs and Palestinians. With regard to the main historical event of the conflict – the 1948 Palestinian exodus – 39% of Israeli Jews surveyed believe expulsion by Israel was one of the factors

leading to that exodus, in addition to Palestinian fear and the call of Arabs/Palestinian leaders to leave. An additional 8% believe the refugees were primarily expelled, adding up for a total of 47% that believe expulsion took place. In contrast, only 41% accept the Zionist narrative that rejects even partial expulsion and claims Palestinians left due to their own accord." (Teachers College, Columbia University 4/6/2009. "Study Surprisingly Finds 47% of Israeli-Jews Believe that the 1948 Palestinian Refugees were expelled by Israel.")

If one listened to Arab radio stations at the beginning of the war, one would have been convinced that Israel's back was against the wall and that the armies of Egypt, Syria and Jordan were about to vanquish the Israeli forces. A telephone conversation between the leaders of Israel's three enemies was broadcast on Israeli Arabic Radio station repeatedly, in which the three Arab leaders stated that they would tear the Jews of Israel apart with their nails and teeth and throw them into the sea. The words were so convincing that many Arabs really believed that Israel was losing the war.

President Abdur Rahman Aref of Iraq joined the leaders of Egypt, Syria and Jordan in declaring war against Israel. The aim of the war was no less than total annihilation of the Jewish state: *"The existence of Israel is an error which must be rectified. This is our opportunity to wipe out the ignominy which has been with us since 1948. Our goal is clear – to wipe Israel off the map."* (*A History of the Israeli-Palestinian Conflict*, by Mark A. Tessler, Indiana University Press, p.393.)

President Nasser of Egypt would never consider a peaceful co-existence with Israel. Israel's neighbours were in a belligerent mood, their aim being total annihilation of the State of Israel.

Just before the war, the Voice of the Arabs radio station blasted: *"As of today, there no longer exists an international emergency force to protect Israel. We shall exercise patience no more. We shall not complain any more to the UN about Israel. The sole method we shall apply against Israel is total war, which will result in the extermination of Zionist existence."*

In reality Israel demolished the Egyptian Soviet-built air force in a brilliant surprise manoeuvre. Sinai fell into Israeli hands within days. Egypt's ability to respond was diminished by fears of betrayal from within. Some Arabs believe that the most senior officers of the three Arab nations were secretly paid off by Israel. Egypt had far more planes, tanks and troops than Israel. Yet Israel's victory was unquestionable and almost absolute.

In the West Bank, the Israelis met little resistance except from a few valiant soldiers. Otherwise, it was almost a walkover into hitherto Jordanian territory. The ease with which Israel conquered the West Bank is reflected in a photograph that prevailed in the Israeli press and is seared into my memory, of the three generals walking, even strolling, into Jerusalem. The image of Moshe Dayan in the middle, flanked by Yitzhak Rabin, later to become Prime Minister, and General Narkiss, is inevitably associated with Israeli superiority. No matter how unfair or unjust Israel may be, there is always a glimmer of fairness and I would venture to say nobility in their conduct. I recall our first post-war visit to my mother's family on the West Bank; somewhere between Jeneen and Nablus is a tank memorial for a valiant Jordanian fighter. He was the exception. Most of his fellow Jordanian soldiers fled without firing a bullet.

I was ten years old at the time and I recall the fear and anxiety on my parents' faces. Why would the defeat of Israel by neighbouring Arab countries worry Christian Israeli Arabs, one might ask. Because the fallout was that some Israeli Muslim Arabs thought that soon they would be living under Islamic rule and that they would have their way. Rumours were flying around that Muslim men, from neighbouring villages, had started earmarking Christian women for the taking, once the three Muslim nations defeated Israel. My father was so incensed that he went and armed himself. He was ready to defend his family with the gun, if the need arose. So real was the fear of such a possibility that a preacher of the Gospel, of no less than thirty years' standing, was prepared to use the gun to defend his family and his honour.

The defeat of Israel's Arab neighbours was so devastatingly convincing that one could sense Israel's confidence wax almost daily after the war. Even I as a child could sense a change in the way ordinary Jews treated us. I recall going with my parents to Acre (Akko, Ptolemeos) where we used to buy our shoes from a Jewish stall. The salesman had always been courteous and polite. On this occasion, shortly after the Six Day War, he was rude and short-fused. He made little eye contact with us. He kept us waiting whilst he served Jewish clients, who arrived long after we had. There were no jokes, banters or quaint stories. It was as if we had suddenly become inferior and we had to thank him for bringing himself down to deal with inferior beings such as ourselves. My father was so displeased that we never returned to that stall again.

There was a sudden hike in Jewish confidence to the point of arrogance. Israel became the superpower of the Middle East and the Arab nations around it became the laughing stock of the world. The USSR, embarrassed by backing the wrong horse, gradually withdrew its support from the Arab nations. This enhanced Israel's confidence. Four nations with a combined population of no fewer than 70 million were totally routed in six days by a nation of three million. Approximately 465,000 Arab troops, more than 2,800 tanks, and 800 aircraft pegged against Israel's 100,000 troop and far fewer aircraft and tanks.

The Arab leaders' excuse for their humiliating defeat was that the USA apparently supported Israel during the war. The accusations went further; American troops were sent to fight Israel's battles. There is no objective evidence to support this claim. At the same time, many Arab nations sent troops to the belligerent Arab countries, and even Pakistan had sent pilots to support the war against Israel. None of this could stop the small Jewish state from achieving total victory within six days. There was only one predictable aftermath for this war: abject Arab humiliation, and boosted Israeli morale.

The outcome of the 1967 war represented a thorough and painful degradation for the Arab nations that they called it "al-

Naksah" (the disaster) and as an Arab, though I did not identify with the Arabs in that war, I felt that humiliation and sensed a decline in my self-esteem. I recall my father shaking his head in disbelief when it was discovered that Syrian officers failed to turn up following their leader's declaration of war. And the Israelis made capital out of it.

During the Six Day War, we as Israeli citizens were expected to lend our cars to the IDF (Israeli Defence Forces). Our women were expected to knit for the soldiers. My father's Jeep was taken away during the war. Sometime after the war it was replaced by the IDF.

Curiously, for a few months prior to the war, we were hosts to an emotional English preacher by the name of Johnson. When the war broke out, he left Israel mysteriously and in haste, never to be seen or heard of again. The best thing that came out of that enigmatic encounter was his leaving me his children's toys. Many of our distant relatives were convinced he was a spy! I do not believe it for one minute. Whom could he have spied upon?! But those were rumours that negatively affected the church's ability to witness. It diminished the Evangelical Church's credibility.

I do not recall any effort by Western Christians to assess the impact of that war on Israeli Christian Arabs. There was no great campaign to provide any support, be it moral or otherwise. We were totally forgotten. The Bible teaches that Christians are one body and that if one part suffers, all members suffer: *"but that the members should have the same care for one another. And if one member suffers, all the members suffer with it; ... Now you are the body of Christ, and members individually."* (1 Cor 12:25-27 NKJV)

This verse was forgotten during the Six Day War – it was just another verse; mere intellectual fodder for Western theologians, without any practical application! We were left to fend for ourselves. We did not feel like members of the body of Christ, but suffered fear and anxiety in isolation as if the body of Christ did not exist outside of Israel.

Any response from the Western churches was centred on the fulfilment of some prophecy. There was more jubilation in

259

Evangelical Zionist churches than there was amongst the Jews. Israel's victory over its Arab neighbours was hailed as the fulfilment of numerous Old Testament prophesies. This interest completely eclipsed any other concern the Western Church should have had for members of the body of Christ in the conquered territories, and indeed in the Arab world. The fact that fellow Christians on the West Bank and Gaza strip may have been dispossessed and/or displaced did not perturb these Christians. There seemed to be a brand of Christianity so obsessed with prophecy that it became totally bereft of compassion, let alone love for their own kind: that is, fellow Christians caught up in the conflict. Evangelical Zionists would rather spend hundreds of dollars reading prophecy books on Armageddon and the last days than give a dime to help a fellow Christian in the Middle East. Hal Lindsey is said to have sold 50 million copies of one of his books on Armageddon. Such is the importance of this sensational material in American Evangelicalism that huge resources are dedicated to it. Yet, we Christians can do nothing about prophecy. We can only wait and see. Prophecy is really appreciated retrospectively, and not so much prospectively. This must be particularly true of the unpredictable second coming of Christ, who himself said:

"Therefore, when they had come together, they asked Him, saying, 'Lord, will you at this time restore the kingdom to Israel?' And He said to them, 'It is not for you to know times or seasons which the Father has put in His own authority. But you shall receive power when the Holy Spirit has come upon you; and you shall be witnesses to Me in Jerusalem, and in all Judea and Samaria, and to the end of the earth.'" (Acts 1:6-8 NKJV.)

Christ's plain instruction is not to be concerned with times and seasons and matters of when this or that prophecy will be fulfilled. He stated that the church should be more concerned with something else: being witnesses for Christ.

Instead, large parts of the American Evangelical Church has given the world the impression that the Church's primary task is to support Israel and to help their weakling God to fulfil

Old Testament prophecy. It may be unintentional, but to seek to bring about the fulfilment of prophecy, is tantamount to denying the power of God. Besides, where does the witness to the truth of the Gospel rank on their list of priorities?!

Eschatologists are seeking after knowledge of the wrong kind, one that Christ advised against. Yet Christians have been given knowledge of a privileged kind.

"He answered and said to them, 'Because it has been given to you to know the mysteries of the kingdom of heaven'". (Matt 13:11 NKJV)

The mysteries of the Kingdom of Heaven should be the primary and only occupation of the body of Christ. To gain a deeper knowledge of the mysteries of God/Christ, the person of God and His attributes, is far more essential than the pursuit of the thrill and adrenaline fix of end-time theology. To be more interested in the sensationalism of the last days, above the souls of men is to miss the point of being a follower of Christ.

If the consequence of the Six Day War was victory for Israel and jubilation for the Evangelical Zionist churches, these were short-lived. The humiliating defeat of the war, al-Naksah, weakened the Arab regimes and increased the popularity of alternative powers. The Arab street had no option but to look elsewhere for representation. Someone else had to redeem the reputation of the Arabs. Though the PLO had existed for four years prior to the Six Day War, and though it had been active for four years, it really only became a force to be reckoned with after al-Naksah. The PLO filled a niche created by the defeat and humiliation of the Six Day War. The PLO was the only Arab force engaged in real war with Israel. Their small successes against Israel, allied with the desperation of the Arab street for the restoration of Arab dignity and recognition and respect on the international arena, increased the popularity of the PLO. In that respect, the PLO has done more damage to Israel than entire three Arab Israeli wars put together.

The PLO was born out of loss of confidence in the impotent Arab regimes who seemed to only pay lip service to the plight of displaced Palestinians. It was also born out of despair, out of loss of confidence in the Israeli intent for a settlement of the conflict. The Palestinians could no longer trust Israel's claims of pursuing peace as more than just hollow words for public consumption, and a tactical delaying strategy.

Zionists have a cynical view of a peaceful settlement of the conflict: *"In 1923, radical Zionist Ze'ev Jabotinsky – spiritual father of not only of Israeli Prime Minister Menachem Begin but of Brooklyn Rabbi Meir Kahane – wrote that the 'sole way' for Jews to deal with Arabs in Palestine was through 'total avoidance of all attempts to arrive at a settlement' – which Jabotinsky euphemistically termed the 'iron wall' approach. Not coincidentally, a picture of Jabotinsky graces Prime Minister Ariel Sharon's desk."* (*The Village Voice*, "Death Wish in the Holy Land," Dec. 12, 2001.)

Worse still for Israel, al-Naksah gave birth to a reactionary force that has snowballed ever since and continues to do so: that is, Islamic fundamentalism. Israel's disingenuous claims of wanting peace and its allies' failure to be open and honest about their real intentions provided the battle cry for Muslim fundamentalism. Whereas before the Six Day War the conflict was an Arab-Israeli conflict; following the war it gradually and surreptitiously metamorphosed into an Islamic-Israeli war. From a Christian Arab point of view, this has been the most serious and damaging development of the post-1967 Middle East.

It should be noted that American support for Israel became more material following the 1967 war. The Israelis believe that the USA began to seriously support Israel after the 1967 war because the war was testing ground from which Israel emerged as a powerful nation worthy of an alliance with the mighty. (The Washington Institute, "Consequences of the 1967 War", David Makovsky, January 12, 2004.) With that inflated sense of importance, Israel became more arrogant and intransigent towards its Arab neighbours, not least the Palestinians, and uncompromising when dealing with her Western friends, who may half-heartedly appeal to Israel for moderation of its stance towards the Palestinians.

The Six Day War was a triumph not only for Israel, but also for dispensationalism, the belief by some Evangelicals that the future is divided into stages, or dispensations, all revolving around the return of the Jews to Palestine, soon to be followed by the rise of the antichrist and the second-coming of Christ before the end times. The outcome of the Six Day War was to expand the borders of Israel, and bring closer to reality the re-establishment of the greater Israel of Solomon. For dispensationalism, the Israeli victory was a shot in the arm for their hitherto relatively unpopular theology. Nelson Bell, Billy Graham's father-in-law, writing shortly after the Six Day War in *Christianity Today*, declared that *"for the first time in more than 2,000 years Jerusalem is now completely in the hands of the Jews gives the student of the Bible a thrill and a renewed faith in its accuracy and validity."* It saddens me to be at odds with a medical colleague and an influential Evangelical. But those sentiments are insensitive and un-Biblical.

The Six Day War was a watershed in the history of the Evangelical Zionist church, as it moved a dormant giant (Dispensationalist Evangelicals) into action on all fronts in favour of Israel against the Arabs, in the hope that they may sooner bring about fulfilment of their dispensationalist theology. This is the pivot around which the Dispensationalist Church has been revolving since. From this day on, one saw a constant rise of political, economic and moral support for Israel, amongst some western Christians with a concomitant indiscriminate demonization of Arabs.

The Jewish state welcomed this climate change in the Evangelical church, and responded by opening its gates to celebrated leading dispensationalists. These leaders were invited by the Israeli ministry of tourism on promotional visits to the Holy Land (free of charge). In return, the beneficiaries of Zionist hospitality led hundreds of thousands of their followers to the Holy Land.

For dispensationalists the new honeymoon with the Zionist State became their prophetic telescope. The more deeply involved they became with Israel, the better they could see the future, and the more they could contribute to the fulfilment of prophecy. A dispensationalist American organisation, Bridges for Peace, used this slogan in their advertising: *"Don't just read about prophecy when you can be part of it."*

Dispensationalists would get carried away and became deeply involved with Zionist organisations such as the Temple Mount, a movement founded by Gershon Salomon, one of the Israeli soldiers who seized the Temple Mount during the Six Day War. He found a ready audience amongst Dispensationalists visiting Israel.

Dispensationalist dollars flooded into Israel and their flow has only waxed stronger with time. International Fellowship of Christians and Jews is a Zionist organisation headed by a Zionist, Rabbi Yechiel Eckstein, who revealed that *"We get 2,000 to 2,500 pieces of mail a day, most of them with cheques,"* mostly from Evangelicals. *"Eckstein, an Orthodox rabbi, has broadened the organization's mission and in the last decade has collected more than $100 million in financial support for Israel. Last year, the fellowship contributed $20 million from a donor base of 365,000 individuals and groups, most – if not all – of them evangelical Christians, Eckstein said.*

"... Although no one tracks all evangelical contributions to Israel, Eckstein believes the figure could exceed $25 million annually... Evangelical leaders such as the Rev. Jerry Falwell began lobbying for greater political support of Israel from the U.S. government and urging financial support from the rapidly growing evangelical movement... The 1977 election of Likud Party leader Menachem Begin as Prime Minister marked a new era in evangelical-Israeli relations. Begin was so pleased with Falwell's pro-Israel activities that in 1979 he gave the evangelical leader a Lear jet.

"The Zionist charm seemed to spare no Evangelical leader, whose coffers were wide open for Zionists to dip into for all sorts of Zionist causes. In January, the Israeli Parliament created a Christian Allies Caucus to coordinate activities with its Christian friends... On Feb. 15, Israeli Tourism Minister Benny Elon honored Pat Robertson at the National Association of Broadcasters Convention in Charlotte.

He praised Robertson's leadership of a movement that has 'saved Israel's tourism from bankruptcy' by promoting pilgrimages to the Holy Land despite U.S. government travel warnings after the Sept. 11, 2001, terrorist attacks and renewed hostilities between Israelis and Palestinians... Each year, the church contributes $100,000 to welfare projects in Israel, with most of the money going to a centre for children with disabilities in the West Bank settlement of Ariel." (By Bill Broadway, Washington Post Staff Writer, Saturday, March 27, 2004; Page B09.)

These dispensationalists were opposed to any move that would steer events from the dispensationalist agenda. The return of land (seized by Israel in 1967 and 1973) for peace was strongly opposed by dispensationalists, who could not bear to see the momentum of the Six Day War victory be slowed down. The Oslo Accords ensured that Israel returned some land to the Palestinians. Shortly after the accords, the Christian Friends for Israeli Communities was founded in 1995 following the transfer of land by Israel to the Palestinian Authority. In 2004, the Christian Friends was supported by 2000 Evangelical donors.

"'These are deeply religious people who read the Bible, take it literally and enjoy seeing the Bible coming alive,' Baras said by phone from the northern West Bank (Samarian) settlement of Karnei Shomron. 'They are very connected to prophecy and understand events happening today in fulfilment of prophecy.'" (By Bill Broadway, Washington Post Staff Writer, Saturday, March 27, 2004; Page B09.)

Not only are these dispensationalists willing to support the Zionists, but they are willing to do so at the expense of the Christian mission, Jesus' last command to go to Jerusalem and to evangelise. "Baras said none of the Christian support organizations she knows in Israel allow donors or workers to evangelize – despite the fact that those who come are the most ardent believers in end-time prophecies predicating the second coming of Jesus on the return of Jews to Israel."

Once Evangelicals abandon the core theology from which they derive their name, in order to pursue sensationalist dispensationalist causes, all their other foibles pale into insignificance. Once evangelisation has been sacrificed by an Evangelical, they have betrayed their faith and missed the point. Once an Evangelical has crossed the line of abandoning the cause of evangelising, there is no limit to their perfidy. The support for Israel by some Evangelicals can be extreme and blind: *"Evangelical Christians in the United States are even more supportive than Israelis themselves of Israel's targeted attack on Sheik Ahmed Yassin, leader of the terrorist group Hamas and architect of 425 terror attacks that killed more than 375 Israelis and wounded nearly 2,100.*

"Of 1,630 evangelicals who responded to an online poll conducted Monday and Tuesday, March 22 and 23, by the International Fellowship of Christians and Jews, 1,457, or more than 89 per cent, said they supported Israel's decision to kill Yassin. The poll showed 41 evangelicals, or 2.5 per cent, opposing the attack and 132, or 8.1 per cent, unsure how they felt.

"Meanwhile, the Israeli newspaper Maariv reported Tuesday that its own poll showed 61 per cent of Israelis in support of the Yassin killing and 21 per cent opposed to it." (International Fellowship of Christians and Jews, Wednesday, March 24, 2004.)

The defeat of the Arabs at the hands of the Zionist State, the empty rhetoric of Arab leaders and the increasingly unquestioning support of the USA to Israel, particularly the ardent support of the dispensationalist Evangelicals for the Zionist State, all conspired to fuel the small embers of Islamic fundamentalism into the all-consuming flame we witness today. Those looking for a reason why Al-Qaida came into existence, why the Khumeni was so successful, and why Hamas is so popular, or why the Taliban have not been defeated, or why the "Twin Towers" were destroyed, should begin their search in the post-1967 war Arab psyche, and the arrogant and entrenched Zionist and Evangelical Zionist position that ensued.

The simple adage of *"keep your friends close, and your enemies closer"* was not heeded by the Americans. The distance between the Islamists and the Americans has been widening. Any contact between the two was meant to help the Americans defeat the Russians in Afghanistan or the Iranians in the Iraq-Iran war. Both contacts have backfired. ("The Muslim Terrorist Apparatus was Created by US Intelligence as a Geopolitical Weapon, The CIA's Founding' of Al Qaeda Documented", *Veterans Today*, originally published 15-21 January 1998.)

The consequence of the rise of Islamists is not merely political. It has had consequences for Christians in the Arab and Muslim world. I know many Christian families in the West Bank and on the Gaza Strip who have been pressurised by Islamists to leave their homes and flee to the West. I have fond memories of staying with a Baptist Christian family in Gaza in 1974/5 just before leaving to pursue my university education in England. Even then, one could sense their isolation and fear. That church continues its witness, despite the harsh conditions.

The rise of Islamic fundamentalism has made life for Arabic-speaking Christians very difficult. Increasingly, and more brazenly, the accusation has been levelled against us of being Zionists. Evidence of our Zionism is (Christian) America's blind support for Israel despite atrocities committed against innocent Arabs. This has been seen as solid evidence that Christians in general and especially Evangelicals are Zionists. Examples abound of attacks on Arab churches in the Middle East, by Muslim fundamentalists, who seek to retaliate against American policy towards Israel, by punishing Arabic-speaking Christians.

In Egypt, where Christians constitute a significant minority, Christian churches and individuals are subjected to assaults of a physical and sexual nature on a regular basis. This is punishment by proxy. One of the Islamists' favourite methods is to kidnap Christian young ladies and force them to marry Muslims. This is designed to inspire fear amongst Christians in Egypt.

The consequence of the negative events of the last sixty years in Israel is that Christians have dwindled from 18% to 1.9% of the population.

Except for the occasional lone voice speaking on behalf of the Arabic-speaking Christians, for the most part the Western Church has remained silent and has done little to assist members of the body of Christ in the Middle East. Yet Evangelicals, particularly American Evangelicals, pour millions of dollars into Israel every year in support of the State of Israel and in support of new Jewish immigrants, who are settled on Palestinian land, acquired by the Zionist State through dishonest means. Zionist military success in 1967 has been seen as the star pointing the way for Evangelical Zionists to increase their support for the Zionist State.

Chapter X

The 1973 War

"What Israel needed was not a new tank but a new take on its Arab neighbours."

Six years following the Six Day War, once again Israel found itself at war with its Arab neighbours. In the third war, Israel used the element of surprise against Egypt, thus securing victory. However, in 1973 the tables were turned against Israel. The belligerent Arabs attacked Israel on one of its holiest days, Yom Kippur, the Day of Atonement, when no work can be done by Jews. What added to the surprise element is the coincidence of Yom Kippur with the Muslim holiday of Ramadan, when Muslims were presumed to be on holiday. Israel had fortified its Suez front with the most up-to-date equipment and fortification. This was the $500m Bar-Lev Line, a most impressive defence line in those days.

The 1973 war triggered an awakening, a new Arab Israeli consciousness, even a new identity. Therefore, the significance of the 1973 war exceeds its military vital statistics, as is reflected in the subtitle of this chapter.

Earlier on, the point had been made about how arrogant Israel had become following the relatively easy victory of the 1967 war. One of the weakest points of Zionism is that whilst Zionists refer to the Scriptures to prove ownership of the land of Palestine by divine right, they have not learnt the Scriptural adage that pride comes before a fall. Zionists have always looked down on Arabs as inferior beings, less intelligent and less capable creatures. Some analysts believe that Israel was caught out by Egypt, not by dint of the attack taking place on a holiday, but rather because of its arrogant disregard for the Arabs. Egypt and Syria exploited Israeli complacency, bringing their enemy to near defeat, leading Defence Minister Moshe Dayan to warn that *"The Third Temple is falling"*.

Why did Israel neither strike first nor make preparations for a war, which was well predicted by the Israeli secret service, and well prefaced by public threats of an Egyptian invasion?

The hawks felt *"the lack of preparation at the front revealed a near-fatal complacency, a failure to take seriously the continuing existential threats to the Jewish state"* ("A Lesson From the Yom Kippur War for a Perilous Time", Yossi Klein Halevi, *The Wall Street Journal*, Oct. 3, 2013.) Surprisingly the doves in Israel did not offer a radically different analysis : *"For dovish Israelis, the sins that led to the failures of the Yom Kippur War were arrogance and an excessive reliance on military power. They recall how, in the aftermath of the 1967 Six Day War, Israeli leaders dismissed Arab fighting capability and reassured the nation that Arab armies wouldn't dare attack."* Whether it is complacency or arrogance, they both stem from a low opinion of Arabs, who according to the Israeli government of the day *"dare not"* attack Israel, whose military was far superior.

JewishHistory.org, gives several factors bringing about the Yom Kippur war and determining its outcome: *"Here it was a combination of Nasser's death, the rise of Arafat and the PLO, Israeli arrogance, the energy situation in the world."* ("The Yom Kippur War", Jewish History.org.) Once again arrogance is flagged up as a factor!

Amos Gitai, an Israeli film-maker, one of whose films dealt with the Yom Kippur War, believes that the war *"Broke the crest of arrogance after the Six Day War. Maybe it's the moment when the Israelis understood the fragility of military power and had to work out other ways of relating to the region."* (Jonathan Romney, *Guardian*, Friday 21 July 2000.)

And why did Golda Meir fail to respond to overtures of peace from Egypt's president Anwar Sadat, just before the war? Most probably because of the same old arrogance, which imperialist Zionists had inherited from their "superior" European ancestors.

Israel has since committed the same mistake time and again. Their previous involvement in Lebanon, their engagements with Fatah and their most recent Lebanese fiasco show repeatedly that Israel has, to its own detriment, an over-inflated opinion of itself and an unhealthy disrespect for its neighbours. (*The Yom Kippur War: The Epic Encounter That Transformed the Middle East*, Abraham Rabinovich, 56.) Zvi Zamir, Mossad Director-General, admitting that Israel had been forewarned by King Hussein of Egypt's intention to strike, said: *"We simply didn't feel them capable [of war]"* (Rabinovich 57)

This brink-of-defeat experience would have been more plausible had Israel not received numerous warnings from Egyptian informants, and most surprisingly had Israel not received a personal warning from King Hussein, who flew into Israel to warn Golda Meir that Syria and Egypt were about to mount a war against Israel. Both Israel and its Christian allies would do well to learn from this mistake: Pride comes before a fall.

The mighty Bar-Lev line was washed away with powerful water jets prepared by the Egyptian army. The Israeli army, often boasting the best intelligence, was taken by surprise and reacted by sending in its powerful tank units. The Israeli intelligence service did not grasp the fact that the Egyptians had been building up a powerful infantry unit, armed with shoulder-launched anti-tank missiles. These missiles penetrated the heavy armour of Israel's tanks with devastating effect. Israel lost hundreds of tanks and thousands of personnel. Why? Because Israel was too arrogant to show healthy respect for her Arab neighbours.

Ironically, Israel's answer to its near defeat in 1973 was not a new attitude, but new technology, the Merchava tank, a brand new, all-singing, all-dancing, newly-fangled Israeli tank, hailed as the best tank in the world, costing the small Zionist State nearly $6 billion to develop. The hubris of the Zionist

State meant that the folly that nearly brought her to her knees in 1973 did not furnish her with a valuable lesson, at least not one that the Zionist State was willing to learn. What Israel needed was not a new tank but a new take on its Arab neighbours. The Merchava was eventually, in 2006, rendered totally useless in the Israeli-Hizbullah Lebanese war. The best tanks in the world were so vulnerable, they were equally easily destroyed by Hizbullah infantry with equipment not dissimilar to that used by the Egyptian infantry in 1973. "Pride comes before a fall" has rarely been so precisely fulfilled.

Israel had never been so close to losing a war as it was in 1973. Its only saving grace was the fact that the Egyptians, who surpassed themselves by penetrating the Bar-Lev Line, were not prepared for such success. They could only penetrate into Israel as far as their military cover permitted. They would have to wait for their cover to be moved deeper into Sinai before they dared advance. I recall being glued to the radio as I listened with my father to the Arab stations claiming that Egyptian forces were a matter of hours from Tel Aviv. My father, who was often sceptical about anything broadcast by the Arab stations, seemed uncharacteristically convinced that Israel was on the brink of defeat. I had grown to trust his judgement, and now I know that he had reason to believe the Arab broadcasts about the near-conquest of Tel Aviv by the Egyptian forces.

Israel desperately needed America's support. America responded with supplies and, some sources would add, manpower. Indeed one of my friends, who was working as a nurse in a local hospital, had to treat some American soldiers wounded during the 1973 war. They may have been American Jews.

A massive American airlift of equipment and weaponry rescued Israel from the jaws of defeat. In addition, the American fleet was engaged in a face-off with the Russian fleet. ("The little-known US-Soviet confrontation during Yom Kippur War", Abraham Rabinovich, Global Post Blogs, October 26, 2012 05:24.)

Just as religion played a role in 1967, so too it did in 1973. The USA's involvement in the 1973 war, the US being a largely churchgoing nation, was heavily influenced by religious fervour. A Pew survey in 2003 found that 36 percent of US adults believed that the creation of the State of Israel is a necessary precursor for the second coming of Jesus Christ.

The recent Pew survey showed that Britons and Spaniards were more supportive of the Palestinians, whereas Germans and Russians were more sympathetic to Israel. The French were evenly divided.

A Pew Research Center survey of residents of 15 countries (19 July 2006) demonstrated that Americans had the most sympathy toward Israel. Pew analysts Jodie T. Allen and Alec Tyson recently wrote that 48 percent of Americans supported Israel, compared with just 13 percent of Americans who supported the Palestinians.

In the USA, Evangelicals were undoubtedly behind Israel. Some Churches were public in their support, equating lack of support for Israel with lack of commitment to Christ. Some churches paid for whole-page advertisements in newspapers calling Evangelicals to support Israel.

Soon after the Yom Kippur war the Muslim world declared an oil embargo on all who supported Israel. America suffered. The Rev Jerry Falwell stood by Israel, quoting Genesis (12:3), he explained that God *"will bless those who bless the Jews and curse whoever curses the Jews"*.

There is no easy position for a Christian Arab to take vis-à-vis Israel. If you support Israel you offend Arabs and Muslims alike and you are labelled a traitor. If you support the Arabs you will offend the Jews. Considerations of pleasing one side or the other is therefore innately futile. One should side with the truth without fear or favour. This will always come at a price. Egyptian pastor Emil Boutros, declared his support for Israel in an interview with the *Jerusalem Post*: *"God allowed Israel to be surrounded by Arab nations, but at the same time God is also defending Israel."* What did such a stance cost him? I have visited his church. The building is far too small for the congregation. The authorities will not permit the construction of a new church building. Members of his congregation are often threatened by Muslim neighbours.

I experienced the internal conflict of a Christian with respect to Israel bitterly in 1975, two years after the Yom Kippur war. I was only seventeen and was helping at a Christian Camp in Bethlehem. It was my pleasure then to meet one of the most beautiful daughters of Palestine. She was one year younger than me. Not only was I drawn to her physical beauty, but I was also impressed with her intellect. She was a Christian who possessed a different understanding of the Old Testament. Her views were coloured by the bitter experience of living under Israeli military occupation. Mine was shaped by my being the son of an Evangelical pastor and an upbringing steeped in traditional Brethren pro-Israeli teaching. I felt hugely drawn to her. If only I could persuade her that Christians have to support Israel. Sadly, the seedlings of love were stifled by our differences over Israel. This small sacrifice on my part may be minor, but for me, it was akin to the little boy giving his lunch to Christ for the feeding of many. A small sacrifice for many, but it was no small sacrifice for the little boy.

To some Evangelical Westerners, this war was another dice throw on their eschatological game board. It did not touch them at all. By contrast, Israeli Arab Evangelicals, and Christian Arabs in general, had to live through that war. Once more, our car was taken away by the Israeli military. I recall the moment we learnt about the war. I was 15 years of age. I was preparing to go to a church service with my father, when a visiting Pentecostal preacher dropped in, and with some excitement shared the news that Israel was under attack and that Egyptian forces were advancing into Sinai. Somehow, he soon returned back to the USA. Again he was accused of being a spy. As his credibility suffered, so did ours by association.

Although Israel emerged from the Yom Kippur War victorious, and although Israel's IDF could have marched into Cairo and Damascus, Israel had never been so close to defeat. Whilst Israel emerged victorious, it was shown not to be so invincible as Israel would like its neighbours to think. Though defeated, the Arabs drew some comfort from bringing Israel to the brink of defeat. This positively affected Arab self-esteem. Israeli Arabs began to feel some pride. At least the sense of shame that had plagued us from the days of the Six Day War began to lift like fog dispelled by the sun of courage and near-triumph.

Who Are These Israeli-Arabs?

Palestinians who neither escaped nor were expelled from Palestine during the 1948 war, al-Nakbah, were given Israeli citizenship. They lived under Zionist military rule till the mid-1960s.

The 1973 war and the near loss Israel experienced caused a boost in Arab self-confidence, which bore practical consequences. There were meetings in Nazareth and other large Arab towns demanding equality for Israeli Arabs, particularly in education and the provision of infrastructure. I recall the road to Nazareth from my village was a terrifying experience. My father drove an old Jeep. The centre of the road was at least twenty inches higher than either side and the jeep always felt on the verge of keeling over onto its side. I was so afraid that I would always sit on the higher side in order to counter gravity and reduce the risk of the Jeep keeling over. My father spent more time driving on the mud paths next to the main road than he did on the road. By contrast roads connecting Jewish centres of population were far superior. Yet we paid taxes like any Israeli citizen. Why were our roads so poor?!

Our schools were disgraceful. I recall there were no windows in my classroom and the floor was made of rough concrete, the chairs never sat evenly on the floor. In winter the wind would drive the rain into the classroom and there would be puddles of water on my classroom floor. My feet were so cold that I bled from my chilblains.

Shortly after the war, our school arranged an exchange with a Jewish Kibbutz school. I hosted two Jewish boys. They were impressed by our simple way of life and the close-knit family unit. We had no television, though this was partly due to my father's personal philosophy. They appreciated the family unit and the nourishing family atmosphere which the Kibbutz did not provide. We had discussions covering various topics especially religious and political topics. My two Jewish guests definitely felt superior and behaved as if they were superior to us. My guests did not express any empathy with my argument that though we were citizens and though we paid tax, it seemed unfair that our infrastructure was so much poorer than that of Jewish settlements. And when it came to discussing opportunities for further education, there was complete silence. I did not feel that they were silent for lack of arguments against mine, but rather out of politeness. They did not believe in equality of the two races, and were too ashamed or afraid to speak out.

More meetings and gatherings took place. Israeli Arab youth demanded equality. It was often pointed out that whilst Israeli Arabs formed 20% of the population, less than 1% of places at medical school were available to Israeli Arabs.

The lack of educational opportunities for Israeli Arabs went unheeded by Western countries. What a missed opportunity for Evangelism. The opportunity to right injustices by giving victims of discrimination another chance is a unique platform on which to showcase the brilliance of the Christian faith. My own battle was to find an alternative university abroad. Most students of my generation joined the Communist Party who paid for their education in communist countries such as Russia, East Germany, Czechoslovakia or Romania. All one had to do was join the Communist Party and they would take care of the rest. Consequently the Communist Party grew in popularity amongst Israeli Arabs and its membership rose exponentially. Of course, my family would never sign up to Communism. Ironically, I was subsequently accused of being a communist by a group of visiting Evangelical Zionists, when I preached on the ethos of equality in the Scriptures. I was even sent anti-Communist material to help elute communism out of my mind!

My own battle to study medicine proved a very disappointing one. To date I have not been able to understand or digest the treatment of fellow Western Evangelicals of me. My father was an Israeli Arab Evangelical pastor. He was a free Evangelical and as such had no salary. We lived by faith literally and we never knew where our next meal was coming from. My parents had always freely hosted Christians from the West. I never recall an evening when my mother was not cooking for some Western Christian visitors. I remember some visitors would tarry for weeks, and my parents would never complain.

As I approached my seventeenth birthday, I had to decide what and where I was going to study. Most of my classmates had secured their further education through their membership of the Communist Party. I wanted to study medicine. What better than approach a medical missionary society? After all, one of its chief doctors was a close friend of my father's. He and his family had enjoyed hospitality at our house on many occasions. Surely they would not flinch from helping me fulfil my calling.

My father dictated and I translated and wrote a letter to the mission headquarters. To our disappointment, the response was discouraging. In short the chief doctor advised my father, as a friend, not to send me to the United Kingdom. Yes, the mission still had influence (some five places per year were preserved for the mission at a medical school), but the mission did not have the money to support me and the United Kingdom was far too expensive a place to live. We wrote back trying to persuade the mission's chief doctor to rethink.

The reply was more robustly negative. The advice, and we were not looking for advice as much as support, was not to send me to the United Kingdom.

Somehow, and with the help of a most remarkable Evangelical Anglican vicar and his family, I went to live and study in the United Kingdom. Had the mission supported me, I could have commenced medical school at the age of 19. Instead, the first year was spent working in London Bible College as an assistant maintenance officer and cleaner. I then spent three years in pre-university studies. In other words, what should have taken me one year, actually took me four years. In the meantime, the Anglican vicar pleaded with the medical missionary society to support me in any way they could. The chief doctor was adamant. Indeed he even refused to support me through designated gifts from my friends, who supported the mission.

Within ten months of being in the UK, I went on a tour of the British Isles with the son of my surrogate parents. We visited the hometown of the mission. The chief doctor of the mission asked to see me. I was invited to meet him at the mission's headquarters. He kept me waiting for thirty minutes. He never invited me to his home, but chose to see me in his office. He was extremely officious and cold, which saddened me greatly. This man had lived amongst us for many years. He had enjoyed Christian Arab hospitality for many years. He had feasted in my own house on many occasions. My mother looked after his ill wife and his children for a long period. Why did he not afford me the courtesy of a slightly less chilly welcome? Then he proceeded to interrogate me. He pulled out a file from his filing cabinet and proceeded to read it to me. *"On such and such a date, I advised you never to come to the United Kingdom... why did you ignore my advice? this is most unwise... you will never make it here."* It was such a perfect psychological demolition job that I felt I was in the presence of an enemy and not a close family friend. Why did I deserve such humiliation? Contrast this treatment with that received by converts to Communism. People who had never done any service to the Communist Party were taken in without questions and supported financially all the way to graduation. And I, the son of an Evangelical minister, am being subjected to such humiliation by a fellow Evangelical, who is supposed to be a close friend of my father. Is it any surprise that many Christian youths joined the Communist Party? To date I have no answer for such a paradox, though I have an inkling.

One year previous to my departure for the UK, I had a clash with the wife of the American Chaplain of the mission hospital in question. He had organised a summer camp in

Bethlehem. I was invited to teach. I was also invited to recruit young people. I saw this as an opportunity to reach out to members of other denominations. Though difficult, I managed to enlist some Episcopalians and managed to fill all the places allotted to me. On arriving in Bethlehem, the wife of the American chaplain accused me of taking liberties and of bringing more young people to camp than she had allotted me. She was wrong. I tried to remind her of conversations we had had. She accused me of impudence and suggested that I had to send two young ladies home instantly. This was ridiculous, as it was too late in the evening and they were under twelve years of age, and there was no transport available. Somehow, this woman had held it against me all this time and had written to the mission advising that they should not support me. The mission's chief doctor who pulled out a letter from the folder and started reading to me her account of that incident. The words that stuck in my mind were *"he is not reliable"*.

I am sure this sort of treatment would not have been meted out to a fellow American or an Anglo-Saxon or indeed a Jew. This was racism at work; the American Evangelical superiors dealing with an Arab inferior.

When I was 16 years of age, I fell in love with the relative of a European missionary. She would beg me for a kiss, and I would refuse on the basis that we were Christian and outside wedlock. I had been brought up to think that a kiss was reserved for married people. That is what my Christian Arab parents had taught me. She, however, persuaded me to accompany her to watch sunrise on top of a hill in Bethlehem. All the way to the hilltop, she begged for a kiss or even for me to hold her hand. I refused on the grounds given above. Yet her missionary relatives who had lived amongst Christian Arabs for years rebuked her severely for having any feelings for m, telling her that Arab men only have one thing on their minds!!

Israeli Arabs, often called Arab Citizens of Israel, should not be presumed to be equal to Jewish Israeli citizens. Indeed the basic law of Israel does not guarantee equality for Israeli Arabs. It talks of high values: of dignity, liberty and freedom. However, nowhere does it guarantee equality for non-Jews or

Gentiles. Curiously, when tested in the High Court, the Basic Law of Israel has been interpreted in such a way as to presume equality for Israeli Arabs.

According to the Minorities At Risk Project, Israeli Arabs *"suffer political discrimination based on decades of social exclusion."* Israel is referred to as an *"ethnic democracy"*. It states that Israel's claim to democracy is marred by *"the nationalism inherent in Israel's foundation as a 'Jewish state' is at odds with its political basis of democratic governance vis-à-vis the Arab minority."* In other words, Israel being a Zionist State in which Jewishness is essential, automatically alienates and even excludes Gentiles, of whom Arabs are the majority.

One irony of Israeli society is that Arabs who work, pay taxes and are forced to contribute to the war against their Arab brothers, are denied basic rights to education and public services, whilst Hassidic Jews can have all these facilities at their disposal, though they do no work whatsoever. Their *raison d'être* is to feed, breed, and creed. Their lifestyle is greed and selfishness. Yet they have more rights than Arab citizens of the State of Israel.

I personally believe that Israel wants to be democratic, but feels hindered by its history which imposes upon it an urgent sense of self-preservation dictating that the Jews should be in the ascendancy in order to avoid another holocaust. This is embodied in Netanyahu's controversial remarks: *"If there is a demographic problem, and there is, it is with the Israeli Arabs who will remain Israeli citizens,"* he said. *"The Declaration of Independence said Israel should be a Jewish and democratic state, but to ensure the Jewish character was not engulfed by demography, it was necessary to ensure a Jewish majority."* (*Haaretz*, 18/12/2003.)

In Western terms these are first-rank racist remarks, which automatically dispossess their owners of any claim to democracy. Netanyahu believed the answer to the demographic problem of modern Israel would be the *"integration"* of Israeli Arabs. He did not elaborate, but it is implied that integration means Judaising Arabs. This is what I experienced as a pupil in an Arab Israeli school. The sort of

Hebrew we studied consisted of Jewish history and tradition, which was passed on to us as fact, not as a version or a view. I always found it curious that we had to learn the Old Testament and Jewish traditions, whereas Jewish children did not. And what history did we study/learn? Mainly Jewish history. We learnt about the ancient Arabs, but briefly. Most of our history was about European history. Little of it was about modern Arab history. We studied the history of the State of Israel. We learnt nothing, at school, about the Palestinian side of the story.

Jewish paranoia about being overtaken by Israeli Arabs is nowhere better reflected than in its willingness to give up a strategically important territorial prize, taken from Jordan almost by force, at least threat of force, so as to redress the balance in numbers in favour of Jews. This prize is Wadi Ara, which is *"full of Arab communities, including Umm el-Fahm, the second largest Palestinian town inside Israel's pre-1967 borders."* (*Washington Post Sunday*, August 14, 2005.) Apparently, Ariel Sharon, whilst still Prime Minister, was keen to progress this swap with the Palestinian authorities despite the residents of Wadi Ara's opposition to the idea.

When I was a child, it was anathema for an Israeli Arab to call themselves Palestinian, for fear of consequences from the Israeli authorities, who denied the existence of a Palestinian people. Now that Israel is worried about its demography, and fears the loss of Jewish majority, even its most right-wing politicians are keen to recognise that Israeli Arabs are Palestinian. This would prepare the way for the transfer, eventually, of Israeli Arabs out of the State of Israel.

Golda Meir once declared that her party's aim is to eventually have a pure Jewish state. Such an idea has found a bold expression in the politics of an increasingly more popular extremist Jewish politician Avigdor Lieberman, who leads the Israel Our Home party. He proposes to redraw Israel's map in a way that excludes Israeli Arab settlements from Israel.

On October 30 2006, Lieberman was appointed Israel's Minister of Strategic Affairs and Deputy Prime Minister. He categorically stated his keenness on a pure Jewish state, totally clean of Arabs: *"It's not only an issue of territory and borders..., but of the character of the state – will it be a Zionist State, a Jewish state, or a state like others? I want it to be a Jewish state."* (*Guardian*, Jonathan Steele, November 3, 2006.)

"Lieberman's party stands for one thing: an Israel finally cleansed of the remainder of the indigenous Palestinian population." (*Counterpunch*, Saree Makdisi, "The Ethnic Cleansing Party Outpaces Likud," March 31, 2006.). Lieberman has recently published his own peace plan reiterating the option for Israeli Arabs and Palestinians to move to surrounding Arab states. ("Lieberman 'peace plan' would pay Arabs to leave Israel; FM's party manifesto calls on Arab-Israelis to decide if they want to be part of the State of Israel or a future Palestine"; TIMES OF ISRAEL November 28, 2014.)

Whilst the need of a purely Jewish State to be rid of its Arab citizens makes Zionist sense, it completely bypasses the sensibilities, religious and national, of Muslim and Christian Arabs. Why would a Christian Arab want to leave Bethlehem or Jerusalem?!, Why would a Muslim leave Hebron or Jerusalem?!

Understandably Lieberman has been accused of *"race hatred"*. (*Guardian*, Jonathan Steele, November 3, 2006.) He has been known to have spoken of Palestinian prisoners with extreme disdain for human life: *"It would be better to drown these (Palestinian) prisoners in the Dead Sea if possible, since that's the lowest point in the world."* (*Guardian*, July 25, 2003).

This leading Zionist politician is hardly the best face of country that claims to be democratic. And who has objected to this man's appointment, let alone his spiteful and hate-laden mind and utterances?! Whilst the Israeli judicial system makes gestures towards the Arabs, by standing up to non-consequential people and institutions, it has failed to make a stand against this leading politician who is essentially a racist.

"The attorney general ruled that an anti-Arab slogan used by militant rightists constitutes incitement to racism, an offence punishable by five years in jail, the justice ministry said." (By Joel Greenberg (NYT). Published: February 1, 2002, New York Times.) Does the ministry of Justice have the moral fibre and courage to apply the same standards to Lieberman and men of such calibre?

Israel's claim to democracy is further limited by its "leom" rights, nationality-based rights, or rights that only apply to Jews. Such rights are the monopoly of the Jewish sector of Israeli society. Examples are presented by Phyllis Bennis:

"Other rights are defined as nationality rights, and are reserved for Jews only. If you are a Jew, you have exclusive use of land, privileged access to private and public employment, special educational loans, home mortgages, preferences for admission to universities, and many other privileges.

"Many other special privileges are reserved for those who have served in the Israeli military. And military service is compulsory for all Jews (male and female), except for the ultra-Orthodox who get the same privileges as other Jews, but excludes Palestinians, who do not." (*Colorlines Magazine*, December 15 2000.)

This is the reason why thousands of Israeli Arabs of my generation felt compelled to join the Communist Party and to seek education abroad. The Druze, who also serve in the Israeli army should have more privileges than ordinary Israeli Arabs. But even they are discriminated against.

In her report *"Israel's Two-Tiered Citizenship Law Bars Non-Jews From 93 Percent of Its Lands"* Roselle Tekiner explains: *"Zionist uses of the term 'nation,' 'national,' and 'nationality' are indeed difficult to understand and to explain because they derive from concepts that are unfamiliar to Americans. Moreover, their true meanings are deliberately obscured by usually incorrect translations from Hebrew into English.*

"The prime example of deception, from which the others flow, is the accepted translation of Israel's Law of Citizenship

as 'Nationality' Law. In the original Hebrew text, the word is ezrahut, the correct translation is 'citizenship.'

Whereas in the West 'nationality' and citizenship may be synonymous, in Israel they convey different meanings and confer different rights and privileges. Citizenship (Ezrahut) is the right of all Israelis, whereas nationality (leom) is the preserve of Jews only. This reality was reaffirmed by the Supreme Court in 1972 which emphasized the interdependence of Israeli nationality and Jewishness. No Israeli nation can exist outside the Jewish people. This automatically excludes all non-Jews, primarily Israeli Arabs from nationality rights." (Roselle Tekiner in "Washington Report on Middle East Affairs", January 1990, p.20)

In the West, freedom implies freedom of speech. The basic law of Israel guarantees freedom for its citizens. In reality, Israeli Arabs have to fight in the Supreme Court for their freedom of speech:

"In June, Arab Knesset Members Ahmed Tibi and Taleb el-Sana were censured by the Knesset Ethics Committee for harshly criticizing IDF operations in Gaza. The Committee banned Tibi and el-Sana from attending Knesset sessions for 1 and 2 days, respectively.

"In September, the Supreme Court upheld its original ruling overturning the Film Council's ban on the screening of the film, 'Jenin, Jenin,' which depicts fighting in the West Bank refugee camp in Jenin during April 2002. In its decision, the Supreme Court reasoned that a ban on the film was an undue infringement on freedom of expression." (US Department of State Country Reports on Human Rights Practices – 2004, Released by the Bureau of Democracy, Human Rights, and Labor, February 28, 2005).

The report concludes: the Israeli government *"did little to reduce institutional, legal, and societal discrimination against the country's Arab citizens."*

In terms of Arabic political parties and the chances of representation in the Knesset, Israel has raised the threshold: *"The question is particularly acute because the threshold for getting into parliament has gone up to 2% of the national vote.*" (*The Economist*, March 23 2006). This takes advantage of a divided Arab Israeli population with multiple parties, diluting the Arab Israeli vote and making it harder for Arab parties to achieve a seat in the Knesset.

The inequality pervades all levels of Israeli society. Israeli Arabs are less likely to find work. In 2003 *"Peace and Social Justice Organization Report Shows 16% Unemployment Rate in Israel and 20% Unemployment in Arab Sector."* (Arab Association for Human Rights (HRA) Weekly Press Review No. 156/7 – February 13, 2004).

The 2004 US State Department Country Reports on Human Rights Practices notes that:

- *"According to a 2003 Haifa University study, a tendency existed to impose heavier prison terms to Arab citizens than to <u>Jewish</u> citizens. Human rights advocates claimed that Arab citizens were more likely to be convicted of murder and to have been denied bail."*

- *"The Orr Commission of Inquiry's report... stated that the 'Government handling of the Arab sector has been primarily neglectful and discriminatory,' that the Government 'did not show sufficient sensitivity to the needs of the Arab population, and did not take enough action to allocate state resources in an equal manner.' As a result, 'serious distress prevailed in the Arab sector in various areas. Evidence of distress included poverty, unemployment, a shortage of land, serious problems in the education system, and substantially defective infrastructure.'"*

- *"According to a report by Mossawa, racist violence against Arab citizens has increased, and the Government has not done enough to prevent this problem. The annual report cited 17 acts of violence by Jewish citizens against Arab citizens.... A Haifa University poll released in June revealed that over 63 percent of Jews believed that the Government should encourage Israeli Arabs to emigrate."*

- *"Approximately 93 percent of land in the country was public domain, including that owned by the state and some 12.5 percent owned by the Jewish National Fund (JNF). All public land by law may only be leased, not sold. The JNF's statutes prohibit the sale or lease of land to non-Jews. In October, civil rights groups petitioned the High Court of Justice claiming that a bid announcement by the Israel Land Administration (ILA) involving JNF land was discriminatory in that it banned Arabs from bidding."*

- *"Israeli-Arab advocacy organizations have challenged the Government's policy of demolishing illegal buildings in the Arab sector, and claimed that the Government was more restrictive in issuing building permits in Arab communities than in Jewish communities, thereby not accommodating natural growth. In February, security forces demolished several homes allegedly built without authorization in the Arab village of Beineh."*

- *"In June, the Supreme Court ruled that omitting Arab towns from specific government social and economic plans is discriminatory. This judgment builds on previous assessments of disadvantages suffered by Arab Israelis."*

- *"Israeli-Arab organizations have challenged as discriminatory the 1996 'Master Plan for the Northern Areas of Israel,' which listed as priority goals increasing the Galilee's Jewish population and blocking the territorial contiguity of Arab towns."*

- *"Israeli Arabs were not required to perform mandatory military service and, in practice, only a small percentage of Israeli Arabs served in the military. Those who did not serve in the army had less access than other citizens to social and economic benefits for which military service was a prerequisite or an advantage, such as housing, new-household subsidies, and employment, especially government or security-related industrial employment. Regarding the latter, for security reasons, Israeli Arabs generally were restricted from working in companies with defense contracts or in security-related fields. The Ivri Committee on National Service has issued official recommendations to the Government that Israel Arabs not be compelled to perform national or 'civic' service, but be afforded an opportunity to perform such service."*

- Human Rights Watch has claimed that cuts in veteran benefits and child allowances based on parents' military service discriminate against Arab children; however, *"The cuts will also affect the children of Jewish ultra-orthodox parents who do not serve in the military, but they are eligible for extra subsidies, including educational supplements, not available to Palestinian Arab children."*

Silver Plated Equality

Friends of the Jewish state are quick to point out that Israel is the only democracy in the Middle East and that Israeli Arabs enjoy better freedom of speech than Arabs in Egypt and Saudi Arabia. It is odd, however, to lay a claim to being the only democracy in the Middle East whilst simultaneously seeking a comparison with inherently undemocratic states. So Israel is more democratic than Saudi Arabia. Yes Israel is more democratic than Egypt and Saudi Arabia, Yemen or Iraq. Is this such a great achievement?! The second question that comes to mind is, if Israeli Arabs are citizens of the State of Israel, why should they only aspire to Saudi Arabia's standards? Does the State of Israel measure the rights and liberties of its Jewish citizens by Saudi standards?!

It is also pointed out that a few positions in the military, Supreme Court, the Israeli football team and even a few diplomatic offices are held by Israeli Arabs. It must be remembered, however, that such positions are few and far between and do not proportionately represent the percentage of the Israeli population, that is the Arab citizens of Israel. Nor are Israeli Arabs allowed to compete on merit.

The appointment of the first Arab Minister Ghaleb Majadele was postponed because of racist remarks by Tartman, Secretary of Yisrael Beiteinu faction (the party of Lieberman, Israel's "Strategic Threats Minister"). She was reported to have said of the intended appointment that it was like *"swinging an axe at the tree called Judaism,"* and that *"we need to uproot this terrible evil from among us."* (Haaretz.com, January 17, 2007). Lieberman did not dissociate himself from such racist remarks. *Haaretz* commented about the meeting between Lieberman and Condoleezza Rice, American Secretary of State, which took place soon after those racist remarks were made. *"Rice's meeting with Lieberman was like giving a stamp of approval to the racist positions he and his party have adopted. It is not clear why the Secretary of State saw a need to hold this meeting, which is not part of the standard protocol for her visits to Israel. Her meeting with Lieberman thus constituted a kind of American recognition of his status and his stances. Instead of the United States denouncing his racist positions, it has given them support, in the form of a well-publicized and unnecessary meeting. Rice, who came to the region to 'strengthen the moderate forces,' thereby in fact lent her hand to strengthening the extremists, at least on the Israeli side."*

The above anti-Arab position is to be contrasted with the freedom British Jews enjoy in the United Kingdom, which I have made my home, a country of which I am proud. Britain, who has a Jewish population of approximately 300,000 had a Labour government, under Blair, with a Protestant Prime Minister, and two Jewish ministers (actually brothers, the Milibands). That is democracy. Israel cannot claim to be in the same league of democratic nations. As I put the finishing touches to this manuscript, one of the Miliband brothers is leader of the labour party, and if his party win the elections in May 2015, could be our next Prime Minister. Israel has never given its Arab citizens this sort of equality. It does well to compare itself with Saudi Arabia.

Iran, a Muslim dictatorship has a Jewish population of 25,000, a fraction of one percent. Yet it has one Jewish MP, Maurice Motamed, one of 290 Majlis members (June 28, 2006, *Guardian*). He publicly criticised Ahmadenajad for his denial of the Holocaust. Motamed was not penalised. Israeli Arab representation in the Israeli Parliament is well below that of Iranian Jews in Iran. Also by contrast, Israel allows its extremist Jewish MPs and cabinet members to express racist anti-Arab ideology, whilst simultaneously penalising Israeli-Arab MPs for meeting with Palestinian politicians.

The Zionist's claim to democracy is only superficial. There is no more truth in it than there is silver in a silver plated ring. According to Moshe Sharett, Israel's first Foreign Minister, Israel has to play games of deceit in order to survive. *"I have learned that the State of Israel cannot be ruled in our generation without deceit and adventurism."* (Simha Flapan, *The Birth of Israel*, 1987, p. 51).

A web page by B'nai Brith Canada challenges the claim of Palestinians that they have a right to return to Palestine/Israel on the grounds that:

"The claimed Palestinian right of return is not a 'right', since it is recognized neither in Israeli law nor in international law. Nor is it about 'return', since it is applied to millions of people who have never set foot in Israel. There are reportedly 6.5 million Palestinians around the world who trace their descent from Arabs who lived in Palestine before 1948 and who identify themselves as Palestinians." ("Israel and the Palestinians: myths and realities" by David Matas, LLB, MA, Senior Legal Counsel, B'nai Brith Canada).

The above illustrates Zionist's inability, or perhaps unwillingness, to deal fairly with their Palestinian cousins. There is no such thing as equality in their thinking.

What the Zionists claim for themselves, they deny others. If being born to parents who had lived in Palestine does not give a Palestinian the right of return to Palestine/Israel, how is it that Zionists have awarded themselves the right to return because some of their forebears, with whom they may have a tenuous genetic link at best, lived in Palestine some 2000 years ago?!!! To Zionists, what is sauce for the goose is not sauce for the gander. They believe they are racially superior and inherently possess more rights than their Arab cousins.

It is difficult for Israel to make a credible claim to democracy. Arab representation in the Knesset is well below the 20 percent commensurate with the percentage of Arabs in the population, or when 20 percent of academic positions are filled by Israeli Arabs, when 20 percent of its cabinet is occupied by Arabs, when 20 percent of seats in the Supreme Court are filled by Arabs etc, etc, etc. By claiming to be democratic, Israel self-imposes an obligation to act democratically towards its Israeli Arab citizens. When Israel fails the tests of democracy it should blush before the democratic civilisations of the world and relinquish its void claim to democrarcy. It should eat a humble pie and go back to the drawing board and try and do better. Its friends ought to coax her to do better. Israel, with an increasing proportion of religious Jews, ought to be reminded of God's instructions through the prophet Micah:

"He has shown you, O man, what is good;
And what does the LORD require of you
But to do justly,
To love mercy,
And to walk humbly with your God?" (Mic 6:8 NKJV)

Rattner, Arye and Gideon Fishman, in their *Justice for All? Jews and Arabs in the Israeli Criminal Justice System,* state: *"the authors demonstrate that Arabs have their criminal files remain open for a longer period than Jews; that an Arab defendant with no prior history of criminal activity is more likely to be convicted than a Jewish defendant with a similar record; and that Arabs are more likely to be convicted to a prison term than Jews. The results also indicated that in general, there is a higher probability of Arab defendants receiving a harsher sentencing across particular categories of criminal acts that range from violent crimes to property offenses."* (Robert Hazan Metropolitan State College of Denver)

The authors also concluded that Arabs *"are not treated as equals"* (p. ix): *"... the Israeli criminal justice system has neglected one of its cornerstone duties – distributing justice to all people."*

"Being an Arab may lead to a presumption of guilt without facts and the rules of evidence." (p. 115). (System. Westport, CT: Praeger Publishers, 1998, p.138).

A poll carried out amongst Israeli Jews about their attitudes towards their Israel Arab fellow citizens showed that 18% felt hatred when they heard another person speak Arabic. 34% believed Arab culture to be inferior to Israeli culture. Taleb El-sana, an Israeli-Arab MP, commented that when Jews are subjected to anti-Semitism abroad the reaction in Israel is palpable objection and loud protests. *"Yet when it happens at their home, they're quiet, and that's why this is a twofold failure – they are racist, and they're also not attempting to address their own racism."* (*The Sunday Morning Herald*; by Chris McGreal in Jerusalem, March 25, 2006).

The inclusion of Swan, an Israeli Arab footballer from Sakhnin, in the Israeli national team, may be a sign of Israel's desire to be inclusive. However, football is one arena where feelings are difficult to conceal. Swan has been subjected to racist remarks simply for being an Arab. Supporters of a rival team to Swan's team were on record saying:

"'We hate Arabs and Muslims,' shouted 19-year-old fan Eliran, a member of Beitar's La Familia hooligan gang. 'If any Arab played for Beitar, we'd burn their ass and burn the club. They're our enemy.'" (*Guardian Unlimited*, November 26, 2006).

If Evangelical Zionists really love Israel and the Jews, they owe them this much: they should open their eyes to the fact that God loves mercy and justice and expects his people to act in like manner.

"Therefore circumcise the foreskin of your heart, and be stiff-necked no longer. For the LORD your God is God of gods and Lord of lords, the great God, mighty and awesome, who shows no partiality nor takes a bribe. He administers justice for the fatherless and the widow, and loves the stranger, giving

him food and clothing. Therefore love the stranger, for you were strangers in the land of Egypt. You shall fear the LORD your God; you shall serve Him, and to Him you shall hold fast, and take oaths in His name." (Deut 10:16-21).

There can be no greater foundation for Israel in its dealings with her Arab citizens than the above Scripture. It is the best guide on the muddy path of inter-race relations. This should be the yardstick by which Israel should measure itself. It is the minimum standard Western Evangelicals should demand from their Jewish friends, particularly vis-à-vis Christian Israeli Arabs. The God of Israel loves the stranger giving him food and clothing. Israel has failed to meet the standard of her own God, the God of Abraham, Isaac and Jacob. Israel cannot claim to love the strangers in her midst. Or are Zionists and Evangelical Zionists only interested in those parts of the Scriptures that support their theology and political views?!

Why does Israel not love the strangers in her midst? Is it because Israel is more evil than its Arab neighbours? Certainly not. The Bible teaches that we have all sinned. All human beings are equal in this respect. What is the reason, then, for Israel failing to love the strangers who dwell in her midst? It is my conviction that Israel, the Zionist State, is largely driven by fear and by greed. Yes, there is ambition and the drive to succeed by any means. But Israel also acts out of fear. The Zionist movement was born out of the pogroms of Europe. The Zionists capitalised on the fears of European Jewry caused by the heinous actions of the Nazis. The *raison d'être* of Israel is that the Jews having their own state will never be subjected to such cruelties and abject deprivation as they had for almost two thousand years in Europe. And yet the instruction to love the stranger, in Deuteronomy, is preceded by the motive force to fulfil such a command: *"for you were strangers in the land of Egypt."*

What will enable you to love the stranger in your midst? What will dispel your fears that the stranger would take advantage of you? What would mollify the anxiety that your love would be mistaken for weakness? The resounding definitive answer is plainly this: *"For the LORD your God is*

God of gods and Lord of lords, the great God, mighty and awesome." In other words, if you really believe in Jehova, Elshadai, the mighty one, the Lord of Lords, you have nothing to fear. With such a God on your side, watching over you, a God who never sleeps nor slumbers, you can afford to take risks with your *"strangers"*, and act justly and show mercy and love towards them. You can afford to obey His command. Your obedience may make you vulnerable. But His love, power and fitfulness should give you security.

Israeli Jewish fear about the next holocaust underpins their relationship with their Arab cousins. I am often chagrined by the way I am treated in Tel Aviv airport. Israeli airport security is so proud of keeping terrorism to an absolute minimum, that they attribute it to their interrogatory methods. There is a palpable attempt to harass, insult, undermine, and bully any Israeli Arab passing through Tel Aviv airport. I recall my first return to Israel in 1979, after an absence of four years. I was so looking forward to returning to my country and my family. When I left the plane, I felt strangely reassured by the typical pungent smell of the Yarkon River. *"What an excuse for a river,"* I laughed to myself, *"but it's my river, and it'll do. I am home."* The warmth of the air was to provide such a sharp contrast to the frosty reception at the passport control. Security men walked along the queues of arrivals, picking Arabs out of the queue for questioning. I got off lightly, with a few annoying but bearable questions. However, next to me was an elderly Arab man, dressed in a pin-striped suit and tie, who possessed an aura of intelligence and gravitas. They treated him like a dog. I could not restrain myself. *"There used to be a Hebrew word for please a few years ago,"* I said to the security officer. He looked puzzled. *"What's become of it?"* I asked facetiously. I remonstrated with him that the old man next to me had been humiliated, made to carry his luggage from one corner to another, been ordered (not asked) to do this that and the other: *"bring your bags, wait here, give me your passport."* Never a word of "thank you" or "please". The tone of voice was worse than the verbal discourtesy. He was made to stand up and was never offered a seat. *"Where is courtesy?"*

I asked in vain. Perhaps I had been living in England for too long. I would hate my father to be treated like this.

The most humiliating experience I have had in Tel Aviv airport was in the early 1980s. I was returning to Israel for a two-month stay and taken all my medical textbooks with me. In addition I had taken all my Russian novels with me, the works of Tolstoy and Dostoyevsky. This meant that I was carrying a heavy suitcase. At the end of my holiday, I returned to Tel Aviv airport by bus. The bus was stopped at the entrance to the airport. Soldiers boarded the bus and started staring into people's faces. Those who looked like Arabs were asked for their passports. Yours truly was singled out for special treatment. *"You. Come,"* they ordered with a digital gesture. They asked me to take my luggage out of the bus luggage compartment, which greatly inconvenienced the driver. *"Take it out."* I was accustomed to the English phrase 'please'. *"What's the matter with these people? Don't they have 'please' in Hebrew? Of course they do. Bevakashah, I still remember",* thought I. I was asked to open my suitcase on the pavement, in sight of all bus passengers on my side. *"Open,"* ordered the soldier as he kicked my suitcase. *"Open,"* he repeated with urgency and loudly, as my driver remonstrated with him. Then I was ordered to carry my heavy bag to a special cubicle some 200 yards away. The bus driver looked embarrassed and confronted the soldier: *"I cannot let you treat my passengers like this. Let's put the suitcase back on the bus, and let me drive the distance."* The soldier soon let the bus driver know who was in charge. I was marched 200 yards and made to open my suitcases again. What was this about? Security? I doubt it. It was about humiliation. By their own account, part of the Israeli security approach is to unsettle prospective terrorists by provoking them, in this instance with physical and psychological means. Israel's secret service is second to none. They know everything they need to know about me and my family. They should have no reason to suspect that Emil Shehadeh is a terrorist.

As I recall this negative life event, I am not angry, but filled with pity towards a people who are so unintelligent that they believe they can better protect themselves by being rude and insulting to their friends and neighbours. They are too fearful or too full of hatred to conceive that treating people badly can only create bitterness and enmity.

On returning from Israel to Scotland after my wedding in 1990, I remember my bride and I were searched at least three times, and almost missed our flight. The security men could not give a monkey's about the consequences. I begged them, reminding them of who my family was. Surely, the Mossad is the best secret service around. *"Surely you know who I am?"* Do you really believe that I am a threat to your security? Is it not enough that you have searched me once, twice? Why a third time, not to speak of the vehicle search outside the airport? The exasperation, the tension, the disturbance, the humiliation and diminution of self-esteem are indescribable. And yet, all they achieve is just that, not to speak of an increased alienation of Israeli Arabs.

On one occasion in 2005, I was travelling back to London with one of my relatives, who is a doctor of theology. He had been on good terms with the authorities as he was advisor to the government on Christian affairs. He assured me that we would receive VIP treatment, because of his contacts. When we arrived at the airport we waited for half an hour for his contact to come and greet us, following which we simply ended up in the queue with everyone else, except we had been delayed by half an hour. So much for VIP treatment. I saw the humour of the situation as one would appreciate honey coming out of a rock. It was a welcome relief from the tension of the moment.

More recently, I embarked on a project to collect as many family photos of at least six generations and save them on a CD. This involved scanning photographs. I had purchased a powerful Epson scanner from London and took it with me to scan more photographs. On my return journey, I was searched as usual. This time the scanner was the subject of great security attention, which caused me a delay of at least one hour. *"It's a scanner,"* I said. *"It has been through the x-ray machine. Is there a problem with it?"* The security officers could not tell me, but they had to retain it for further tests. No matter what I said, they had made up their minds to retain it. Having resigned myself to being parted from my newly acquired equipment, I then tried to ensure that it would be returned to me undamaged. I asked them to post it back in a secure hard box. They reassured me that they were professional and that they knew how to handle such equipment. I pleaded with them several times to ensure that they took great care in packaging it. Eventually, when it arrived at my home address, it was boxed in a large flimsy card-board box. It was scratched, broken and totally out of order. I wrote to the security people, who blamed it on the airline, who also blamed it on the airport security. To date, the relevant correspondence lies on a shelf in my study as a constant bitter reminder of Israeli security disrespect and utter disregard for Israeli Arab citizens. Such treatment can only be possible in the presence of either fear, disrespect or both. My feeling as an Israeli Arab is that Israel suffers from both fear of and disrespect for its Arab citizens.

In terms of the future, are things getting better or worse. Is this disrespect for Israeli Arabs dissolving or caking up on the faces of Jewish Israeli citizenry? Let a Jew answer this: *"We are sliding fast, yes, and it will soon be much, much worse; Israeli Jews are abandoning their identity as Israelis and retreating to a tribal and religious Jewish identity, incapable of tolerance, and drawing from proto-Nazi sources within Judaism, which speak of the destruction or enslavement of the other nations; but that is not reason enough to fabricate a mythical, liberal Israel that never was. "* ("The NY Times has it wrong: Israel's roots are not liberal", by Yossi Gurvitz, +972 Magazine, published July 24, 2012.) This brings to mind the restriction on freedom of expression for the Christian Arabs of Israel in particular. I am here referring to the "anti-missionary laws". This puts Israel's claim to democracy and tolerance to the test. Let the furnace of experience tell us whether these claims are gold or dross.

One of the cardinal signs of democracy is freedom of speech, for which Mr Netanyahu so heroically marched in

Paris, in the wake of the Charlie Hebdo massacre. The freedom to express an opinion without being persecuted is an essential constituent of democracy. The freedom to exchange ideas is a sign that a society is mature, democratic and vibrant. Conversely, most non-democratic societies suppress expression of opinion or exchange of ideas, which often results in one ruling or one dominant party claiming all powers to itself whilst curbing any opposite opinions from being expressed.

The last command of Christ to all His followers was to share the Gospel with the world, otherwise known as Evangelism, which in its purest form is a civilized peaceful activity based on sharing of ideas in the hope that the other person may come round to a particular point of view. In a democratic society, sharing must be a banal activity. Sharing of ideas must be an integral part of the humdrum of normal life in a democratic society. Indeed there is no backlash in the media against political parties trying to share ideas with members of opposite parties. However, when it comes to religion, at least in some countries, sharing of ideas is frowned upon, and even legislated against.

Evangelism has been met by Israel with laws restraining the freedom of Christians to share their faith. On December 25, 1977 the Israeli Knesset passed an anti-missionary law, penal law 5737-1977. This played into the hands of extremist Jews who believe that any conversion from Judaism to Christianity, any apostasy, is a great loss to the nation. Shas leader, Rabbi Ovadia Yosef, reportedly stated that *"Every time he (Rabbi Ovadia Yosef) hears of a case where someone falls into missionary hands, he feels great sadness and asks us to try and save at least one soul in Israel"* (Neta Sela. Published: 03.14.07, Israel News.) Note the expression *"falls into missionary hands"*. This conveys such negativity about the concept of freedom to share ideas, let alone the freedom of an individual to choose what they believe. There is a sense of paranoia that sharing ideas is tantamount to tricking or trapping innocent unthinking people, who are incapable of listening to ideas, assessing them and making up their own minds. Is that an accurate description of the average Jew? Surely not. Why then this misrepresentation of evangelism?! Is it a visceral hatred and fear of anything non-Jewish?!

Let the Rabbi himself answer these questions *"Whether it's Christians coming from abroad or Jewish converts working in Israel, they all have the same agenda – to destroy every trace and memory of the people of Israel, and they plan to do this by converting Jews. These bodies are operating mainly among the Jewish population which is under physical, social and spiritual distress."*

The Supreme Court judge, Dr B. Halevi, describing Christian missionaries, said: *"The Christian missions are a cancer in the body of the nation and are trying to carry forward the aim of physical liquidation [of the Jewish people], which had been furthered by the Catholic Church since it was established."* (*The Tablet*, p.18, 7th January 1978.)

There is a stark and unfortunate confusion here between sharing the Gospel and converting a Jew. Sharing is a matter of someone expressing their view to another. Conversion is not something that someone does to another. It is not a passive process on the part of the convert. When a Jew converts to Christianity, he or she have not had their hands and feet tied, nor a gun put to their head, nor have they been threatened with violence unless they accept the Gospel. Jews converting to Christianity do so of their own free will. It is the Rabbi who is trying to deprive them of that freedom to listen to another opinion, and the freedom to choose for themselves. The truth is Judaism, does not believe in choice. And the anti-missionary laws have played into the hands of non-democratic extremist Jews.

No Christians called for the Jews involved to be penalised. And what of the Supervision of Housing places Act, which, by laying down in effect that Jewish parents could not send their children to Christian-run boarding schools, forced the closure of some badly needed institutions, to which parents had continued to send their children in spite of harassment by Jewish extremists?!

By contrast, the BBC permits Jewish Rabbis, not infrequently, to participate in "Thought for the Day" morning programme.A Facebook link sent to people in Israel tells the story of a Jew who converted to Christianity. I have copied it for illustrating a few points:

"IRVING SALZMAN who went to a Lubavitch Yeshiva found Yeshua.

"Irving Salzman's father had survived the Holocaust, and was committed to raising 'good Jewish boys.' So Irving went to synagogue, attended Hebrew school, and was observant to kashrut (the 'kosher' dietary laws) and went to a Lubavitch Yeshiva. He became very active in synagogue life, apprenticing with the local cantor and learned how to be a Torah reader, a position he held for fifteen years. To meet new friends, Irving was on a chat line one evening, and talking with a born-again Believer. The two told each other about their respective faiths. Every week, this young man would share with Irving the Messianic prophecies from the Hebrew Scriptures. Irving took all of this with a grain of salt as he trusted the wisdom of the rabbinical interpretations of these prophecies over this born-again Christian's understanding.

He thought to himself, 'Who is this Gentile Christian and what does he know about the Messianic Jewish prophecies?' Irving later found out that his friend spent hours and hours in the Jewish public library researching all the questions that came up in their weekly conversations. For an entire year the two debated on the phone, but Irving's trust was solidly in the rabbinical authority. 'Can I read to you from the New Testament?' Irving's young friend asked one day. Irving agreed, as he had never heard a word of the New Testament. He was then treated to the entire Sermon on the Mount, when Yeshua (Jesus) spoke the life of faith to the multitudes. 'I had not seen anything like this in the rabbinic writing of my youth. I was overwhelmed by the authority, wisdom, and compassion of Yeshua in the Sermon on the Mount,' said Irving. 'Could we have all been wrong?' This was a hard pill to swallow. It would mean that the Jewish people had seen their Messiah and denied Him and for 2,000 years we have all been telling our people a lie [that Jesus is not the Jewish Messiah]. And so Irving began his own study of the Messianic prophecies. 'I vowed I would not allow the rabbinic interpretations to influence, but let the text show me who He was. After a couple of months I knew that Jesus of Nazareth was the only candidate who fulfilled the prophecies. It was a matter of fact, so I accepted Him as my Savior.' Irving Salzman is now a Messianic Rabbi in New Jersey. He has been an outreach worker with Chosen People Ministries, reaching hundreds, maybe thousands of people with the truth of Yeshua, giving them the opportunity – much like he had – to find their Savior."

The reaction of a conservative Jewish blog was *"Missionaries waging war upon the Jewish people: illegally targeting Jews in Israel"*. The blog refers to an interview by journalist Dan Wooding of Dr Oren, Israel's ambassador to the USA, which took place after an address by Oren to an Evangelical Californian congregation, in which he thanked the American Evangelicals for their support of Israel. When asked whether Oren was concerned about the growth of the Messianic community in Israel, the ambassador replied, *"I have no statistics on the size of the Messianic community, but I think certainly that the State of Israel wants the Jewish people to remain Jewish…"* While noting that *"Israel greatly values its relationship with the evangelical community and other Christian communities in the world,"* Oren cautioned that *"we are very sensitive to the notion of proselytizing – very sensitive."* ("Ambassador Oren cautions against Messianics and proselytizing"; Jewish Israel on February 18, 2010.)

For Israel the essential democratic freedom to think for oneself and to change one's religion poses an existential dilemma. What if the majority of Jews in Israel convert to Christianity? This bypasses the question of whether conversion is a passive or active process, whether those converting are mature enough to make their own decisions. The scenario of mass conversions to Christianity threatens the security of Israel. This explains the extreme reactions of Rabbi Yosef and the extremist Jewish bloggers. This is why Oren said *"we are very sensitive to the notion of proselytizing – very sensitive"*.

Apart from the Israeli anti-conversion stance being undemocratic, it is an insult to its citizens' intelligence. Can individual Jews think for themselves? As Irving Salzman said above, he *"had never heard a word of the New Testament"*. Indeed many Jews are brought up with very negative images and language about Christians. By contrast, the Jewish religion was rammed down our throats in Israeli Arab schools. Where is the sense of equality here?! How can an intelligent population make a decision about a whole religion, without the freedom to read and enquire for themselves?!

The undemocratic aspect of the anti-missionary Israeli lobby aside, the lack of fair play in the anti-missionary camp is astounding. By contrast with the anti-missionary law, Jews are happy to accept converts from other religions. Many a celebrity have converted to Judaism from Christianity, including Madonna and Sammy Davis Junior. Throughout history Jews have proselytised Gentiles. During the days of Christ, 10% of the Roman Empire was Jewish by proselytization, thanks to the evangelistic zeal of Jewish middle-class women. The conversion of the Khazars to Judaism, in the eighth century AD, is another case in point.

Israel is co-signatory to the Universal Declaration of Human Rights, article 18 of which states: *"Everyone has the right to... change his religion... and freedom... to manifest his religion or beliefs in teaching, practice, worship and observance."* It needs to be borne in mind that Israel, at every turn possible, claims to be the only democracy in the Middle East. Avraham Benjamin, Israel's First Secretary (Information) said in 1980 that Israel is a *"country universally known for its religious freedom, tolerance, and plurality of views..."* (https://truthtellers.org/alerts/christiandeportedfromisreal.htm)

The first application of the anti-missionary law took place against a German graduate student, Barbara Ludwig, who was woken up at 6:30 and taken to prison, then deported because she was accused of doing missionary work ("German student to be deported for alleged 'missionary work'; Barbara Ludwig, 32, says 'I was born in Germany, but I found my identity in Israel.'"; *Haaretz*; by Ofri Ilani | May 29, 2008). The German student, who obtained an undergraduate degree in philosophy in Israel and who was working on her master's degree in religious studies at the Hebrew University, said: *"I go around with Jews, with Christians and with Messianics, and I read books about Christianity. So what? That's not a reason to deport me."* The interior ministry insisted that Ludwig was being deported because she had no residency status and had overstayed her welcome in Israel. Yes the truth is that as the head of the Population Administration's central region, Elinor Golan, stated in two letters to Ludwig's lawyer, *"Ludwig's repeated requests for residency status had been denied because she was 'doing missionary work'"*. This concords well with Michael Decker, Ludwig's lawyer, stating that in 2004, *"a hearing held on her case in 2004 in the Interior Ministry was a 'humiliating religious interrogation,' including asking whether she believed Jesus was the messiah"*.

It boils down to a question of trust. I do not mean trust between neighbours. I mean Trust in God. If the God who commands the Jews to love the stranger in their midst is so mighty, do they trust Him enough to obey Him? The Psalmist has something to say on this subject: *"Trust in the LORD, and do good."* (Ps 37:3 NKJV)

One cannot do good unless one trusts in the Lord. One cannot do the right thing if one is always wondering about the possible negative consequences. If God, who is good, has commanded it, then it can only bring blessings to obey His command. Only then would a believer be freed from their fears and liberated to do good, to do justly and love mercy. This should be the basis of any dialogue between Western Evangelicals and their Jewish friends. The thrust of any Evangelical activity should be generally to bring people closer to God, to encourage people to walk with God and obey His commands, and ultimately and more specifically to trust in the saving grace of God, through Jesus Christ. The question must be asked of whether the millions of dollars donated by Evangelicals to Israel every year have achieved any of the above. I doubt that very much. But if anyone should claim the contrary to be true, they must explain why Jesus did not supply his disciples with gold when he sent them on their mission?!Why did He never leave them worldly riches?!

The current Evangelical stance does not draw the Jews closer to God. It draws them closer to Evangelicals. That's about it, closer to Evangelicals, but not an inch closer to God. The result is the Gospel is forgotten, is side-lined, and is sacrificed on the altar of deference.

In 2003, 60 percent of Israeli Arab children were below the poverty line. What have Western Evangelicals done about it? Nothing. Is this not one of the lost opportunities to share the love of God?! Evangelical obsession with Israel is backfiring. Evangelicals are totally hamstrung by their mistaken theology on Israel. Some Evangelicals are better defined by their fanatical support for Israel than by their zeal for the Gospel.

Instead, what Evangelical Zionists have done, for almost a century, is to invite Jews to trust the Evangelical dollar and to arm themselves with Evangelical political support, and to fortify themselves with blind Evangelical zeal for Israel. The Evangelical Zionists have transformed themselves into a surrogate God for the Jews. The Lord God almighty has been marginalised and the great Evangelicals have stolen the limelight. It seems to the untrained eye that God does what Evangelical Zionists tell Him to do. Evangelical Zionists do not do what God tells them. They are more pro-Jewish than pro-God. The consequence is for the Jews to totally ignore the injustices they are committing against the stranger who dwells in their midst. In this sense, Evangelical Zionists have been partners in crime with Israel and deserve the same criticism and rebuke from the world at large and Israeli Arab Evangelicals in particular.

Israel needs the wisdom of Solomon whose main attribute was justice. Israel needs to act justly towards its Arab citizens and its Palestinian neighbours. The longer the injustices of inequality persist, the more negative consequences Israel stores for the future. All civilisations based on the superiority of one race over another have imploded. Israel's injustice against its Arabs is its own suicide bomb, made in Israel, by Jewish hands, and ready to explode in the heart of the nation.

The injustices against Israeli Arabs, alluded to above, have long been recognised by Israeli Jews, both lay and officials. From the outset, there have been Jews who have opposed the Zionist acts of hostility against the indigenous Palestinians:

"An article by Yitzhak Epstein, published in Hashiloah in 1907... called for a new Zionist policy towards the Arabs after 30 years of settlement activity... Like Ahad-Ha'am in 1891, Epstein claims that no good land is vacant, so Jewish settlement meant Arab dispossession... Epstein's solution to the problem, so that a new 'Jewish Question' may be avoided, is the creation of a bi-national, non-exclusive program of settlement and development. Purchasing land should not involve the dispossession of poor sharecroppers. It should mean creating a joint farming community, where the Arabs will enjoy modern technology. Schools, hospitals and libraries should be non-exclusivist and education bilingual... The vision of the non-exclusivist, peaceful cooperation to replace the practice of dispossession found few takers. Epstein was maligned and scorned for his faintheartedness." (Israeli author, Benjamin Beit-Hallahmi, *Original Sins*.)

Epstein shows more sympathy, understanding and wisdom that the children of the Kingdom of God, who support Israel's pugilistic stance against the Palestinians. Jeff Halper, the Israeli anthropologist, describes the treatment of Arabs/Palestinians by Israel and how ethnocratic Israel is defined by its oppressive relationship with Palestinians. (*An Israeli in Palestine: Resisting Dispossession, Redeeming Israel*, paperback – 5 Jul 2010, by Jeff Halper.) Speaking of a personal experience of witnessing the demolition of his Palestinian friend's house, he wrote: *"As the bulldozer pushed through the walls of Salim's home, it pushed me through all the ideological rationalizations, the pretexts, the lies and the bullshit that my country had erected to prevent us from seeing the truth: that oppression must accompany an attempt to deny the existence and claims of another people in order to establish an ethnically pure state for yourself."* This experience made him a post-Zionist, which he neatly defines as *"a Zionist who has witnessed a house demolition."*

Indeed, there is an increasing amount of sympathy and empathy for the plight of Israeli Arabs/Palestinians amongst the Jews of Israel. Not so amongst some fundamentalist Evangelicals, particularly those of North America. They often behave and speak as if they are more Jewish than Jews. By their excessive zeal for Israel, some Evangelical leaders are making fools of themselves professing to be more Jewish than Jews, then having to waste precious time apologising for doing so. *"Pat Robertson is back in the news with another mean-spirited, cold-hearted pronouncement. This time the '700 Club' host declares that Israel's Prime Minister Ariel Sharon has had a stroke because God hates him for pulling Israel out of the Gaza Strip."* He later had to eat a humble pie, or rather eat his words and apologise for such excessive zeal. Should that energy and zeal not be invested in sharing the Gospel of Jesus Christ with the Jews and/or strengthening the hands of Christian Israel Arabs in God?!

Ultimately Israel's approach to solving its dilemma of fear of the next holocaust has been to establish a Jewish state to enable them to determine their own destiny. However, by cheating their way to ownership, by dispossessing Palestinians, by expelling them from their homeland, by condemning them to sixty years in refugee camps, Israel has simply created its next enemy from potentially one of its best allies.

What is the State of Israel? It is an island of Jews surrounded by Arab states, who will soon have the power to annihilate six or more million Jews with one blow. Is this what the Zionists have striven for? Is this the culmination of sixty odd years of atrocities? Has this been worth achieving? Has Israel made Jews feel more secure? Never in a million years.

Iran, more than likely, will soon possess a nuclear weapon, if it has not already done so. Pakistan, the hot seat of Muslim fundamentalism, already possesses the atomic bomb. It will only require a change of regime and Israel could be annihilated in one minute. In a volatile region such as the Indian subcontinent, a change of regime is not such an unlikely scenario.

In other words, if the *raison d'être* of Israel is to protect Jews, the Zionists have failed abysmally. All they have achieved is to move a few million Jews to a vulnerable crucible in the Middle East, where they are sitting ducks for an atom bomb to annihilate them anytime soon. And what is more disappointing is that the Zionists, through their brutality, injustice and rapacious appetite for land, have given Muslim fundamentalists the motive to use the atom bomb. Only fools should feel secure in Israel. The sooner Israel makes peace with its neighbours, the sooner it will feel secure. This is within the grasp of the Zionists, if only they can be cured of their greed and racism. All they have to do is acknowledge their misdeeds, apologize and make recompense. Peace will follow as surely as day follows night, though consequences of past misdeeds may still have to be borne.

Alas, apologizing is not part of the fabric of Zionism. Ayelet Shaked (Habayit Hayehudi), one of the most successful politicians in Israel at present, has recently stated: *"This election is between those who apologize and those who are proud"*. A columnist for *Haaretz* hit back at Zionist obstinance with the following rebuke:

"As a rule, in Israel people don't apologize for anything, not in the occupation nor on the road. Here only nerds apologize. Guilt feelings are an embarrassment, and apologizing is for those with no backbone. That's why Bennett's election slogan: 'Stop Apologizing. Be Proud' will become so catchy and popular: the 'apologizers' vs. 'the proud,' the 'objective ones' vs. 'lovers of the country.' I'm proud to belong to the former group.

"I would like to apologize, if that would be of any significance, to the entire Palestinian people, throughout the

generations. For 1948, for 1967 and for everything that happened in their wake. An apology for 1948 would not have made the state that was established less just – it would have become more just. For the mass expulsion and for preventing the return, for the ethnic cleansing in several districts and for several acts of slaughter, which may be part of every war – we can and should apologize.

"We can and should apologize for the fact that what happened in 1948 has never ended. That the spirit of 1948 has not passed, and continues to this very day in the State of Israel's basic attitude toward the Palestinian inhabitants of the land, in its sense of ownership and superiority, in its aggressiveness and violence, in its ultranationalism and racism.

"Nor has anything changed in the policy of dispossession: Take what you can – then as now, when the State of Israel is already a regional power. We should apologize for that. We should apologize for the innumerable dead killed for no reason, for the endless lies and deception. For tyranny in the territories and for apartheid. For trampling a nation's dignity, for suffocating its freedom and for separating it and breaking it up into tiny nations. For erasing its heritage and disdaining its culture. For short-changing Israeli Arabs and for demonstrations of racism against them. For the 'price tag' crimes and the Operation Protective Edge crimes. For all of them we should apologize." ("I love Israel – and I apologize; Apologizing would not solve anything or atone for anything, but it could signal a genuine intention to turn a new leaf." By Gideon Levy; *Haaretz*; 01.01.15)

If Israel cannot see the error of its ways, admit its mistakes and apologize for the past, then the victory of 1973 has been in vain. It remains arrogant, not proud, and more vulnerable than ever.

Chapter XI

Sabra and Shatila Massacre
16.09.1982

"Israeli forces enabled the entrance of the angry Kataeb Party group to the refugee camps, by providing them transportation from outside Beirut and firing illuminating flares over the camps."

In 1975 Lebanon was thrown into civil war, lasting several leading to utter devastation of the country. The PLO had been using South Lebanon as a base from which to launch assaults on Israel. The latter would retaliate and naturally inflict damage on the Lebanese population as much as on PLO positions.

Eventually, Israel invaded South Lebanon with a force of 60,000 troops. Through US intervention, Israel agreed to withdraw from Western Beirut and built an alliance with the Maronites. The leader of the Maronites, Bachir Gemayel, was killed in a massive explosion of his headquarters. The Israelis and Maronites blamed the PLO (though it transpired later that the PLO were innocent). Israel broke its promise to the USA and invaded West Beirut again. Her forces totally surrounded and sealed the Palestinian refugee camps, Sabra and Shatila. The allies agreed for Israel to provide cover (sealing the perimeter, ammunition and supplies), whilst the Maronite militia would eliminate PLO resistance from the camps.

In the event, whilst Israel provided the means, the Maronites massacred between 700-3500 innocent Palestinian women and children and, under the watchful gaze of Israeli forces.

The following account from Wikipedia gives a brief account of Israel's involvement in the massacre.

"For the next two nights, from nightfall until late into the night, people reported seeing illuminated flares above the camps, allegedly fired by the Israeli military.

"On the evening of September 16, 1982, the Phalangist militia, under the command of Elie Hobeika, entered the camps. For the next 36 to 48 hours, the Phalangists massacred the inhabitants of the refugee camps, while the Israeli military guarded the exits and allegedly continued to provide flares by night.

"A unit of 150 Phalangists (including some SLA fighters, according to Saad Haddad as quoted by Robert Fisk, and also other sources) was assembled at 4:00 p.m. These militiamen armed with guns, knives and hatchets entered the camps at 6:00 p.m. A Phalangist officer reported 300 killings, including civilians, to the Israeli command post at 8:00 p.m., and further reports of these killings followed through the night. Some of these reports were forwarded to the Israeli government in Jerusalem and were seen by a number of Israel's senior officials.

"At one point, a militiaman's radioed question to his commander Hobeika about what to do with the women and children in the refugee camp was overheard by an Israeli officer, who heard Hobeika reply that 'This is the last time you're going to ask me a question like that; you know exactly what to do'. Phalangist troops could be heard laughing in the background. The Israeli officer reported this to his superior General Amos Yaron, who warned Hobeika against hurting civilians but took no further action. Lt. Avi Grabowsky was cited by the Kahan Commission as having seen (on that Friday) the murder of five women and children, and gave a hearsay report of a battalion commander saying of this, 'We know, it's not to our liking, and don't interfere.' Israeli soldiers surrounding the camps turned back Palestinians fleeing the camps, as filmed by a Visnews cameraman.

"Later in the afternoon, a meeting was held between the Israeli Chief of Staff and the Phalangist staff. According to the

Kahan Commission's report (based on a Mossad agent's report), the Chief of Staff concluded that the Phalange should 'continue action, mopping up the empty camps south of Fakahani until tomorrow at 5:00 a.m., at which time they must stop their action due to American pressure.' He stated that he had 'no feeling that something irregular had occurred or was about to occur in the camps.' At this meeting, he also agreed to provide the militia with a tractor, supposedly to demolish buildings.

"On Friday, September 17, while the camps still were sealed off, a few independent observers managed to enter. Among them were a Norwegian journalist and diplomat Gunnar Flakstad, who observed Phalangists during their cleanup operations, removing dead bodies from destroyed houses in the Shatila camp.

"The Phalangists did not exit the camps at 5:00 a.m. on Saturday as ordered. They forced the remaining survivors to march out of the camps, randomly killing individuals, and sending others to the stadium for interrogations; this went on for the entire day. The militia finally left the camps at 8:00 a.m. on September 18. The first foreign journalists allowed into the camps at 9:00 a.m. found hundreds of bodies scattered about the camp, many of them mutilated. The first official news of the massacre was broadcast around noon."
(http://en.metapedia.org/wiki/Sabra_and_Shatila_massacre)

Eventually journalists had some access to the aftermath. Much of what had gone on had been concealed and evidence destroyed. However, what was left was shocking enough. Anyone looking at pictures of the eliminated victims would think they are in Auschwitz or Dachau! And the Israelis just stood and watched! This defies imagination.

There was a huge international verbal response to this massacre and anti-Israeli sentiments ran high in the media. There is no doubt that at best Israel knew what was going on, and at worst Israel supported, abetted and according to some witnesses participated in the massacre of women and children in Sabra and Shatila. And what was the USA's response? Hardly audible or palpable. And implicitly supportive of Israel.

"Israeli forces enabled the entrance of the angry Kataeb Party group to the refugee camps, by providing them transportation from outside Beirut and firing illuminating flares over the camps. The Phalangists stood under the direct command of Elie Hobeika, who later became a long-serving Member of Parliament and, in the 1990s, a cabinet minister." (http://www.princeton.edu/~achaney/tmve/wiki100k/docs/ Sabra_and_Shatila_massacre.html)

Much has been written and there have been some inquiries into Israel's culpability in this massacre. Even Sharon, at the time Israel's defence minister, was indicted in Belgium for his alleged war crimes against the victims of Sabra and Shatila. The Belgian court would also indict American President George Bush Senior. However, the mighty arm of the USA has dismantled the Belgian justice machine and the case has fizzled out into oblivion. This is politics. However, how about justice and fairness? Do not those innocent victims deserve some justice? I suppose they are just Palestinians, dispensable Arabs. Who gives a damn?!!! Isn't that the logical conclusion of what happened, or rather what had not happened? The USA has the moral obligation to pursue the truth of this massacre, and it has failed in its duty. Its failure is twofold, by virtue of its being a Christian country with a powerful Evangelical lobby and electorate. Whilst man may hide the truth and play dirty political games with the truth, God will judge all men one day and those players will have to give account before God. I wonder what defence they have prepared *"Can any hide himself in secret places that I shall not see him? saith the Lord. Do not I fill heaven and earth? saith the Lord."* (Jeremiah 23:24; King James Version)

And what of the Evangelical Zionists in the USA? What might one expect from them? Compassion? Love and some form of effort to aid the surviving relatives of the victims? Pigs might fly! The reaction of some Evangelicals was so uncharitable it makes one ashamed of sharing that adjective.

"Some evangelist leaders had enthusiastically supported Israel's wanton atrocities against the Palestinians, such as the Sabra and Shatila refugee camp as well as the Jenin Refugee

Camp massacre in the Spring of 2002 on the ground that such events ushered the near second coming of Jesus." (Pat Robertson: "Road Map" is a 'Satanic Plan'", Oct 4, 2004, 17:10, *Daily News*.)

Yet other Christians took a more enlightened and fair-minded approach, calling a spade a spade:

"However, the United Nations Human Rights Commission strongly condemned what it called 'Israel's responsibility for the large-scale massacre in the Sabra and Shatila refugee camps, which constituted an act of genocide.' The current Prime Minister of Israel was deemed to bear personal responsibility for the massacres by an official Israeli inquiry and under the IV Geneva Convention as the highest-ranking military officer in command, General Ariel Sharon, may be deemed guilty of war crimes." (Christopher J Davey, 9 February 2004, "The Israel-Palestine Conflict: reality and the demise of Evangelical Christianity".)

Chapter XII

The Dialogue of the Deaf

"He who has ears to hear, let him hear." (Mark 4:9)

What I enjoyed most about my university career in Scotland was the opportunity to share my intellectual and social life, and my dreams and aspirations, with so many young people. The most exciting parts were the extracurricular activities, particularly the ability to cross intellectual swords with students of other disciplines, virtually at any time. Someone once said: *"Blindness cuts you off from things; deafness cuts you off from people."* I believe most people would identify with this. Deafness can limit our ability to interact and share with others in a unique way. Though physical deafness is a tragedy for many ordinary people, for others there is a worse deafness with more serious consequences. Victor Hugo once said: *"What matters deafness of the ears, when the mind hears? The one true deafness, the incurable deafness, is that of the mind."*

As Jesus so often said, there are people who have ears, but they are not for hearing. The art of hearing, or better still actively listening, is fast disappearing from the Middle East. And there lies the secret of success of any prospective peace effort.

Whilst engaged in a debate at university, I found myself uttering one of the most cynical statements I have ever made. I said to my closest friend: *"Here on earth, there is no such thing as justice, just influence"*. What I meant was that though there are people genuinely interested in justice, ultimately those who win are not necessarily always those who are in the right, or those who have been wronged, but those who have most influence on a decision-making process, or those whom the jury and the judge, for better or for worse, favoured over the other side. Anyone who knows anything about corporate law knows that it is almost impossible to successfully sue giant multinational companies, because of the foreboding legal costs and the influence they can exert over the legal scene. Thus justice is only enjoyed by those with bank accounts fat enough for phenomenal legal fees. Some people are only interested in winning, not in justice, and therefore they have ears, but only to prop up their spectacles.

Human beings' capacity to do justice is inherently restricted, by our imperfect human condition, which other than lack of omniscience, includes corruption, collusion, conspiracy, cowardice, selfishness, greed and a host of other negative human traits. It is the equilibrium of these factors that determines the outcome of any case.

President Carter's book *Palestine, Peace Not Apartheid* has provoked angry reactions from American Jewry. In his response: *"As to where the Jewish community should go from here, Kleinberg, the Phoenix rabbi who organized a protest against Carter's book, said the community should realize that 'protest is a good thing to do.'*

"'We should recognize our power to influence,' he said." (*New Jersey Jewish Standard*: **"When words collide"** by Lois Goldrich, published Dec 21, 2006.)

The key word here is influence. Some Jewish reaction to Carter's book stemmed from having ears that do not hear. They are not interested in truth, just in winning, by any means. It is claimed by some Jews that Carter's book is full of errors and misleading statements unsupported by reliable evidence. Personally, I support President Carter. However, Carter is a Nobel Prize winner, well respected throughout the world for his peace effort, and he is an ex-President of the USA. This amounts to influence. The rabbi has to fight influence, not with truth, but with influence. Whether the rabbi's or the President's account wins, will largely depend on who possesses and exerts more influence.

This is no less true of the Arab-Israeli conflict. Up to recently, Israel has been allied to the most powerful and influential nations on Earth. This would explain why UN resolutions, passed over half a century ago, are still awaiting enforcement. Much to my disappointment as an Arab, I still see Palestinians, whose parents own land in Israel, grow up and survive in refugee camps in Lebanon and elsewhere. Why? Because the Jews have the right friends, friends with influence. This may be cynical, but it is also true. It is the reason why many more shocking acts of violence against whole nations, such as the Armenians, remain marginal. Millions of Armenians have been massacred by the Ottomans/Turks. Who cares?! Who knows about it?! Very few people. Why? Because Armenians have no friends who possess any influence.

As long as Israel is in the ascendancy, it has no vested interest in genuine dialogue. This is no reflection on the Jews, as much as on human nature. Had the shoe been on the other foot, I dare say the Palestinians would fare no better. Whilst Israelis may live in fear of Palestinian terrorism and suicide bombing, they have less to fear than Palestinians, who fear violence, poverty disease and deprivation. This is bound to affect the sense of urgency of each group for dialogue. The effect of poverty on the sense of urgency is well expressed in a paper on Canadian involvement in Arab-Israeli dialogues

"A third recommendation is that CFDD [Canada Fund for Dialogue and Development] must fully recognize that Israelis, Palestinians, and Jordanians have different interests in dialogue, and different stakes when participating in joint programs. For example, Israelis can generally dialogue without fear of retribution and are thus generally more interested in the social aspects of joint programs, i.e., getting to know the other.

"However, Palestinians are more interested in political change because of their more immediate problems, and thus they focus on trying to convince their Israeli counterparts to pressure the Israeli government. It is essential for CFDD to ensure that expectations of the joint programs are not presented unrealistically." ("Canadian Peacebuilding in the

Middle East: Case Study of the Canada Fund in Israel/Palestine and Jordan", Tami Amanda Jacoby, University of Alberta, Fall 2000.)

Notwithstanding, there has been no lack of dialogue between the two sides. But, has dialogue produced any positive outcomes? Dialogue has begotten more dialogue, which has begotten more dialogue. Why? Because this is the dialogue of the deaf.

"I spent a day at the Tantour Institute listening to a dialogue amongst Palestinians and Israelis. It reminded me of dialogues we have had ten and twenty years ago. We need to work harder to understand how to hear and communicate with each other." (Middle East Report. Allan Solomonow leads the Middle East Peace Education Program of the AFSC Pacific Mountain Region. Monday, December 21, 1998.)

Putting cynicism aside for one moment, some form of peace has been achieved. There is peace between Israel and Egypt. To the Palestinians, this means that they have lost the support of one nation, Egypt, in their fight for justice. Israel has lost an enemy and gained a non-hostile neighbour. The net effect is that the Palestinians have less influence.

What has characterised all the dialogues between Israel and its Arab neighbours is the tendency for each side to simply state their case and wait for the other side to shift. This is better known as the dialogue of the deaf and just about sums up the history of dialogue between the two parties.

In such a situation the best way to ensure a stalemate, a deadlock and lack of progress, is to take sides. When Evangelical Zionists side with Israel, whether she is right or wrong, they are simply maintaining the status quo of deafness. Some Western Evangelicals have developed a system of theology which revolves round a handful of verses from the Scriptures. They are adept at quoting these verses and even more skilful at reaching the wrong conclusion.

Central to the theology of Zionist Western Evangelicals is the Scripture which says: *"I will bless those who bless you, And I will curse him who curses you".* (NKJV Gen 12:3).

Evangelical Zionists think this verse justifies their bigotry against Arabs and their blind support for Israel. They quote the Scriptures but reach the wrong conclusion. This interpretation is simply tragic because it ignores the rest of God's Word.

The role of Evangelicals in the dialogue of the deaf should be this: *"Pursue peace with all people"* (NKJV Heb 12:14). *"All people"* actually includes Arabs.

Zionists, who enjoy the unconditional support of their Evangelical friends, have no incentive to seek genuine peace. The impact of Evangelical support for Israel is to deepen the deafness of both sides. The impact has been for both sides to be more deeply entrenched in their positions, which has made peace less feasible. Evangelical Zionist support for Israel has led to the burial of the possibilities for peace deeper into the morass of dialogue, so that future generations have to dig deeper for peace and have to unravel a lot more complex material to try and connect for peace.

On 21 December 1973 I recall being so elated when I watched TV news clips of the peace talks between the Jews and Arabs which took place in Switzerland. I, rather innocently, thought that before the day ended, a peace agreement was going to be concluded. At least that is how I perceived it at the age of fifteen. In my naiveté, I expected the two sides to pose in front of the cameras in order to sign a peace agreement that would put an end to Israeli-Arab enmity and wars.

This was the Geneva Peace conference. I recall watching live TV midday at my eldest brother's. I was too anxious for peace and got angry at the prologues and introductions. Then came Henry Kissinger. *"There is an Arab saying, Eli Fat Mat, which means that the past is dead. Let us overcome old myths with new hope. Let us make the Middle East worthy of the messages of hope and reconciliation that have been carried forward from its stark soil by three great religions. Today there is hope for the future, for the conflict is no longer looked upon entirely in terms of irreconcilable absolutes. The passionate ideologies of the past have, in part at least, been replaced by a recognition that all the peoples concerned have earned, by their sacrifice, a long period of peace."*

Henry Kissinger used a well-known Arabic rhyme, which literally means "the past is dead", which is a call for both sides to bury their hatchets and pursue peace. Those words were music to my ears. I kept asking my eldest brother, *"When will they sign the peace agreement?"* Eventually he answered cynically, *"Bilmishmish"* – a cynical expression meaning *"in t neverland"*. It soon dawned on me that the conference could go on for hours, if not days, and that the best we could hope for was words, which may or may not in a few years lead to another conference. I cannot convey today the sense of disappointment I felt on that day. I was so hungry for peace. I so wanted to feel at home with my Jewish neighbours. I was so tired of ostracization, alienation and discrimination. The constant war rhetoric chisels away at the inner parts of one's soul and leaves one broken, wounded and exhausted. I had thought that the Geneva peace conference was a time of healing. Alas, peace had to wait another day, nay another generation. I am in my sixth decade and I am still waiting for peace. Why? Because the past is still alive and kicking. Both Jews and Arabs cling to their share of the past in order to bolster their deeply entrenched positions. The result is the dialogue of the deaf. And what is the role of Evangelical Zionists in all of this? They side with Israel and deepen the deafness of both sides. The dialogue is doomed to failure, as most recent tragic events have shown.

The Israel Gaza Conflict (The Seven Weeks War)

A seven-year-old Israeli blockade on Gaza, allied with shutting the borders with Egypt, has meant that Gazans were hemmed in and besieged, unable to travel or trade. The consequences have been inadequate power and water supplies, with consequent poor health, unemployment and misery. The Gazans say this is what has led them to start the most recent rocket firing campaign against Israel commencing in June

2014. The only ceasefire worth their consideration is one that is predicated upon lifting or easing the siege, to allow Gazans to travel and trade.

Israel's counter-offensive has consisted of air raids upon Gaza, killing hundreds of innocent people, including helpless children. A Norwegian professor of Accident and Emergency Medicine volunteering in Shifa Hospital in Gaza described the outrage, then in the privacy of his room shed tears for the helpless young Palestinian victims whose lives were snuffed out by Israeli shelling. *"And as I write these words to you, alone, on a bed, my tears flow, the warm but useless tears of pain and grief, of anger and fear. This is not happening! And then, just now, the orchestra of the Israeli war-machine starts its gruesome symphony again, just now: salvos of artillery from the navy boats just down on the shores, the roaring F16, the sickening drones (Arabic 'Zennanis', the hummers), and the cluttering Apaches. So much made in and paid by the US."* (Mads Gilbert MD PhD, Professor and Clinical Head Clinic of Emergency Medicine, University Hospital of North Norway, July 20, 2014.)

The international outcry against indiscriminate Israeli bombing of Gazan civilians, has led Israel to risk its own soldiers' lives by sending a land mission to neutralise the underground military capability of the Gazans.

What undergirds all of this is a mentality of accusations and counter-accusations, attacks and counterattacks; a mentality of retribution, an eye for an eye and a tooth for a tooth.

By July 22, 2014 the war had claimed 630 Palestinian lives and 30 Israeli lives, mostly soldiers. This is excluding the 4000 injured in Gaza by Israeli strikes. (CNN News, Michael Pearson, Chelsea J Carter and Ian Lee, July 22, 2014.) In a bid to win over international public opinion, the IDF launched a propaganda campaign, including a constructed image of the British Houses of Parliament being subjected to missile fire. Reporting on this endeavour, the *Independent* quoted a twitter response reminding the IDF that the UK did not bomb Irish civilians when the IRA assaulted mainland Britain. (Adam Withnall, *Independent*, July 21, 2014).

Israeli newspapers, such as the *Haaretz*, reported on Palestinian rockets found in Gazan schools by UNRWA (Barak Ravid, July 22, 2014). This was welcome news for the politically besieged IDF, who have claimed that they had both warned Gazan civilians to abandon their homes, and provided safe areas with directions, so they can target the Hamas militants who use schools and Palestinian homes as shelters. An army colonel, Lerner, speaking on BBC radio, claimed that Hamas forced civilians to stay in their homes, despite these warnings from Israel. Palestinians claimed that due to Israeli indiscriminate strikes, nowhere in Gaza was safe. Once more, the two sides engaged in claims and counter-claims, reprisals and counter-reprisals. Each wished to be heard over and above the other. Each wished to take, and neither intended to give. Each claimed divine rights to own the world. The two sides behaved like anti-social school kids in a school playground, if it were not for the more desperately serious consequences.

Israel took great pains to demonstrate that they would not give in to the pressure from and fear of Hamas rockets killing their civilians, and refused to lift the seven-year-old siege against Gaza. On 22nd July 2014, and despite a crushing blow from the IDF by air, land and sea, the Gazan militants managed to land a rocket not far from the Ben Gurion airport. Anshel Pfeffer, writing in *Haaretz* asked whether this strike, which demonstrated that even primitive rockets used by Hamas can penetrate the much vaunted Israeli home-made Iron Dome anti-missile defence system, would bring Israel to accept Hamas' demands to lift the siege, which had starved Gazans of bare essentials for seven years. *"With a single rocket... Hamas might just have achieved what it failed to do with nearly 2000 rockets fired at Israel since the beginning of this round of warfare 15 days ago."* Fearful prospective visitors to Israel had been reassured by the IDF about the safety of flying to Ben Gurion airport by boasting about the effectiveness of the Iron Dome. My wife seriously considered not flying to Israel on 12th July, where I had been for one week with my children and where we were fairly close to a rocket landing in the vicinity of Nahariya. As I write this, and as many airlines cancel their flights from and to Ben Gurion, my daughter's flight back to London has been cancelled as a result of this strike on Tel Aviv. British Airways were the only non-Israeli airlines still flying to Ben Gurion. The psychological and public relations impact on Israel of such flight cancellations was immense. Would it not have been more sensible to have listened to the Palestinian pleas much earlier?! Sadly, one must remember, this is the dialogue of the deaf, where only aggression and force is heard.

On July 6, 2014, driving from Ben Gurion airport near Tel Aviv, to Kufur Yasief, my home town in Israel, I passed by the Arab town of Tamra. My family and I were perturbed by the sight of a heavy police and army presence at the Tamra junction. As we descended the hill leading to the familiar junction we first noted no fewer than twenty vehicles, military and police, parked on the roadside. Then came the demonstrators on the one side and the armed police and soldiers on the other. I had driven that route hundreds of times, and had never witnessed such scenes. When I reached home, I was told the people of Tamra were demonstrating against the barbaric burning alive of the Arab teenager Abu Khdeir, by vengeful Jews, seeking to avenge the death or killing of three Jewish teenagers.

The Israeli Gaza conflict was complicated by the apparent murder by Arabs of three Jewish settlers, teenagers Naftali Frenkel and Gilad Shaar, both 16, and Eyal Yifrach, 19 (Mail Online, June 30, 2014). The IDF set off explosives, destroying the homes of suspect Arabs, arresting six and killing one Arab boy. The IDF struck 34 targets in air raids against Gaza.

It was interesting to listen to expressions of mistrust by Israeli Arabs about the official version of events. There were suspicions that the bodies of the three Jewish boys were too well preserved for them to have been buried in a hot country under a pile of stones for over two weeks. Had they died in an accident? Had their accident been exploited in a cynical callous and calculating fashion by Israel to justify intensifying raids on Gaza? Rightly or wrongly, Israel blamed Hamas for the murder of the three Jewish teenagers. The snag is that Hamas is normally more than happy to own up and gloat. They did not, which has further aroused the suspicion of Israeli Arabs as to the cause of death of the three Jewish teenagers and the alleged involvement of Hamas.

Further suspicion was aroused when it was announced that Mohammad Abu Khdeir was burnt after he had been killed, later to be countered by medical evidence:

"Palestinian boy Mohammed Abu Khdeir was burned alive, says official. Mohammed al-A'wewy, attorney general for Palestine, makes claims as violence continues in West Bank and East Jeruslaem." (Peter Beaumont in Jerusalem, *Observer*, Saturday July 5, 2014.)

In July 2014, whilst on a visit to Acre, an ancient northern Israeli port town, where Jews and Arabs live side by side, we noticed how lifeless the shopping streets and the old Suk were. One Arab restaurant owner told us that Jews, who had dined in his restaurant for years, have simply boycotted the Arab part of town. *"They are punishing us for the killings of the three Jewish teenagers,"* he added.

Whilst being driven by taxi to a dental appointment in Upper Nazareth, a bus driver on my right signalled for me to wind down my window. I could read the angry expression on his face. The taxi driver advised me to ignore him. But I was curious and wound the window down only to be met by a torrent of racial abuse. My taxi driver told me that since the Israeli-Gaza conflict this abusive behaviour had become all too common.

During the 2014 Israeli-Gaza conflict, an Israeli Arab relative of mine, who is a taxi driver, took two weeks off, in fear he may be kidnapped by a militant Jew. He informed me that an Arab taxi driver had recently been imprisoned for kidnapping and killing a Jewish passenger.

Of course liberal Israeli Jews and Jews outside Israel have been critical of Israel's disproportionate military action against Gaza. Writing in the *Independent*, Mira Bar Hillel gave reasons why she was contemplating giving up her Israeli passport. She found the Israeli government's response to Gazan shelling of Israel disproportionate. She took issue with the right-wingers in Israeli politics, who seem to be unbridled and disinhibited. She further referred to expressions of Arab-hate by Israeli Jews: *"And, as the bombs rain on Gaza, Israeli teens have taken to tweeting scantily-clad selfies alongside their political sentiments. In two now deleted tweets, one wrote "Death to all of you Arabs you transfag", while another proclaimed "Arabs may you be paralyzed & die with great suffering!" Another teen simply tweeted "Death to these f****** Arabs", and attached a photo of themselves pouting alongside it.*

Seeing these angelic faces of evil spouting such genocidal rhetoric, I pick up my Israeli passport and a box of matches. 'Not in my name, people. Not in my name!'".

("Why I'm on the brink of burning my Israeli passport, I can no longer stand by while Israeli politicians like Ayelet Shaked condone the deaths of innocent Palestinian women and children", *Independent*, 11 July 2014.)

Time to Listen

As an Arab I could confidently state that as long as Israel refuses to contemplate the right of Palestinians to return to their homes in what is now Israel, the citizens of Israel will have no peace. In acting deaf to Palestinian demands for self-determination, and in refusing to contemplate this imperative component of the Arab conditions for peace, Israel has opened itself to accusations of being no better than the Nazis.

"It is appropriate to emphasize that the right of self-determination is designed to liberate and not to enslave. Alleged claims to the right of self-determination which are, however well-disguised, a technique of denying self-determination to others are inconsistent with the United Nations Charter and must be recognized as immoral and illegal. In addition, the United Nations and its member states must take appropriate enforcement measures to ensure that the

non-discriminatory provisions of Article 55 of the Charter are observed in practice. A pre-eminent example of this kind of discriminatory law which violates the Charter is the Israeli Law of Return. Under its terms, a member of 'the Jewish people' as defined in Zionist public law who is born anywhere in the world has a right to immigrate to Israel and to become an instant Israeli citizen upon arrival. Neither this law nor any other Israeli law grants the right to return to a Palestinian Muslim or Christian who is born in the country and is now living in exile, or to the child of such a person. The meaning of the Law of Return, and particularly the Zionist juridical meanings of the term 'Jew' and 'the Jewish people,' has become one of the most important subjects of litigation in the Israeli courts.

"The Zionists regard this type of litigation as necessary to maintain the 'Jewish' characteristics, that is the discriminatory and segregationist features, of the State of Israel. In contrast, Jews recall that Nazi Germany used analogous juridical criteria involving the tracing of ancestry of individuals in ascertaining 'German' and 'Aryan' identification." ("The Role Of International Law In Achieving Justice and Peace In Palestine-Israel", by W. T. Mallison, Jr., and S. V. Mallison; Presented at the Conference on "Human Rights in Palestine" Of the World Conference of Christians for Palestine, Geneva, Switzerland, January 11-14, 1974.)

My family know the pain of separation from loved ones. The establishment of the State of Israel has ripped asunder my family as it has done virtually every Palestinian family. Two of my uncles were trapped in Lebanon and lost their homes in the new State of Israel. I still to date recall my dear father's tears at the death of one of my uncles in Lebanon. Uncle Haleem had been the local headmaster for many years. He was well liked and respected in North Palestine. When the State of Israel was formed, he was on holiday in Lebanon. He was unable to return home due to fears of violence at the hands of the Zionists. And when he did attempt to return to Palestine, the Zionist State forbade him and confiscated his property.

It was painful enough that my father and his brother had been separated for over twenty years. Not to be able to say farewell was too much for my father to bear. My father, a strong character, a man's man, and a man of faith, buckled under this emotional strain and locked himself up for three days and three nights only appearing occasionally and briefly. So great was his grief that he could be heard sobbing and wailing from behind the thick wooden door to his study. That memory is so vivid it still chokes me up and brings tears to my eyes even today. Yet all that time any Jew anywhere in the world, whose only link to Palestine is the claim that his forebears lived in Palestine some two millennia ago, could immigrate to Israel and live anywhere he or she choose to live. My uncles who were born in the land of Palestine and who had built their own homes in Palestine, had no right to return to their families or homes. As long as Zionists are deaf to such Palestinian cries for justice, they will not achieve peace, not because of Palestinian revenge, but because God who is a God of justice, will not give them peace.

Meantime Israel pursues the return of so-called Jewish wealth from Swiss banks and continues to receive compensation from Germany. Why does Israel expect justice from the world, when it is not prepared to act justly towards the Palestinians? The dialogue of the deaf is here to stay as long as Israel is not prepared to deal with these injustices, and as long as its Evangelical Zionist friends pat it on the back as if Israel had not shirked any moral responsibility or breached any moral code.

Chapter XIII

Power Versus Peace

*"The pursuit of peace involves making a sacrifice to the other.
The pursuit of power involves making a sacrifice of the other"*
An Israeli Christian Arab

*"When the power of love overcomes the love of power the
world will know peace."*
Jimi Hendrix

When I was a child, I recall that the walls of my classrooms
were always decorated with a selection of wise sayings or
proverbs. One that stands out to date is *"The Jew is a brother
to the Arab"*. Of course this is historically true as both Jews
and Arabised Arabs are descendants of Abraham, and Eber is
the father of both true Arabs and the forebears of Abraham.
However, fraternal love is very thin on the ground in the
Middle East, and that saying is no more true now than it was
some sixty years ago. It behoves one to ask why is there no
love lost between Jews and Arabs today. The answer is
probably to be found at the beginning of human history. Why
did Cain kill Abel? Selfishness, and the love for domination
and the need to control.

The conflicts of the Middle East can be summarised with a
few words, the love of power, or perhaps more precisely the
perceived need for power. Both Arabs and Jews have sought to
dominate and exercise power over the other. The only
difference between the two sides is that, for whatever reason,
in the twentieth and twenty-first centuries the Jews have been
better at it. But it is this pursuit of power that has dashed the

hopes of many in the Middle East for peace. Both Jews and Muslim Arabs also feel empowered by heaven itself. They both have a system of theology that elevates them above the rest of humanity and entitles them to dispossess others, to rape and claim as theirs what is someone else's property. They both have an overdeveloped sense of superiority and entitlement. They both believe they have the power of God to carry out their greedy designs, which they both attribute to the will of God.

The Double Whammy of a Sense of Superiority and Entitlement

Whilst queuing in the departure lounge of Terminal 3 in Ben Gurion airport, waiting to board the plane to London on 20.07.2014, I could not help noting the discourtesy of some Israelis, who jumped up the queue with complete alacrity and non-compunction. They did it so brazenly, as if it were the normal and decent thing to do. One Hassidic chap slickly inserted himself just in front of my wife. I asked him to kindly do what all decent people do and go back to the tail end of the queue. This passed uneventfully, except he actually simply stood behind us, thus encroaching on the rest of the queue behind us.

Then came another chap wearing a kippa. He slyly stood next to us, waiting for a chink in the tightly-packed queue. As he slowly drifted in front of us, I asked him to please have the decency to queue like all decent people. He apologised claiming he did not jump up the queue intentionally. Then he continued and said, *"There are more important things to worry about right now,"* referring to the Israeli Gaza conflict. I advised him, *"but this is how it all starts; taking people and their rights for granted; having a huge sense of entitlement that over-rides other people's rights."* He sarcastically thanked me *"for the lecture"*, to which, I told him, he was welcome. It is true, however, that major principles are often more clearly and more easily breached in minor day-to-day transactions.

The same underlying attitude and belief in self-aggrandisement and superiority, leads one to violate other people's right of priority in a queue as that which leads them to build on someone else's land, which is essentially what the Israeli-Gaza conflict was all about.

Orthodox Judaism declares Jews to be superior to *"Carrion eaters"* as Gentiles are often called. This haughty stance is reflected very clearly in Rabbi Avraham Yitzhak HaCohen Kook's words (1865-1935):

"The difference between the Jewish soul... and the soul of all the Gentiles... is greater and deeper than the difference between the soul of a man and the soul of an animal."

There is a popular perception that the Hebrew term goyim is a derogatory Hassidic name for Gentiles meaning cattle. In fact the word literally means nations. However, it is Orthodox Hassidic Jews who have given this sense to the term goyim:

"On the house of the Goy one looks as on the fold of cattle." (Tosefta, Tractate Erubin VIII.)

They also believe in the right to possess anything Gentiles own, otherwise known in most civilised societies as stealing.

"When a Jew has a Gentile in his clutches, another Jew may go to the same Gentile, lend him money and in turn deceive him, so that the Gentile shall be ruined. For the property of a Gentile, according to our law, belongs to no one, and the first Jew that passes has full right to seize it." (Schulchan Aruch, Choszen Hamiszpat 156.)

Nor is this an isolated opinion.

"That the Jewish nation is the only nation selected by God, while all the remaining ones are contemptible and hateful.

"That all property of other nations belongs to the Jewish nation, which consequently is entitled to seize upon it without any scruples. An orthodox Jew is not bound to observe principles of morality towards people of other tribes. He may act contrary to morality, if profitable to himself or to Jews in general.

"A Jew may rob a Goy, he may cheat him over a bill, which should not be perceived by him, otherwise the name of

God would become dishonoured. " (Schulchan Aruch, Choszen Hamiszpat, 348).

The legalisation of stealing, under a religious guise, is the natural foul excrement of self-aggrandisement, entitlement and superiority.

These beliefs are embarrassing to many right-thinking Jews. Even Hassidic Jews are aware of the repercussions that may result from such racist bigoted views of Gentiles. *"To communicate anything to a Goy about our religious relations would be equal to the killing of all Jews, for if the Goyim knew what we teach about them, they would kill us openly."* (Libbre David 37.)

This unbridled arrogance is to be contrasted with the sermon delivered by Moses, in Moab (part of TransJordan) before the people of Israel went into Canaan. These words are pre-emptive, designed to nip any sense of self-importance in the bud.

"Do not think in your heart, after the Lord your God has cast them out before you, saying, 'Because of my righteousness the Lord has brought me in to possess this land'; but it is because of the wickedness of these nations that the Lord is driving them out from before you. It is not because of your righteousness or the uprightness of your heart that you go in to possess their land, but because of the wickedness of these nations that the Lord your God drives them out from before you, and that He may fulfill the word which the Lord swore to your fathers, to Abraham, Isaac, and Jacob. Therefore understand that the Lord your God is not giving you this good land to possess because of your righteousness, for you are a stiff-necked people.

"Remember! Do not forget how you provoked the Lord your God to wrath in the wilderness. From the day that you departed from the land of Egypt until you came to this place, you have been rebellious against the Lord." (Deuteronomy 9:4-7)

No human being is inherently better than or superior to another, for as one of the greatest Jewish theologians put it to the Church in Rome, *"all have sinned and fall short of the glory of God"* (Romans 3:23). Therefore the Talmudic Rabbis have missed the point of being a "chosen people".

Of course the Pact of Omar, which the extremist Muslim ISIS is implementing in Iraq and Syria – albeit they are exceeding its tenets – is in the same mould as the Jewish Talmud. It is based on the principle that Muslims are superior to non-Muslims (see Pact of Omar, chapter IV). Once that sense of superiority is accepted, the seed is sown of rapacious actions against non-Muslims. ISIS's behaviour is a natural development of the principles of the Pact of Omar, and the actions taken by Muhammad against the Christians of Najran, the pre-Islamic tradition of protection money or Jizya, are the very template that Abu Bakr Al-Baghdadi has copied and imposed on the Christians of Syria and Iraq.

The Christian Arab is caught in the middle. Christ came neither to build an earthly kingdom nor to conquer. He had neither wealth nor wished to be rich in this world. He was more interested in people than property, more concerned for souls than silver. He had no wives, no concubines, and no slaves. He came to serve and not to be served. He had no army and organised no military campaigns. He had *"emptied Himself, taking the form of a bond-servant, and being made in the likeness of men"* (Philippians 2:7 NASB). He taught that all people are the same in the eyes of God. Christ re-iterated the ten commandments thus: *"The second is this: 'You shall love your neighbor as yourself.' There is no other commandment greater than these."* (Mark 12:31 ESV). The ethos of Hassidic superiority, which entitles Jews to take Gentile possessions, the ethos of Islam expressed in the Pact of Omar, which declares that Muslims have more rights than non-Muslims, contradict the second commandment of the laws of Moses. One cannot love one's neighbour as one's self and declare them inferior, or take their possessions or enslave them! Christianity has no framework for ethnic or religious superiority.

The words of Paul still echo in the churches of the Middle East today: *"There is neither Jew nor Greek, there is neither bond nor free, there is neither male nor female: for you are all one in Christ Jesus.*" (Galatians 3:28 King James Bible 2000.) As for the derogatory term used by Hassidic Jews to describe Gentiles, namely *"carrion eaters"*, the apostle Peter, a Jew by birth and upbringing, had an interesting vision in which he *"saw the heavens opened and something like a great sheet descending, being let down by its four corners upon the earth. In it were all kinds of animals and reptiles and birds of the air. And there came a voice to him: 'Rise, Peter; kill and eat.'"* (Acts 10:11-13.) Peter, a devout Jew, could not encounter eating *"carrion"* or unclean meats. But in the vision, he was instructed to break the mould and eat *"unclean"* meat. And as Peter testified in the House of Cornelius, a Roman centurion of what was known as the Italian Cohort at the great port city of Caesarea, *"Truly I understand that God shows no partiality,"* which is why Peter had no compunction about having fellowship with a Gentile. He learnt from that vision, that in the eyes of God we are all equal. In Christ no individual is superior in rights or entitlement.

In the light of the recent events in the Middle East leading to further departure of Middle Eastern Christians, that moderating presence of non-superior and non-entitled Christians will wane, probably leading to a greater conflict between Muslims and Hassidic Jews. Is that why the West has failed to act to help stem the tide of persecution upon the Christians of the Middle East? Does the West wish Muslim Arabs to self-destruct, leaving their oil supplies to an energy-greedy West?! Perhaps they have simply abdicated their fraternal responsibility towards their Middle Eastern Christian brethren.

Time to Choose

Most of the time life presents us with two choices. When we find it difficult to make a choice we either try to choose two opposites at the same time, or alternatively kid ourselves that there is a third choice, even when it is blatantly obvious that no third choice exists.

Anti-Semitism of any kind is just another subspecies of racism, which simply dismisses a human being because of their race. It expresses itself by exercising power over the object of hatred, by trying to control and manipulate. The only antidote to racism is love, without which all pursuits of peace are rendered futile. In a world riven by racism and sectarianism, the only effective remedy is love. This has to be distinguished from favouritism. Evangelical Zionists do not practice love towards Israel. They practice favouritism, which always turns a blind eye to Zionist wrong doings. By contrast, love dictates that the lover corrects the person they love. This involves causing hurt. Solomon, in his wisdom acknowledged this inevitable unintended consequence of friendship by saying: *"Faithful are the wounds of a friend"* (Proverbs 27:6)

The Middle East only has two options: power or peace. The divisions in this world are only superficially racial. Deep inside, the difference is to do with the condition of the soul and the heart of man. Our world is divided between the power-taker and the peace-maker.

Power seeks to dominate, peace seeks to illuminate. Power seeks superiority, whilst peace seeks equality. Power stems from fear and breeds terror and chaos, whilst peace stems from love and leads to harmony. Power creates winners and losers, peace creates winners upon winners. Power creates slaves and masters, whilst peace creates friends and brothers. Power expresses itself at the expense of others whilst peace is the fruit of self-sacrifice. Power puts itself first, and peace puts itself last. Power crushes and destroys, whilst peace nourishes and builds bridges. If power is a destructive deluge, peace is a reviving river. Peace is warm sunshine. Power is a furnace.

"Where love rules, there is no will to power; and where power predominates, there love is lacking. The one is the shadow of the other." (Carl Jung).

"Whom the gods would destroy, they first make mad with power." (Charles A. Beard).

The pursuit of peace involves making a sacrifice to the other. The pursuit of power involves making a sacrifice of the other. Whilst peace pacifies, power provokes, punishes and pillages. It is the attitude of those who are power-crazed that leads them to racism. They are unable to give, give up or give in. They can only take, take away, take advantage, and takeover, and do so unjustly and avariciously. Those who seek power are incapable of making peace, because they can only take and never give. They only feel secure when they are in control. In vain do they crave after a peaceful existence! Yet peace remains something they crave. But they can never attain it, because of their lust for power.

One of my favourite Jewish cousins, Paul the Apostle, once advised a young Jewish Christian thus: *"pursue righteousness, faith, love and peace"* (2 Timothy 2:22).

Faith, love and peace are a common trinity in Christian thinking, as they are very similar, almost amounting to the same thing. Applied to the Arab-Israeli situation, it could be said that those who desire power as opposed to peace have no faith in the power of God to do justly or to provide for them. They must take things into their own hands and will never compromise. Sadly both Muslims and Jews make much of the greatness of God and His mercy. Yet in their politics, they show lack of faith in divine providence, which they substitute with power, force and violence.

"Power concedes nothing without a demand. It never did and it never will." (Frederick Douglass).

Evangelical Zionists are less likely to fulfil the Scriptures which say *"pursue faith love and peace",* and more likely to fulfil Frederick Douglass's description of power.

In as far as power is both corrupt and corrupting, those who seek it become putrid with evil and commit more evil to conceal their bad odour. This is what happened in Sabra and Shatila. By contrast, peace is open and unconcealed. It works its magic quietly, patiently but openly. Though the impact of power is forceful, the impact of peace is powerful.

"The arts of power and its minions are the same in all countries and in all ages. It marks its victim; denounces it; and excites the public odium and the public hatred, to conceal its own abuses and encroachments." (Henry Clay, 1834).

Zionists did just that, claiming there is no such thing as a Palestinian nation and spreading a negative image of the Palestinians as backward savages, and ruthless brutes, whilst Zionist actions fitted that description more aptly. The Africans, often considered inferior to other races, have taught the world a remarkable lesson, namely "Truth and reconciliation". They deserve the utmost respect from the so called civilised world. One cannot reconcile two sides without the truth being told. Power-lust is antithetical to the truth. Evangelical Zionists ought to take a leaf out of the African Church's book.

Peace and power are the two great contenders for the throne of the human heart, and the main protagonists of the Middle East are no exception. It is for man to give peace a chance and to incarcerate power in a dungeon deep enough to render it harmless. Only when the love of power is so boldly dashed can there be hope for peace.

"When the power of love overcomes the love of power the world will know peace." (Jimi Hendrix).

Before He was taken to the cross, when He was arrested, when He was accused, when He was forced to bear the cross through Jerusalem and He was nailed to the cross, Jesus had the power to fight back, to stop all this. However, Jesus, the Son of the Most High God, chose to conduct Himself like a lamb being taken to slaughter. He pursued peace, even when His own life was at stake. This is the sort of contribution that Evangelical Zionists ought to bring to the Middle East conflict, the pursuit of peace. Instead they have been encouraging Israel to seek power over her Arab neighbours.

Chapter XIV

A Plea from the Heart

"Let not the birthplace of Christ be the burial ground for Palestinian Christianity."

"For mine enemies speak against me; and they that lay wait for my soul take counsel together, Saying, God hath forsaken him: persecute and take him; for there is none to deliver him. O God, be not far from me: O my God, make haste for my help." (Ps 71:10-12)

The journey of this book started with depiction, went onto remonstration and finally it will end with an imploration. At the beginning of this book, I depicted what had been done to Arabic-speaking Christians, by Jews and Muslims. In the middle of this book, I remonstrated with my Semite cousins and the Western world about their acts of commission and omission with regards to the persecution of Arabic-speaking Christians. In this chapter, I wish to make a plea, hoping to appeal to the reader's sense of fairness and brotherhood. The former should bind all humanity. The latter should certainly bind all the children of Shem.

It is hoped that, though this book may have perturbed some readers, it would have at least lifted the lid on the hitherto concealed suffering of the Arabic-speaking Christians. If this book caries a message, it is hoped that the message has become clear; it is this: The Arabic-speaking Christians of the Middle East, the descendants of Shem, have been downtrodden for too long. They have been dispossessed, despised, persecuted, intimidated, raped, subjected to extortion, denied basic human rights and sacrificed like cheap cattle. This is the other anti-Semitism, the anti-Semitism that few have noticed, recognised or attempted to address.

In the heat of the Middle East conflict, the Arabic-speaking Christians have been victimised by three groups: The Evangelical Zionists, Muslims, and Jewish Zionists. The irony is that the Arabic-speaking Christians uniquely share common ground, blood and faith, with all of those three groups. It is mainly to these groups that the author addresses this plea from the heart.

To The Christians

I am using the term Christian in the wider sense of the word. For instance, the majority of British citizens may be glad to call themselves Christian, though they may never see the inside of a church. The fact is that the genotype of the West remains Christian, though its phenotype is fast changing and becoming less Christian as the genotype wanes and loses its penetrance. Perhaps I have given some readers cause to reflect on their Christian heritage. If you do not want a Christian West, what do you want? What is the most viable desirable alternative to Christianity in the West?

I hope by now, Christian readers have developed a closer sense of identity with Arabic-speaking Christians. This is the first step towards corrective action, and by that I definitely do not mean military action. There is no Jihad in Christianity. The author is not calling for the ancient Crusades to be revived. Without wishing to enter into interminable arguments about the crusades, they differ from Jihad in that one is offensive whilst the other is defensive. One, Jihad, is theologically justifiable, the crusades were politically based.

By encouraging this sense of identity with Arabic-speaking Christians, the author hopes that the manner in which the West has been dealing with the plight of the Arabic-speaking Christians, would be radically altered. Douglas Alexander, a senior opposition frontbencher writing in the *Daily Telegraph*, states that the *"mounting persecution of Christians is a "story that goes largely untold"* ("Labour: We must 'do God' to fight anti-Christian persecution", Edward Malnick 21 Dec 2013). Hopefully *The Other Anti-Semitism* has encouraged the reader to ensure that the story is told and that demands are made to put an end to the suffering of Christians, at the hands of Muslims, in the Middle East.

The Muslim Arab view and their treatment of Arabic-speaking Christians has closely paralleled the Muslim view of the West, which to most Muslims is synonymous with Christendom. During the colonial age, when the Middle East was governed by Christian nations such as the British and the French, Muslims looked upon Christians with respect, admiration and a degree of envy. Muslim Arabs would emulate Christians. However, the congruity of the West and Christianity began to abate. The West began to divest itself of its Christian heritage. Left-wing politics, a weak church, a culture of self-blame and self-hate began to gather strength and reached a pitch whereby it became fashionable to blame all the woes of the world on the West's Christian past. In the UK Victorian values became synonymous with child abuse and exploitation, unfairness and all that is evil in any society.

A West that has gradually de-Christianised itself is a West that is morally impoverished. The sexual revolution, secularism, the obsession with minority rights, to the point of unfairness towards the majority, have both made the West look weak and morally bankrupt; nay, corrupt and wanton. Muslim reaction was almost predictable. The image of the West was one of profligacy, sexual immorality and general moral anaemia. This view, coupled with the questionable political adventures of the post-Christian West, made the West look both feeble and repulsive. Since West still equalled Christian, Muslim fundamentalists who sought to fight against the West struck at the nearest Christian target, namely their Christian neighbours, fellow citizens and kinsmen.

As a Muslim friend once put it to me, the West is like a prostitute lying prostrate and naked, screaming *"Take me, take me"*. The simile may be vulgar, but the situation is sufficiently desperate to warrant a frank depiction. Muslim fundamentalists have responded to this open invitation by flooding the West, exploiting its liberal laws, whilst meantime they have tyrannized Christians in their midst.

Raymond Ibrahim, in his excellent book *Crucified Again*, asked: *"And where did Muslims learn to despise the West?"* The answer comes succinctly: *"The same place they had originally learned to respect the West – from the West itself."*

By contrast, the West is both afraid to criticise Islamic violence and keen to appease Muslims by promoting a manufactured image of peaceful Islam. Self-effacing Christendom which has abandoned its faith, and followed hedonism and licentiousness, cowering before an increasingly belligerent Islam, whose followers despise and abuse Christians, amounts to where we are now.

"Far from appeasing angry Muslims, such self-loathing and sycophantic behaviour has prompted even more revulsion to Western culture in the Islamic world." (Raymond Ibrahim, *Crucified Again*, p.17). The 6th and 7th of January 2015 provided prime examples of the striking contrast between the tolerant, indeed overly tolerant West which has generously given home to millions of Muslims wither fleeing Muslim persecution or seeking a new life in the west, and the intolerance of Muslim fundamentalists living in Europe.

A new movement in Germany called PEGIDA, seems to have caught the public imagination. According to *Deutsche Welle*, *"Patriotische Europäer gegen die Islamisierung des Abendlandes" ('Patriotic Europeans Against the Islamization of the West': PEGIDA) is a German political movement based in Dresden. Founded by Lutz Bachmann, it has been setting up public demonstrations since October 2014, warning of the islamisation of Europe."* (*Deutsche Welle*, 07.01.2015)

BBC Radio 4 "Thought for the Day" contributor, Bishop Baines rushed to stem any Islamophobia by saying that he knew many Muslim people who were decent and not violent. But he also stated that not all PEGIDA members, who are dramatically increasing in number, are *"neo-Nazis"*. Cologne is one of the cities to have seen growing protests against what is called the *"Islamisation of the West"*. What began as a small demonstration by a couple of hundred from the East German right wing has grown into marches of up to 18,000 people. And the majority of these people cannot be brushed off as *"wild neo-Nazis"* (BBC Radio 4, Thought for the Day - 07/01/2015 - Rt Rev Nick Baines). The good Bishop warned against generalisations. It cannot be that all Muslims are violent. Of course not. But there is plenty of Muslim violence in Europe, and it is hardly being challenged. The Bishop then referred to the Bible for examples of *"dreadful brutality and fear of those who are different"*. However, it was not clear whether he was referring to fear of Islamic violence and imposition of Muslim values on a Christian West, or whether it was fear by Muslims of being persecuted. The *Telegraph* report on the protests made it clear that *"The new protests, which began in the city of Dresden in the former East Germany, feature no neo-Nazi slogans and have nothing to do with the traditional far right"* ("Germans take to the streets to protest against 'Islamisation'" By Justin Huggler, Berlin, *Daily Telegraph*; 08 Dec 2014.) They simply want to preserve the Judeo-Christian culture of their country.

Angela Merkel is noted for her opposition to David Cameron's attempts to curtail freedom of movement within the EU. However, *"the German debate over immigration has focused on those coming from outside the bloc, and on Muslims in particular"*.

Those fearful of dealing with this political hot potatoes are keen to besmirch PEGIDA. The German political establishment rushed to ward off any accusations of German neo-Nazism. *"Political leaders in Germany, including President Joachim Gauck and Chancellor Angela Merkel, cautioned that PEGIDA protests represent xenophobia and racism"* (*DW*). *Deutsche Welle* compared PEGIDA with the British EDL, but added that the *"English Defence League (EDL)... is not as avowedly anti-violence as PEGIDA"*. However, *"Demonstrations against Muslim immigration in Cologne earlier this year turned violent, but unlike the far-*

right groups and self-proclaimed 'hooligans' behind those protests, PEGIDA insists its movement is peaceful."

In Cologne, the demonstrations triggered a lights out in the Cathedral. *"We don't think of it as a protest, but we would like to make the many conservative Christians [who support Pegida] think about what they are doing,"* the Dean of the Cathedral, Norbert Feldhoff, told the BBC ("Rallies over 'Islamisation'", BBC News, 6 January 2015.)

Nor is PEGIDA in isolation. The CSU in Bavaria had to deal with a proposal that *"Whoever wants to live here permanently should be encouraged to speak German in public and within the family"*, the reaction from our politicians was to condemn violence and warn against islamophobia!!!Is that the most appropriate reaction to the current situation in Europe?!

Ironically, on 06.01.2015, Islamist terrorists stormed into the satirical newspaper *Charlie Hebdo* in Paris, having killed the policeman guarding the headquarters, and killed 12 members of staff and injured 11. The perpetrators fired *"on staff after seeking out journalists by name in France's deadliest post-war terrorist attack... Clad all in black with hoods and speaking flawless French, the militants forced one of the cartoonists – who was at the office with her young daughter – to open the door. Witnesses said the gunmen were heard shouting 'we are from the Al Qaeda in Yemen', 'the Prophet has been avenged' and 'Allahu akbar!' – Arabic for 'God is great' – as they stalked the building."* (*Daily Mail*; by Simon Tomlinson and Peter Allen and Jay Akbarand Chris Pleasance for MailOnline, 7 January 2015.)

Charlie Hebdo had taken a stand against previous Islamist threats and decided to defend their freedom of speech against Islamic terror. Whilst admiring their stance, one has to question the civility of mocking a religion. True liberty cannot be unbounded. What is to be achieved by mocking something sacred to fellow citizens. Honest disagreement is one thing. But mockery of a religion is another. The freedom to express an honest difference in opinion is not in the same league as the freedom to mock another man's religion. Perhaps it is a symptom of how far we have become irreligious in the West. Freedom to mock religion is a mockery of freedom. However, nothing justifies the murder in cold blood that was committed in the name of Islam on that day in Paris. This sort of barbaric behaviour does not befit a European citizen.

Recognising the rise of Muslim Fundamentalism in Europe, *"Jacques Myard, French MP with opposition party UMP, said: 'We knew something would happen. The (security) services used to say to us it's not if but when and where. We know that we are at war. The Western nations – like Britain, France, Germany – we are at war.'"* (*Daily Mail.*)

What is striking is the alacrity of Western politicians to ward off "islamophobia" when the main problem is actually Islamic terror in Europe, by European Muslims. One must also decry the paucity of Muslim voices condemning the Paris massacre. Notwithstanding, Mr Talha Ahmad, speaking on behalf of the Muslim Council of Britain, speaking on Sky News 07.01.2015, said he was *"appalled and sickened by these barbaric and heinous acts"*. Although he expressed fear of rising Islamophobia, he added that the primary concern and *"focus should be with the families (of the bereaved)"*.

Professor Sean Hand of Warwick University pointed out that *Charlie Hebdo* had lampooned the Catholic Church for years. They have recently lampooned the Jewish Shoah, a very sensitive subject. Yet neither the Catholics nor the Jews have threatened or carried out any acts of violence against the satirists. In Judeo-Christian Europe, we do not silence people because they express ideas unacceptable to some people. If Muslims want to live in Europe, if they want equality, the least they can do as newcomers to a Judeo-Christian region is to respect that freedom of expression is the norm. They must abandon their violent ways and learn to engage in dialogue in order to express their views.

Perhaps the Norwegian Prime Minister has an answer for Muslim violence in the West. Erna Solberg commenced a programme of deportation of Muslims with terrorist association. *"Norway's government has ruled that 7,100 people will be deported in 2014. At the end of October, PU had deported 5,876 people so far this year.* ("Political Ears", November 15, 2014.) Why have not more Western governments used deportations of violent elements more widely?!

Therefore to the Christians of the West my plea is this: Love your own people first and evangelise them. Help your fellow citizens rediscover their Christian heritage. Do not throw away your Christian heritage. Do not commit spiritual adultery with Islam, by cowering and failing to stand up for your belief in your own house. Some Muslims are not afraid of expressing their repulsion for anything Christian. Why should you not be equally honest and bold with Muslims, *"speaking the truth in love"*? And indeed with Zionists.

Mr Eric Pickles, Communities Secretary, called on Muslims to do more to stem the rising tide of extremism amongst British Muslims. Predictably, he was criticised by spineless compromisers, and some Muslims leaders. However, David Cameron stood by him *"David Cameron has hit out at criticism of a letter sent to Muslim leaders by Eric Pickles in the wake of the Paris attacks, saying anyone opposing it "really has a problem"* (David Cameron says anyone criticising Eric Pickles' letter to Muslims 'really has a problem', Lizzie Dearden The Independent, Monday 19 January 2015). What is astonishing though is the vacuous claim that Islam is a religion of peace, repeatedly claimed by Muslim and non-Muslim leaders alike. Criticising the Muslim perpetrators of the Charlie Hebdo atrocity, Mr Javid, tipped to be the next leader of the conservatives, married to a Christian, claimed *"It is no good for people to say they are not Muslims, that is what they call themselves. They do try to take what is a great peaceful religion and warp it for their own means"* (The Telegraph, By Steven Swinford, Senior Political Correspondent 12 Jan 2015). When both Muhammad and his Caliphs wielded the sword in order to spread Islam, when the entire Christian Middle East was forced to Islamise by Muhammad and his successors, when for centuries after,

Muslims persecuted Christians and non-Muslims in general, when most of the violence today is perpetrated by Muslims, when ISIS rules parts of Iraq and Syria, we are supposed to believe that Islam is a religion of peace. Is it ignorance or diplomacy that prevents our politicians from telling it as it is. Islam promotes violence. Mr Sisi, the Egyptian president, believes so. He has asked his Muslim theologians to start a reform of the faith. Why do our politician cower before Muslim fundamentalism.

The West is spiritually bankrupt, thanks to the failure of the Church to evangelise. The Church in the West has been too busy appeasing other faiths (and people of no faith), not least Islam, by giving up spiritual territory. Our children cannot even enjoy the school nativity in a Christian country, in case Muslims, Hindus and Jews take offence! How much more ground are we prepared to give? Our church buildings are being sold to other faiths. Has the church lost its vision?!

The Western church has enough on its plate discharging its spiritual duties to its own people, and should desist from playing political Zionist and Muslim games abroad and at home. It should desist from playing games of appeasement within the so-called multi-faith society. Whilst evangelising at home, the Western Church needs to have fellowship, in all its fullness, with its suffering brothers and sisters in the Middle East, who can strengthen the faith of the church in the West. There is a sad irony in the contrast between the Christians of the Middle East who are dying for being faithful to Christ, and Christians of the West who are giving up their freedom for a lost cause. One is keeping the faith at pains of death, the other is gladly abandoning the faith despite no risk of death. How hurtful this is for the Christians of the Middle East?!

There are times when King David felt literally God-forsaken. All his enemies around him were growing stronger. He felt no one cared about him, and most of all he felt God had forsaken him. This is the feeling of the persecuted church in the Middle East. It has to be stated, though, that the church goes on in faith. The feeling is that Western Christians, and the world community at large, have forsaken this tiny, yet key, part of the body of Christ, a significant part of the Semitic nations. The greatest disappointment is that Western Christians have rarely if ever intervened in a palpable or impactful way to protect Christians in the Muslim world. One does not need to mount another Dark Age-style crusade in the Middle East. However, Christian nations need to make a stand together and demand justice for their brothers in the Middle East. The West has intervened on behalf of the Muslims in Bosnia, and the Tibetans in China; rightly so. It is disappointing to see that they do not show a similar intensity of interest in the welfare of Arabic-speaking Christians.

With all the above persecution, Arabic-speaking Christians often wonder what it is that accounts for Western Christian indifference. Lack of knowledge? But access to information in the West is unrestricted. Anyone can go on the internet and search under Christian *and* Arab, and read hundreds of reports of persecution. Lack of love? But that is impossible! Lack of love for one's brethren is incompatible with being a Christian. Lack of compassion and mercy? Again, fundamental qualities in Christians. Lack of pride?

The Church in the Middle East should be entitled to love and compassion from Christians worldwide. It is a duty of faith that every Christian everywhere owes to their suffering brethren elsewhere. If the Western Church cannot love the Arabic-speaking Church, perhaps they can pity her and instead of love, show some mercy. *"I seem forsaken and alone, I hear the lion roar; And every door is shut but one, And that is Mercy's door."* (William Cowper)

Is it possible that Western Christians have lost their sense of pride? The Christian West is only nominally Christian. Although 70 percent of Brits call themselves Christian, only a small proportion attend church. Notwithstanding, Western countries have numerous Christians in influential positions. Americans in particular lack no Christians at the top of the power pyramid. Most presidents in recent memory have been confessing Christians: Bush (father and son), Clinton, Ronald Reagan, Jimmy Carter and Obama.

There seems to be no sense of pride in the Christian world. I found a quote about pride which, for a moment made me rethink my view of Western Christianity vis-à-vis Arab Christians. *"But some emotions don't make a lot of noise. It's hard to hear pride. Caring is real faint – like a heartbeat. And pure love – why, some days it's so quiet, you don't even know it's there."* On second thought, however, pride may be quiet, but it is certainly visible. One can tell when a man is proud because of his poise, demeanour and conversation. Western Christendom seems generally diffident, and detached from their Arabic-speaking Christian brethren. By and large Western Christianity, with few exceptions, has been ashamed of calling Arabic-speaking Christians brethren, and wants to keep them at arm's length.

If there is no love for Arabic-speaking Christians, is there at least no sense of ownership of the Holy places. Palestine must be the most important land for Christians. Syria, Egypt and Iraq are historically vital centres of Christianity. Many of the Biblical events were staged in these countries. Yet the West stands and watches unmoved whilst Bethlehem is stripped of its Christians and is almost totally Islamised. The birthplace of Jesus Christ has fallen hostage to extremist Muslims. The extent of this infamy is such that whilst no Christian can set foot in Mecca, Muslims control Bethlehem and are talking about charging visiting Christians tax (Jizya).

A Muslim city councillor of Bethlehem, Hassan al-Masalmeh, stated that there are plans to implement Sharia Law in Bethlehem, according to the *Qur'an*: *"We in Hamas intend to implement this tax someday"*. Injustice apart, this is supremely humiliating. Where is the Christian sense of pride? *"We welcome everyone to Palestine but only if they agree to live under our rules."* The injustice of it aside, the humiliation felt by Christians is beyond description. Where is pride and honour amongst Christians?!

And what of Nazareth, being gradually taken over by Muslims? Has any political influence been used on behalf of the Christians of Nazareth to preserve their city and their ancient traditions?!

Christian nations should stand together and facilitate, by peaceful means, the return of property to Christians. Western nations have influence to exert over leading Muslim nations to ask them to reverse the deliberate takeover of Christian towns, such as Bethlehem and Nazareth. Muslims should be asked to respect the importance of Bethlehem and Nazareth to Christians and should volitionally keep these cities Christian, just as they expect Christians to keep out of Mecca. This is the least Palestinian Christians should expect from their brethren in the West. Land, property, shops and other possessions taken from Christians by force or extortion or any illegal means should be returned. Bethlehem should be returned to its rightful owners, the Christians of Palestine. Nothing less would suffice. Inaction by the West is only an encouragement for the Fundamentalist Muslims to go even further. I reiterate, that I am not calling for military action, but for dialogue and political pressure to ensure that the non-Christians of the Middle East deal with their Christian brethren fairly. The West has the political influence to bring this about peacefully.

If no Christian visitors are tolerated In Mecca, why is it that we accept Muslim takeover of Bethlehem and perhaps Nazareth?! The Christian West should negotiate incentives for voluntary exit of Muslims from these two cities as a matter of respect for the sensibilities of their Christian kinsmen

The indifference of Western nations towards the suffering of the Arabic-speaking Christians is akin to a man waiting for something, perhaps a sign, perhaps a whistle, or a secret nod or something invisible. Whatever you are waiting for, you have waited too long. Here is your nod or sign or whisper: the flame of Christianity in the Middle East is about to be snuffed out. The cradle of Christianity has been captured by violent men, by force, by intimidation, through unjust laws and through terror. For God's sake stand up and act for your faith, for your heritage, for your brethren, and for the values of democracy and the dignity of mankind. If you remain passive and sanguine, this evil will only be multiplied, repeated and magnified, and you will be the next victims. Do not let this happen.

Do not let Bethlehem become Matthew Arnold's *"Home of lost causes, and forsaken beliefs, and unpopular names, and impossible loyalties!"* Let not the birthplace of Christ be the burial ground for Palestinian Christianity.

Parts of the Western, particularly the American, Church have for too long been acting on the whims and wishes of the Jewish lobby. Professor Slezkine, Professor of History at U.C. Berkeley, wrote: *"I am aware how almost impossible it is in this country to carry out a foreign policy [in the Middle East] not approved by the Jews. Former Secretary of State George Marshall and former Defense Secretary James Forrestral learned that... terrific control the Jews have over the news media and the barrage the Jews have built up on Congressmen... I am very much concerned over the fact that the Jewish influence here is completely dominating the scene and making it almost impossible to get Congress to do anything they don't approve of. The Israeli Embassy is practically dictating to the congress through influential Jewish people in the country."* (*The Jewish Century*, Princeton University Press, 2004 (from Introduction)).

Expressing the same sentiment in the 1950s, Secretary of State John Foster Dulles said: *"I've never seen a president – I don't care who he is – stand up to them [the Israelis]. It just boggles your mind. They always get what they want. The Israelis know what's going on all the time. I got to the point where I wasn't writing anything down. If the American people understood what grip those people have on our government, they would rise up in arms. Our citizens don't have any idea what goes on."* (Donald Neff, Fallen Pillars, p. 99))

Arabic-speaking Christians deserve at least as much attention from the Christian West, particularly the Americans. There is a desperate need for a shift in American focus. There is a great need for action on behalf of Arabic-speaking Christians. This should take precedence over any Zionist agenda. The Christian West needs to take stock of the years of negligence and make restitution. They should extend their mighty political and financial arms and exert pressure on Jews and Muslims alike to do right by Arabic-speaking Christians everywhere. What does it take to motivate the Western Church to demand basic human rights for their own kind in the Holy Lands?!

My plea is this, let this book not be just another shout in the forest. Can anyone hear me? Let your love for your Christian Arab brethren be at least equal to the love of the Good Samaritan for the wounded Jew. Do not just pass by.

"But a certain Samaritan, as he journeyed, came where he was. And when he saw him, he had compassion. So he went to him and bandaged his wounds, pouring on oil and wine; and he set him on his own animal, brought him to an inn, and took care of him. On the next day, when he departed, he took out two denarii, gave them to the innkeeper, and said to him, 'Take care of him; and whatever more you spend, when I come again, I will repay you.'" (Luke 10:33-36 NKJV).

If the Samaritan could put aside the natural enmity between his people and the Jews and show compassion towards a Jew in need, why can't Western Christians have compassion on their own spiritual flesh and blood, the Arabic-speaking Christians of the Middle East?!

I have carried out a survey of Evangelical Israeli Arab opinion of how they are regarded by Western Evangelicals (July 2005). The questionnaire used is as follows:

Survey of Evangelical Israeli-Arab opinion about the contrast of attitude of Western Evangelicals towards Jews and Arabs.	
1. Most Western Evangelicals are surprised to know that Evangelical Israeli-Arab Churches exist.	A,B,C,D,E
2. Those Western Evangelicals, who know of the existence of Evangelical Israeli-Arabs, do not care about them?	A,B,C,D,E
3. Western Evangelicals are overly pro-Israeli.	A,B,C,D,E
4. Western Evangelicals are not interested in Israeli-Arab Evangelicals.	A,B,C,D,E
5. Western Evangelicals favour Jews in general over Israeli-Arab Evangelicals.	A,B,C,D,E
6. Western Evangelicals show no respect for Israeli-Arab Evangelicals.	A,B,C,D,E
7. Western Evangelicals show no love or care towards Israeli-Arab Evangelicals.	A,B,C,D,E
8. If a disaster were to befall Israeli-Arab Evangelicals, most Western Evangelicals would do nothing to help.	A,B,C,D,E
9. Foreign Muslims care more about Israeli Muslims than Western Evangelicals care about Israeli-Arab Evangelicals.	A,B,C,D,E
10. Western Evangelicals should be ashamed of themselves.	A,B,C,D,E
A= Strongly agree B= Agree C= Equivocal D= Disagree E= Strongly disagree	

The results are summarised below, and I offer them without comment, except to plea that the reader listens with their heart as they pause to contemplate these results.

Response		B	C	D	E
Statement					
1.	56	36	9	5	6
2.	45	30	12	17	6
3.	67	13	14	11	4
4.	49	29	12	14	7
5.	55	25	17	8	5
6.	40	24	25	15	5
7.	42	34	14	12	5
8.	45	29	12	21	6
9.	79	19	12	2	1
10	59	26	15	9	0

An interesting report in *The Times*, regarding a gathering of religious leaders and people of many faiths, hosted by His Royal Highness Prince Charles, conveys his deep concern about the way Christians were suffering persecution at the hands of their Muslim fellow Arabs, during the so-called Arab Spring. What is heart-warming is how His Royal Highness identifies with persecuted Christians of the Middle East by referring to them as his *"brothers and sisters in Christ"*.

Further, he said he had been deeply disturbed by their plight. (*Daily Telegraph*: "Christianity beginning 'to disappear' in its birthplace, warns Prince of Wales"; John Bingham, Religious Affairs Editor, 17 Dec 2013.)

As a British Christian Arab, this intervention warms the cockles of my heart. The Prince conveys a sense of urgency that is not evident in the Christian West: *"It seems to me that we cannot ignore the fact that Christians in the Middle East are increasingly being deliberately targeted by fundamentalist Islamist militants... Their church communities link us straight back to the early church as I was reminded by hearing Aramaic, our Lord's own language spoken and sung just a few hours ago...*

"This has an effect on all of us, although of course primarily on those Christians who can no longer continue to live in the Middle East.

"We all lose something immensely and irreplaceably precious when such a rich tradition dating back 2,000 years begins to disappear."

The Church in the West needs to listen to His Royal Highness, to follow suit, and openly identify with, show concern for, and speak up against the atrocities that are being committed against Middle Eastern Christendom. All of this needs to be done with a sense of ownership and a sense of urgency.

In an ideal world, I would call for Christian nations to take a united non-military stance to defend and protect their Christian brothers and sisters in the Middle East. I do not mean military action. But it is hard to know whether Western nations identify themselves as Christians. Therefore, I would rather call on churches, Christian organisations and Christian individuals to exert any influence they can, to mobilise their resources in order to defend their Christian brothers and sisters in the Middle East. Christians should ask that their government take a humanitarian stance on this issue.

It would be a good start if Christians everywhere started an International Christian Fund, whose aim is to buy back land and property in Nazareth and Bethlehem and sell it or rent it to returning Christian families. This would only work with support from right-thinking Muslim leaders. It would also be an encouraging expression of unity if such a fund went towards an organised removal of persecuted Christians to temporary safe havens, and assisted in their repatriation when conditions improved.

Kairos Palestine is a Christian Arab organisation calling upon Arabic-speaking Christians not to surrender or give up. An International Christian Fund would go a long way to reinforcing that message.

To The Zionists and the Jews in General

Zionism must not be confused with Jewry. This book has shown Zionism to be a cruel, cold and calculating movement, whose members show no respect for human life, even the lives of innocent Jews, whom they have willingly sacrificed in order to achieve their Zionist aims. A sampler of the heartless determination of Zionists comes from Ariel Sharon's mouth:

"I don't mind if after the job is done you put me in front of a Nuremberg Trial and then jail me for life. Hang me if you want, as a war criminal. What you don't understand is that the dirty work of Zionism is not finished yet, far from it." (Former Prime Minister of Israel, Ariel Sharon, speaking to Amos Oz, editor of Davar, on Dec. 17, 1982.)

This plea is first addressed to liberal Jews, and there are many such Jews around the world. Remember that Jews and Arabs share one common origin. Your father Eber is our father too. Abraham is our cousin and father to many Arabised Arabs. Neither Eber nor Abraham would be too pleased with the discrimination you have exercised against your Arab Brethren. There is a need to put suspicion, fear and greed aside. Look upon the Israeli Arab Christian as a kinsman, a brother and a potential partner. Think of how much can be achieved through fair and just treatment of this forgotten, but key minority.

To the Zionists and fundamentalists, what would Eber or Abraham say about your Talmud, the way you despise your Christian Arab cousins?! What would they say about your dispossessing your Palestinian cousins of home and field?

It is to be pointed out that your own law, an eye for an eye and a tooth for a tooth, has brought you nothing but wars, suffering and bitterness. All you have done is fight one war after another, and there are more wars to come. You have created thousands of widows and orphans, and for what?! Are you really more secure now than you were in Europe?! You, more than ever, live in insecurity. The threat of a nuclear bomb from Iran or Pakistan, or even Lebanon in due course, must hang over your worried heads like Damocles' sword, and is potentially worse than any Holocaust you have endured.

Your treatment of the early Christians has come home to roost, by your own law, and your own example. Yes, the pogroms in Europe, worst of all the Holocaust, fail the basic Christian law of "love your enemy", and can only be condemned by Christian standards. Yet the Jewish law of an eye for an eye and a tooth for a tooth can only justify it. There is a need in the Middle East for new thinking. How many teeth and how many eyes will suffice? Is it not obvious that this is a self-perpetuating formula for war and retaliation and counter retaliation?!

Worse still, to be hostile towards those who have done you no harm is to win you enemies when you desperately need friends. The Christian Israeli Arabs/Palestinians have never done the Zionists harm. Consider how strong you would be if instead of raising your arms against them, you reached out and put your hand in theirs in the spirit of fraternity and co-operation.

Where is your sense of pride and self-respect? Is it only right to take from Christians as you do from Evangelical Zionists?! Is it not equally proper to give?! Give equality and fairness to Arabic-speaking Christians at least, if not to all Arabs living in your midst. Give equal citizenship, and make friends, and be strengthened by their friendship. Return land you have taken by force and deceit, to its rightful owners.

To Muslim Arabs

The author is an Arab, who happens to have been born in Palestine after 1948. He is proud of his Arab heritage, and repudiates the ignorant Arab archetypes that prevail in the West. However, Islam and Arab nationhood are not to be confused. Whilst most Arabs are Muslim, not all Muslims are Arabs. The Arab family includes religions other than Islam. This reality needs to be accepted and acknowledged.

Some of my friends advised me that this chapter is futile. There is no way that an Arab Muslim world, in the grip of fundamentalism, can be interested in such a plea, they opined. However, I am driven by a powerful sense of optimism, which springs from my village of Kufur Yasief, of which I am extremely proud. I am particularly proud of how exemplary we have been in terms of friendly respectful co-existence between Christians and Muslims. In feudal days, our Christian family was allied with Muslim families. My nephews and nieces had Muslim nannies, who to date are considered as family members. Muslim teachers were amongst my favourite, including Uztath Adnan, Uztath Jameel and Uztath Ahmad. In the local elections, Muslims are allied with the son of the Greek Orthodox priest. This leads me to hope that Muslim Arabs elsewhere may adopt this attitude towards their Christian Arab neighbours.

He who denies his roots has no pedigree

Arabs were worshippers of stones and wood, before most were Christianised. Some Muslim Arabs living today are descendants of Christian Arab tribes. What would your Christian ancestors think of your attitude towards Christians today?! The Arab adage says *"Man Nakara aslahu, fala asla lahu"* (which translates into: He who denies his roots has no pedigree) and that is a shameful thing in Arab culture. You can deny that many of your forebears have been Christian, but you only bring shame upon yourselves.

If you hate your Christian Arab neighbours, you hate your ancestors. If you despise your Christian Arab brothers and sisters, you hate your ancestors. Remember the old Arab adage *"Man Nakara aslahu, fala asla lahu"*: He who forsakes his origins, has no pedigree.

Though to the outsider there seems to be greater distance between Muslims and Christians than between Jews and Christians, in reality the reverse is true. Yes, Christians and Jews share the Old Testament, but Jews deny Christ any recognition, let alone show him respect. As shown earlier, the Talmud is rife with vulgar references to Christ and Christians. It expresses shameful disregard and disdain for Christ and His followers.

By contrast, according to the Qur'an, Jesus is a prophet. Though he is not acknowledged as the son of God, he is revered as a messenger from God. It is also believed that Jesus will come back to kill the antichrist. *"Then he will kill the pigs, break the cross, demolish oratories and churches and kill Christians except those who believe in him"* (extract from the Hadith). Therefore Muslims give Christ a status not to be sneered at. By contrast, Jews not only fail to acknowledge Him, they actually despise Christ and revile him and his followers by words and deeds.

Muslims need to foster new attitudes towards their Christian Arab and Assyrian brethren. They need to begin to see that Christ and his followers have something positive to add to the Arab and Semitic family. I am encouraged by president El-Sisi of Egypt, who on New Year's Day 2015, addressing a Muslim gathering to celebrate the birth of their prophet Muhammad expressed a desire to see a Muslim revolution: *"I say and repeat, again, that we are in need of a religious revolution. You imams are responsible before Allah. The entire world is waiting on you. The entire world is waiting for your word... because the Islamic world is being torn, it is being destroyed, it is being lost. And it is being lost by our own hands... We need a revolution of the self, a revolution of consciousness and ethics to rebuild the Egyptian person – a person that our country will need in the near future."* ("Egypt's

President calls for a 'religious revolution'"; by Dana Ford, Salma Abdelaziz and Ian Lee, CNN; January 6, 2015.) He further condemned the Extremist Muslim mentality that says only 1.5 billion Muslims deserve to live and the remaining 5.5 billion of humanity deserve death.

On 6th January 2015 El-Sisi visited the Coptic Cathedral in Cairo and said a few encouraging words to the congregation gathered to celebrate the birth of Christ, in the presence of the Coptic pope. The visit of President Abdel-Fattah El-Sisi marked *"the first attendance ever made by an Egyptian president to the religious occasion"* (Ahram Online, Tuesday 6 Jan 2015); *"crowds cheering as El-Sisi entered the Cathedral with churchmen and saluted Pope Tawadros II"*. El-Sisi invited Egyptians to rise above sectarianism: *"'Let no one say, "What kind of Egyptian are you?"' he said. 'It's not right to call each other anything but "the Egyptians." We must only be Egyptians.'"* (Al Arabiya News Wednesday, 7 January 2015.) *"The congregation shouted, 'We love you Sisi.' He replied, 'We will love each other for real, so that people may see.' Sisi said: 'A happy year for you and all Egyptians!' This is the latest expression of an alliance between El-Sisi and Pope Tawadros II, aimed at defeating Islamic fundamentalist violence."* (*New York Times*, January 6 2015.)

Another encouraging example of relationships between Muslims and Christians comes from Sheikh Dr Ahmad Al-Taib, Al-Azhar Sheikh, speaking on the Nile channel, and reading the Sermon On the Mount, word for word, directly out of the New Testament. He said that when he reads Jesus' Sermon on the Mount, his eyes tear. The sermon he said was *"beautiful and tender"*. He stated that Jesus came to change society. He said that the words of the sermon *"represented the superior spirituality of our Master Jesus Christ peace be upon Him. It shakes great foundations."* (ART, 02.06.2014.)

If Muslims revere Christ, what treatment should they reserve for his followers, the Christians? Remember that Arabic-speaking Christians are your flesh and blood. They are Arabs and Semites and at that, important Arabs. We are True Arabs mostly, as opposed to Arabised Arabs, such as your revered prophet. We are the tree into which you were grafted. It is just inappropriate for you to treat us as aliens. Christian Arabs invented the Arabic Script, and spread the art of writing, and contributed the most able poets and translators, physicians, architects and scientists. Thus your Christian Arab brethren have always made an important contribution to Arab culture, language and society.

If you value roots, as does Arab culture, the discovery of the one and only God was made by Arabic-speaking Christians six hundred years before Islam. Persecute Arabic-speaking Christians and you inflict a self-injury. Kill them and you have committed fratricide. Rob them and you have impoverished yourselves. Beat them to pulp and you have bruised your own flesh, broken your own bones and shed your own blood.

Religion is a personal choice and no one should be hated for their choice of faith. Nor could anyone convert to Islam any soul, through hatred, extortion, sexual violence, denial of human rights or any other form of persecution. Muslim harshness towards Arabic-speaking Christians can only distance its victims from Islam. The lesson of history is this: persecution has only fuelled the fires of Christianity and caused it to spread faster than at times of peace. This is the lesson of Jerusalem and Rome. The first century church in Jerusalem was persecuted by the Jews. The consequence was the fastest advance of that religion in its history. Nero's Rome was another example of impetus generated by persecution of the Church.

God, who sees all things, from whom no secrets are hid, will reward you accordingly. The cry of God to Cain should resound in your ear, every time you persecute one of your Christian brethren:

"Where is Abel your brother?" Gen 4:9 NKJV

"And He said, 'What have you done? The voice of your brother's blood cries out to Me from the ground.'"

The voice of every Christian Arab, Egyptian or Assyrian martyred by Muslim zealots cries to Almighty God from the sands of Arabia, Egypt, Syria, Iraq and North Africa. "Where is your Christian brother?"

If you really fear God, remember these words every time you consider the shedding of the blood of an Arabic-speaking Christian : *"The voice of your brother's blood cries out to me from the ground"*.

If Arabs have an ounce of national pride left, let the Muslim amongst them volitionally move out of spiritually sensitive spots, such as Bethlehem and Nazareth, and make way for the Christians to inhabit their own Mecca and Medina. You should wish for your brothers what you claim for yourselves. To fail to do so is tantamount to self-condemnation. By contrast, to act in such a fair and equitable manner would be a positive testimony to some of the claims of Muslims being a peace-loving people. It would lend meaning to the much vaunted and hitherto hollow Arab nationalism. There can be no more powerful expression of Arab Nationalism than when a Muslim Arab willingly makes way for a Christian Arab.

The most accurate summation of what Arab nationalism has achieved so far comes from the pen of the late Christian Arab poet, Gibran Khalil Gibran, in his *Pity The Nation*:

> *"Pity the nation that is full of beliefs and empty of religion.*
> *Pity the nation that wears a cloth it does not weave*
> *and eats a bread it does not harvest.*
>
> *Pity the nation that acclaims the bully as hero,*
> *and that deems the glittering conqueror bountiful.*
>
> *Pity a nation that despises a passion in its dream,*
> *yet submits in its awakening.*
>
> *Pity the nation that raises not its voice*
> *save when it walks in a funeral,*
> *boasts not except among its ruins,*
> *and will rebel not save when its neck is laid*
> *between the sword and the block.*
>
> *Pity the nation whose statesman is a fox,*

whose philosopher is a juggler,
and whose art is the art of patching and mimicking

Pity the nation that welcomes its new ruler with
trumpeting,
and farewells him with hooting,
only to welcome another with trumpeting again.

Pity the nation whose sages are dumb with years
and whose strongmen are yet in the cradle.

Pity the nation divided into fragments,
each fragment deeming itself a nation."
("The Garden of The Prophet")

The division, violence, the capriciousness, and the cowardice in the face of evil is reminiscent of the state of the Arab nation at present under the reign of fundamentalist Islam that destroys all that does not conform to its twisted template of what is righteous. Is it too late to change?!

Muslim tradition records the words of Abu Bakr Al-siddiq, the first Caliph and father-in-law of your prophet Muhammad, with which he instructed his military chiefs before the invasion of Palestine:

"When on your way, you will encounter those who have shut themselves up in monks' cells; do them no harm and permit to devote themselves to their chosen paths."

Some tradition ascribes these instructions to your prophet himself. If you have any respect for your own prophet, or his Caliph Abu Bakr, why are you targeting Christians, Christian communities, monasteries and churches for violence, destruction, looting and murder? In the name of your prophet, cease from your murderous acts towards your Christian kinsmen.

Deal with the Arab Christians amongst you fairly and justly, reap the fruits of justice and peace, enjoying the sweet reward of a clear conscience and the pleasure of Almighty God, whose name is to be praised.

A Semitic Dream

All great ideas begin with a dream, whose natural development is only hampered by fear of failure. The biggest guarantee of failure, the greatest obstacle to success is fear of failure. Martin Luther King was not afraid to dream, even though his dream might cost him his life; but he was no coward. He did not give in to fear. Because he dared to dream, race relations in the USA and throughout the world have moved in a positive direction. His dream lives on and continues to bear fruit even today.

The Semitic nations, those of Muslim, Jewish, and Christian faiths, should consider a shared dream rooted in the following principles:

1. The brotherhood of Semitic peoples is paramount and must transcend all considerations.
2. Total agreement is not a pre-requisite to peace, nor is lack of it a cause for war. Diversity is a sign of vital pulsating society.
3. Religion is a matter of personal choice. If God is sovereign, if He is great, He does not need self-appointed judges to condemn people for what they believe. All three Semitic faiths preach mercy and compassion. So it is a small step from preaching to practising both mercy and compassion. Differences must never, can never, be resolved through bloodshed.
4. Semites should have total freedom to share or change their faith as often as they choose. God is the only judge. People of conviction should be free to express their opinion without any aggression or negative repercussions from any side. Freedom of the mind must not lead to fear of fanatical actions.
5. No force should be utilised to persuade people to change their creed.
6. It is better to forge friendship than to engender enmity.

If leaders of the three Semitic nations can agree on these basic principles, then we are not a hundred miles away from forming a Semitic political union in the Middle East, based on tolerance and mutual respect, in which Semitic people enhance one another and desist from seeking to weaken or detract from one another, in which no one is superior or inferior, greater or lesser, master or slave.

The dream begins with a moment of courage; courage to close one's eyes and imagine a Middle East in which the three Semitic nations work together, employing the strengths and gifts of each nation for the common Semitic good, finding a common enemy to fight together, the enemy of ignorance, poverty, intolerance and violence. The Middle East had been a bedrock of faith, science and trade for many millennia. Selfishness and violence have ensured a regression of the Semitic nations by a few centuries. The Semitic dream would reverse this regressive trend and ensure a powerhouse of creativity and commerce, for the benefit of all Semitic nations and indeed the entire world. This dream would transform Semitic division to Semitic dynamism and Semitic afflictions to Semitic affluence.

Gibran Khalil Gibran once wrote: *"Yesterday is but today's memory, and tomorrow is today's dream"*. If the peoples of the Middle East want tomorrow to be free of yesterday's fear, fighting and factions, they should choose the right dream today, a Semitic Dream.

END

Index

253, 254, 255, 262, 264,
265, 267, 269, 271, 289,
292, 305, 306, 317, 324,
325, 334, 336, 342, 352,
353